Ritschl: A Reappraisal

A Study in Systematic Theology

Ritschl:
A Reappraisal

A Study in Systematic Theology

———◆———

James Richmond

COLLINS

Published by Collins
London · Glasgow
Cleveland · New York · Toronto
Sydney · Auckland · Johannesburg

First published in Great Britain 1978
© James Richmond 1978

UK ISBN 215714 4

Set in Monotype Times
Made and printed in Great Britain by
William Collins Sons & Co Ltd, Glasgow

First published in the USA 1978
Library of Congress Catalog Card Number 78-69701
USA ISBN 0-529-05622-4

for Ewan and Ruth,
companions in Göttingen

Contents

Preface

This work could not possibly have been written without encouragement, help and financial assistance from others, which it is a pleasure to acknowledge here. The initial impetus to compose it derived from my appointment as Kerr Lecturer at the University of Glasgow for the period 1972–5, and I wish to record my deep gratitude to the Kerr Lectureship Committee for the great honour it conferred upon me in this appointment. The lectures were delivered at my *Alma Mater* in the Michaelmas Term of 1975, when my host was Professor Allan D. Galloway (the Convener of the Committee), whose efforts to ensure that my visit to the Faculty of Divinity was not merely congenial, but also memorably enjoyable, far exceeded the limits of his duty. Any doubts that I might have entertained about the relevance of my subject to contemporary systematic theology were swiftly dissipated not only by my lecture-room audience, but also by the useful informal discussion sessions that followed each of the seven lectures. Most of the reading for, and much of the writing of this work was done in Ritschl's old city of Göttingen, in 1973 on the Hagenberg, and in 1975 in Gross Schneen *bei* Göttingen. Neither of these periods of residence would have been possible without the generosity of the British Academy (which at that time had not suffered the grievous loss caused by the death of its helpful and sympathetic Secretary, Dr Neville Williams), which awarded me in 1973, and again in 1975, European Exchange Grants for periods of research at the University of Göttingen, which I now acknowledge with heartfelt gratitude. It is also a pleasant duty to acknowledge my immense gratitude to the *Deutscher Akademischer Austauschdienst* (especially to Dr Martin L. Mruck and his colleagues in London, and to its President, Professor Dr Hansgerd Schulte, and his colleagues in Bonn – Bad Godesberg), for a Resident Fellowship tenable in the Theological Faculty in Göttingen. In 1973 and again in 1975 I was welcomed to Göttingen by Professor Dr Georg Strecker (in 1973 Dean of the

Theological Faculty), whose warm cordiality to my family and myself was exceeded only by his readiness to be helpful in any way which was open to him. I remain extremely grateful to him. Both in 1973 and 1975, I was given free access to the Lower Saxony State and University Library at Göttingen by its Director, Professor Dr Wilhelm Grunwald, whose staff cheerfully inconvenienced themselves on countless occasions to satisfy my needs. As recorded elsewhere, I was invaluably informed in private discussion with Professor Grunwald on the topic of the intellectual history of his university in the second half of the nineteenth century, about which he knows so very much. But during both periods of research, I was inexpressibly fortunate to make the acquaintance of *Bibliotheksdirektor* Dr Hans-Joachim Kiefert. I am more grateful than I can say to Dr Keifert, not merely for his untiring readiness to help a visitor in a large and complex library which he knows so intimately, but for the enthusiastic interest which he took in my subject, expressed by his eagerness to track down whatever I sought, no matter how obscure. I shall not quickly forget the way in which he, a senior member of the library staff, relentlessly searched, on my behalf, in the crammed and dust-laden cellars of the library under the Prinzenstrasse, for a copy of Johannes Meyer's little history of the theological faculty. It is such as he who make research in a foreign library not a tedious chore but a pleasurable experience.

On this side of the North Sea, I am greatly indebted to Mrs Geraldine Towers, whose skill in accurate typing is surpassed only by her uncomplaining ability to decipher a heavily corrected manuscript containing countless German words, phrases and titles. Finally, I am heavily indebted once more to my wife who, for my sake, added to her list of accomplishments by twice transforming herself into a *Hausfrau* in a linguistically demanding situation, and by general encouragement together with painstakingly careful work has materially assisted in the early production of the final version of this book.

I have only one minor regret. It has been pointed out to me that it might just be possible to read this work as some kind of attack upon, or attempt to discredit, the historical work of my late teacher, Professor Karl Barth. This has filled me with dismay, for nothing was further from my intention. Apart from the obvious fact that Barth's historical work is far too great to be 'discredited' by any one book, however incisive and perceptive, it is worth pointing out to the discerning reader that on the countless occasions where I have dared to dissent from Barth's rather dismissive judgements of Ritschl, I have tried to do so in an objective, scholarly way, by citing his *ipsissima verba* and setting down the precise grounds of my disagreement. Hopefully, too, the careful reader will not overlook those numerous occasions where I have judged that Barth's usually penetrating, if harshly expressed, judgements of Ritschl were more or less justified. It is perfectly true that I have committed myself on many occasions to severe criticisms of 'Barthian' viewpoints and of the 'Barthian' or 'neo-orthodox' schools. But then those of us who were privileged to sit at Barth's feet cannot easily forget his reiterated and vehement claim that *if* a Barthian school existed, he was not a member of it! Not only would I heartily concur with the papal judgement that Barth was the greatest systematic theologian since Aquinas, but would unreservedly endorse the judgement of R. R. Niebuhr and others, that all researchers into nineteenth-century German theology are incalculably indebted to him for the ways in which, in his nineteenth-century history book and other writings, he kept dialogue with the nineteenth-century theological giants in the forefront of theological debate. Indeed, I would go further – when the final, definitive history of nineteenth-century German theology (in several weighty volumes, I would predict) comes to be written, the unenviable author will now have the awesome task of working through and assessing the formidable references to and judgements of nineteenth-century authors contained in the successive volumes of Barth's *Kirchliche Dogmatik*! Such is one measure of the greatness of the man. But, having said that, I would not now wish to retract or qualify any of the judgements contained in the pages that follow.

September 1977   James Richmond
University of Lancaster

CHAPTER I

The Ritschl Renaissance

Our dictionaries tell us that the word 'renaissance' denotes a 're-birth', a 'springing up anew', a 'being reborn'; culturally, it denotes 'a period of intellectual revival', a resurgence of interest in a special kind of learning. But what is reborn or springs up anew cannot do so unless it has been dead, unless it has been ignored, unless it has been destroyed or banished. These reflections apply very aptly to the theological thought of Albrecht Ritschl: once it was alive and vigorously flourishing, then it was banished (almost, it seemed, from the face of the earth), almost buried; now it is springing up again, being reborn; a revival of interest in Ritschl's work has already begun. In order to understand why and how this is so, it is necessary to know something of the man, his work, and that great movement which attracted the name 'Ritschlian', the precise reasons for the apparent demise of this several generations ago, and why it is that during the past decade or so there has emerged a desire to re-examine the man and his writings, to reappraise these, and to enter into a dialogue with a theologian who, for good or ill, about a century ago stood at the centre of the Western theological endeavour.

Albrecht Benjamin Ritschl was born on 25 March 1822, in Berlin, of a family of considerable academic and ecclesiastical distinction, his father being a bishop (or superintendent) of the Prussian Reformed Union Church. He received a fairly typical nineteenth-century German theological education, at the universities of Bonn, Heidelberg, Halle and Tübingen. The most important influence upon him at Heidelberg was that of the distinguished theologian and ecclesiastical lawyer, Richard Rothe (whose work is discussed in Chapter VI below). The most significant influence at Bonn was from the radical speculative theologian, Karl Nitzsch, the distinguished disciple and interpreter of Schleiermacher. But of course during the 1840s in Germany it would have been almost impossible to find any systematic

theologian who did not teach and write under the impact of the
German *Aufklärung*, in the light of the writings of Kant, Hegel
and Schleiermacher. But by far the mightiest influence upon the
young Ritschl came from the great Tübingen theologian and
historian, Ferdinand Christian Baur, whom Ritschl joined as a
student in 1845. The intellectual *affaire* between Ritschl and Baur
lasted for just over ten years, until the final break in 1856, after
the former had become a professor at Bonn. The friendship and
collaboration between these two is one of the most important
and interesting in the history of nineteenth-century German
theology, but its intricate details must lie beyond the scope of
this work. It is hopefully enough to say that from the beginning
the junior Ritschl was simultaneously attracted to and repelled
by the Tübingen theologian. The attraction and repulsion experienced by Ritschl during this period contained deep implications for his life's work. On the one hand, Ritschl was deeply
impressed and attracted by Baur's brilliant gifts as a meticulous
and creative historical critic, and Ritschl's training by and
emulation of the latter is evident in his own later highly gifted
historical work, on the history of the doctrines of justification and
reconciliation, of the emergence of the Old Catholic Church, and
of post-Reformation pietism. But, on the other, more negative
side, from the outset Ritschl was suspicious of Baur's alleged use
of Hegelian speculative categories in his historical investigations,
categories which, in Ritschl's view, were bound to distort the
data of which the theologian is vocationally committed to make
sense. In 1850 Ritschl's thesis and first book, *Die Entstehung der
altkatholischen Kirche*, was published – written under Baur's
supervision and influence, and completed while Ritschl was in his
first teaching job as a *Privat-Dozent* in Bonn. This was the first
and last of his works which exhibited any influence from speculative metaphysics, using as it does Baurian categories to explain
the emergence of the Old Catholic Church of the second century
as the compromising but developing reconciliation of apparently
opposing and contradictory tendencies and attitudes. For no
sooner had the first edition appeared than Ritschl began to
reconsider its main theses, a reconsideration of inestimable importance for his later career, a reconsideration which lasted until
the middle of the fifth decade of the century. While this scholarly

overhauling of his position was proceeding Ritschl was promoted to the rank of *ausserordentlicher Professor* in 1853, the year in which he began to move away from purely historical to systematic and dogmatic theology in his teaching. The appearance of the second edition of *Die Entstehung der altkatholischen Kirche* in 1857 announced to academic Germany Ritschl's break with Baur which had taken place the year before. The work made clear without the shadow of a doubt Ritschl's abandonment of the categories of speculative idealism in his historical theology. To put this another way, no longer is the emergence of the second-century Catholic Church regarded as the quasi-Hegelian *Aufhebung* of apparently contradictory and mutually incompatible movements and beliefs – rather, the second edition strongly hints at Ritschl's later and very complex theory that the contradictions in second-century Christianity are more real than apparent, that early in its history Christianity 'fell from grace', because of its adulteration by alien, nonreligious, speculative elements, an adulteration which was in later centuries to become strongly cumulative and which became encapsulated in the Catholic Church of the late Middle Ages, a process which led eventually to the Reformation and to the twin conceptions of *ecclesia reformata* and *ecclesia semper reformanda*.

But several footnotes must be appended to this all too brief account. It is an interesting and important question as to how far Ritschl failed to appreciate the genius and method of Baur, and how far a sentence of 'guilty' must be pronounced on Ritschl and his school for grave injustices perpetrated upon the name and reputation of a thinker of Baur's genius and originality. More precisely, it is to be doubted whether Ritschl realized how firmly grounded Baur's historical conclusions were on his objective and unbiased examination of the data themselves, and that Baur's so-called 'Hegelianism' was embraced as a result of Baur's *a posteriori* recognition of similarities between historical processes he had carefully analysed and the so-called Hegelian dialectic, rather than as an *a priori* attempt to force the abstract and unempirical categories of a metaphysical system upon objectively given historical data, distorting and violating them in the direction of untruth. (One of the most pleasing characteristics of the contemporary renaissance of nineteenth-century theological studies is the way in which this is being realized, and in which F. C. Baur's creative genius is being rescued from the unscholarly stereotyped description of him as a somewhat wooden and unyielding disciple of Hegel, forcing historical raw materials into the inexorable and impersonal pattern of thesis, antithesis and synthesis.) It would be ironical if it could be shown that Ritschl and his school had vigorously assisted in the discrediting of Baur in a way not altogether dissimilar from that in which Karl Barth and his colleagues quite deliberately and systematically tried to discredit Ritschl's theological work almost sixty years ago. At any rate, what is beyond doubt is that just as some are now successfully trying to rehabilitate Baur after a period of undeserved obscurity, others of us are trying to do something of the same sort for Ritschl. Further, it cannot be seriously doubted that Ritschl's break with the Tübingen school and its so-called 'Hegelianism' occurred partly for reasons which had little intrinsically to do with Baur and his disciples. These reasons had much to do with a fairly general and widespread intellectual dissatisfaction with Hegelianism as a satisfactory philosophical resting-place, a disillusionment that began to be apparent from the mid-eighteen forties, and from which those theological systems closely integrated with Hegelianism had much to fear. The reasons for this incipient decline of Hegelianism in Germany just before mid-century are exceedingly complex, but it can with some confidence be stated that they were rooted, roughly speaking, in two factors: first, in fatal tensions within the Hegelian school itself,[1] and, second, in the incredible advances being made in the nineteenth-century natural sciences.

As regards the first of these, it need only be noted that before mid-century the Hegelian movement had become hopelessly divided into a right wing and a left wing, each of these incompatible with the other. The former of these, which included philosophers like Bruno Bauer and the theologian Philipp Marheineke, clung to Hegelianism in the hope that it might continue to provide some supernaturalistic picture of the world and interpretation of human experience. The latter, which was held to include Ludwig Feuerbach and the theologian D. F. Strauss, tended towards a quite immanentist, and, in the case of Feuerbach, materialistic viewpoint. (It was indeed Feuerbach's materialism, heavily qualified and much radicalized, which provided Marx and Engels a little later in the century with their classic critique of religion.) But the second factor, the advances made by the nineteenth-century natural sciences, was probably more potent for the demise of Hegelianism as a coherent and attractive philosophical framework in mid-century Germany. For these advances had been made possible, it was swiftly recognized, through the meticulously careful examination of natural phenomena on the smallest observable scale, combined with microscopically accurate measurement, both of which provided scientists with predictions which could with a hitherto unheard-of degree of accuracy be verified or falsified in strictly controlled conditions. In a society whose members came to be awestruck by such work, concentrated as it was on empirical phenomena on the smallest scale, on the partial, on the highly concrete, on highly individual things and classes of things, on the particular, it was little wonder that much Hegelian talk of the unobservable, imperceptible, tantalizingly elusive but somehow all-inclusive Absolute came to lack much of its conviction. In a society which was becoming increasingly scientific men were less likely to be impressed by the Hegelian's disdain for the particular and the concrete, by his somewhat cavalier dismissal of all contradiction, negation and difference as illusory rather than real, by his claim that truth becomes apparent only when the observer elevates himself out of the particular and the local and the time conditioned into that lofty realm where he might glimpse the One and the All within which merely temporary mundane antinomies and contradictions are left behind and done away. Such a stance, it was felt by many mid-century Germans, was bluntly incompatible with the vocation of the laboratory and the hard knowledge that it could bring.

It is quite inconceivable that the junior Ritschl in the fifth decade of the nineteenth century could have been unaware of the strong wave of anti-Hegelian disillusionment which swept through the German universities and intellectual classes. It was at this time, as already noted, that Ritschl washed his hands of Hegelian idealism, and with this idealism, of all speculative metaphysics as a significant source of theological truth. Almost thirty years later, in 1881, Ritschl could write: 'The absolute! How exalted that sounds! I can still recall, if only dimly, how that word occupied me in my youth, when the Hegelian terminology threatened to draw me, too, into its vortex. But that was long ago. Now, since I do not find any far-reaching ideas designated by it, the word has become largely alien to me.'[2] But the demise of Hegelianism as an attractively coherent system was by no means an unmixed blessing for theologians of Ritschl's stamp. For German historians of ideas are agreed that the sudden collapse of Hegelianism (like the sudden collapse of many other coherent ideological systems in human history) left behind a large and dangerously hungry vacuum. This is because it is in the nature of any vacuum to suck violently into itself what exists in its immediate environment. And what existed in the environment of the space left behind by Hegelianism were convictions and philosophies that can only be described as materialistic, naturalistic and positivistic. Of course, it was only natural that these should have existed in West European societies which, as we have just observed, were undergoing a process of rapid secularization based upon reverence for scientific method and its fruitfulness. Only such societies could have produced the positivists Ernst Mach in Germany and Auguste Comte in France, and the materialists Ludwig Büchner, Jakob Moleschott and Ernst Haeckel in Germany. Indeed, so rapidly did scientific materialism develop and spread through the German intelligentsia in the 1850s, that in 1855 academic Germany was scandalized by the dismissal of Büchner from Ritschl's old university at Tübingen (on the grounds of the publication of the former's *Force and Matter*), and the unsuccessful attempt of the university authorities at Jena to get rid of the zoologist Haeckel.[3] We must keep such facts as these in mind when we read the texts of Ritschl, because one thesis to be defended in later chapters is that any attempt to interpret Ritschl in isolation from this intellectual milieu dominated by materialism and positivism is not merely unscholarly but unjust.

This then is the background against which Ritschl completed his work which emerged as the second edition of *Die Entstehung der altkatholischen Kirche* (1857). But this work is significant for another reason. For in it are to be found the germs of a theological theory which earned the Ritschlian school world-wide fame, or, depending on one's viewpoint, world-wide notoriety. This is the theory rooted in Ritschl's distinction between early (authentic) and later (largely inauthentic) Christianity. The second edition of Ritschl's dissertation pointed forward to his later sharp distinction between the Christianity of Jesus, to be variously described by Ritschl's disciples as 'primitive', 'dynamic', 'Galilean', 'ethico-spiritual', 'practical', and 'mundane', and the largely fallen Christianity of the second and later centuries which came to be described as largely 'inauthentic', 'theoretical', 'christological' (rather than 'soteriological'), gravely infected not only by alien Greek metaphysics but also by otherworldly, ahistorical and amoral mysticism, described by Ritschl as 'neoplatonic' in origin and nature. This distinction and the seeds which produced it in Ritschl's 1857 book are of incalculable significance. For it lies at the heart of much that is to come in the following three-quarters of a century: Ritschl's systematic exposition of the significance of Jesus for modernity, a significance too often overlaid (because perennially *tending to be overlaid*) by inauthentic Church doctrines, piety and practice; his efforts to free Christian theology from metaphysics; his monumental, if excessively hostile, three-volumed *Geschichte des Pietismus*; his biblical work in the second volume of the *Rechtfertigung u. Versöhnung*; his work on the Reformation, with special reference to the significance of Luther and Melancthon; the monumental programme of the *dehellenization* of the history of Christianity and of ecclesiastical dogma by his disciple, the Berlin church historian Adolf von Harnack, in his multi-volumed *Dogmengeschichte*. Programmatically and germinally, much of this work was outlined in the 1857 publication.

In 1859 Ritschl was promoted to the rank of *ordentlicher Professor* in Bonn, and the same year saw the publication across the North Sea of a work whose theses were not merely to strengthen but also to extend those philosophies of scientific naturalism and materialism referred to above – namely, Charles Darwin's *Origin of Species*. While Darwin's book evoked in these islands a melancholy, because emotive and uncomprehending science-religion controversy which is now better forgotten, its swift translation into German enabled materialists like the discredited Haeckel to rebut the charge that they had hitherto been

espousing an arbitrary, antireligious and anti-ecclesiastical metaphysic which lacked any evidential or experimental foundation.
For this reason, in Germany in the 1860s naturalism and
materialism were almost immediately qualified as 'evolutionary'.
The far-reaching consequences of this were twofold. First, the
transformation, consolidation and development of scientific
materialism posed for German Christians, as for British ones, a
dangerous threat rooted in a new understanding of the *world* and
man's relation to it. For evolutionary materialists identified
reality with the material world, contended that human understanding, restricted to the methods of the natural sciences, was
limited to grasping the nature and structure of the physical world,
and portrayed man merely as a part (however interesting or
complex) of the material world, and as such potentially and exhaustively comprehensible by the laws of social and natural
reality. Occasionally, such views were accompanied by denials of,
significantly, the three Kantian postulates of the practical reason,
the freedom of the will, the immortality of the soul, and the
existence of God. Indeed, some materialists went further than
this and followed the line to be taken later by the Vienna positivist
Ernst Mach, teaching in Humean manner a doctrine of the
personal self as a quite spatio-temporal centre of sensations and
perceptions, although, with Hume, they denied the knowability
of the nature and constitution of this *centrum*. Facts such as these
must be kept firmly in mind by the student of Ritschl, because in
his systematic theology, published largely between 1870 and 1874,
it is clear that the problem of *man's relation to the world* lies right
at the heart of it; moreover, there is reason to believe that
Ritschl's doctrine of the personal self, so central to his exposition
of Christianity for modernity, may owe rather more to the
phenomenalism of the 1860s than has generally been recognized.
To these matters we shall return at later points.

A second consequence of the transformation and consolidation
of materialism after 1860 was the emergence in Germany of the
philosophical movement known as neo-Kantianism. The genesis
of this movement can only properly be understood against the
background of that philosophical *impasse* analysed above:
namely, the seemingly impossible situation brought about by the
collapse of Hegelian metaphysical idealism and the tendency

towards its replacement by crudely reductionist antireligious and anti-idealistic materialistic metaphysics. The point is that both of these (Hegelianism and materialism) were thoroughly *metaphysical*: and, it was asked, not unnaturally, had not the great significance of Kant resided in the way in which, with meticulous precision and care, he had mapped out the nature and the limits of human knowledge? To be more precise, if, on the one hand, Kant's analysis in *The Critique of Pure Reason* ruled out of court much of the extravagant, unempirical and rather nebulous talk of the Absolute so characteristic of much Hegelian idealism, it did, on the other hand, forbid the crude, reductionist and often harshly dogmatic talk of evolutionary and materialistic metaphysics. And, moreover, had not Kant, in *The Critique of Practical Reason*, pointed towards an exit from the matter/mind dilemma in his doctrine of the practical reason which led, in his view, towards practical faith in human freedom, the immortality of the soul, and the existence of God? Now the importance of neo-Kantianism in our context is centred on the fact that in quite recent decades we have become accustomed to having Ritschl bracketed with neo-Kantian philosophers and their theological adherents.[4] That it is both false and misleading to do so can be proved from a brief consideration of dates. German historians of ideas are broadly agreed that the movement proper must be dated from 1865 when Professor Otto Liebmann in his work *Kant und die Epigonen* pointed the German intelligentsia 'Back to Kant!', just as Friedrich Albert Lange was completing the manuscript of his very hostile *Geschichte des Materialismus* (1866). And Hermann Cohen, leader of the Marburg branch of the school, was not appointed to Marburg until 1876, and the first volume of his *System der Philosophie* was not brought out until 1902. As for the Baden branch of the school, its acknowledged leader, Wilhelm Windelband (1848–1915), was not born until Ritschl had begun teaching at Bonn; he was not appointed to Heidelberg until 1903, and his *Einleitung in die Philosophie* was not published at Tübingen until 1914. All of this must be clearly understood if injustice is not to be done to Ritschl's writings. neo-Kantianism as a coherent movement was impossibly late to have exerted much influence on Ritschl in the crucial period of 1864–74. Doubtless, as a university theologian, he was keenly interested in the renaissance of Kant's anti-materialistic idealism during the period in question, and even more so later on in 1881, when he composed his little monograph on the epistemology of religion, *Theologie und Metaphysik*. One cause of the misleading application to Ritschl of the label 'neo-Kantian' is doubtless the fact that the work of later Ritschlians, Herrmann of Marburg, and Harnack and Kaftan of Berlin, betrays the clear influence of turn-of-the-century neo-Kantianism (much clearer in the case of the first two than in that of the conservative and mildly metaphysical Kaftan). This application led to the irritating and unscholarly habit of lumping Ritschl together with the 'Neokantians' and the 'Ritschlians', a practice which contributed strongly to the demise of Ritschl's reputation as a theologian of the Bible, the Christian tradition, and the Reformation. No, Ritschl's 'Kantianism', if it is to be called that, has, as we shall see presently, a quite different source, and produced a rather different result. We must get these facts clear because one very marked characteristic of the contemporary Ritschl Renaissance has been a vigorous and proper protest against the way in which the narrow term 'neo-Kantian' has been used heuristically in the discrediting of Ritschl's theological reputation; Ritschl *did not at all* (prior to the production of his theological constructions) take over any abstract conceptual or epistemological schema from any philosophical school whatever, which became determinative for the theological results he reached. The facts of history orient us towards a rather different picture of Ritschl as a 'philosophical theologian'.[5]

The year 1864 was one of great significance for Ritschl's life and work. In that year he was called to succeed the moderately Hegelian theologian Isaak August Dorner in the Dogmatic Theology Chair at Göttingen. He was to occupy this post until his death in 1889 and, as his immediate successor, Theodor v. Haering, tells us, he was thereafter known as *the* Göttingen theologian,[6] a fact of great significance, as we shall see below, for Karl Barth's period of service there from 1921 until 1925. Brief reference must now be made to several aspects of the final, Göttingen period of Ritschl's life.[7] Upon arrival there in 1864 he found amongst his academic colleagues the Oriental philologist and pangermanist political theorist Paul Anton de Lagarde

(Professor of Oriental Languages at Göttingen from 1869 until 1891) and Rudolf Hermann Lotze (Professor of Philosophy from 1844 until 1881). The progressively unfriendly and critical stance of Lagarde to Ritschl (he could not abide Luther or Lutheranism with which, not without cause, he identified Ritschl, and he deplored all attempts at the systemtizing of religion with which again, not altogether wrongly, he identified Ritschl),[8] was much compensated for by the extremely affable welcome extended to him by Lotze not long after his arrival from Bonn in 1864. The relationship, which began as a social matter, was soon transformed into one in which the technically very competent Lotze acted as Ritschl's philosophical mentor in the handling of those philosophical problems which lay in the way of the composition of the latter's main life's work, *Die christliche Lehre von der Rechtfertigung und Versöhnung*. Ritschl was extremely fortunate in having Lotze as friend and mentor during this period 1865–70, for Lotze, who had entered academic philosophy from medicine, *via* poetry, art and literature, had long struggled with problems which were somewhat akin to Ritschl's philosophical ones: the limitation of our metaphysical knowledge; the relation of living things to non-living and of human to non-human being; the nature and limits of a purely mechanical interpretation of the world; the nature of human personality and consciousness with special reference to man's experience of value; the relations between a world constituted by scientific facts and the dimension of values, and the like. Indeed, the third and final volume of Lotze's monumental exploration of such themes, the *Mikrokosmos*, was published coincidentally with Ritschl's arrival in Göttingen in 1864. The most telling result of this friendship which began in 1865 was Lotze's acceptable advice to Ritschl that the key to much that troubled him philosophically lay in a re-reading of Kant's critical and ethical philosophy. Accordingly, when the first volume of Ritschl's *Rechtfertigung u. Versöhnung* appeared in 1870 it contained a long section on Kant, his contemporaries and his immediate successors.[9] But the overall influence of Lotze on Ritschl is hard, not merely to describe, but to understand. What must lie beyond dispute is that the former was vastly superior to the latter in the handling of philosophical ideas, and that one must doubt if Ritschl always or often understood his philosophical mentor. Indeed, early in the present century it was not difficult for one Scottish researcher to demonstrate that when one compared the *system* of Lotze with the *system* of Ritschl and school there were glaring divergences between the two.[10] And when one has read Ritschl's son and biographer, Otto Ritschl,[11] and the detailed analysis of Ritschl's philosophical sources by Paul Wrzecionko,[12] it is hard to resist the conclusion that Ritschl had little or no *intrinsic* interest in philosophical issues; that, like his master, Luther, before him, his dominating interest was the practical religious life of the believer in Church and society; that he *used* philosophical insights (from Kant or Lotze or wherever) when they served his *theological* purposes; and that he tried, without much originality and with a certain reluctance, to overcome philosophical obstacles only either when he had no real option or when they were laid uncompromisingly before him by hostile critics. The classic example of the latter was the little treatise of 1881, already mentioned, his *Theologie u. Metaphysik*: the only explicitly 'philosophical' work he ever composed, it was written hastily between 15 April and 6 June, in response to criticisms of his theological position made by Christoph Ernst Luthardt of Leipzig, Franz Hermann Reinhold Frank of Erlangen, and Hermann Weiss of Tübingen. Even a cursory examination of this text swiftly convinces a modern that it is by now almost impossible to be sure whether Ritschl is at any point dependent upon Kant, Lotze, the early Luther and Melancthon, or (especially when he is dealing with the psychology of the personal self) nineteenth-century phenomenalists and positivists. Facts such as these should assist in undermining the glib and unreflective application to Ritschl of a technical title like 'neo-Kantian'. To these matters we shall return in some detail in the next chapter.

One final point about Ritschl's Göttingen period remains to be made. Students of modern German theology are predisposed, not unnaturally, to be impressed by the history and reputation of Göttingen as a centre of theological study and research. After all, the published faculty lists[13] constitute something of a little history within the history of modern German philosophical theology – containing, as they do, names such as Georg Ewald, Julius Wellhausen, Paul de Lagarde, Hermann Lotze, Ritschl,

Max Reischle, Theodor Haering, Johannes Weiss, Edmund Husserl, Rudolf Otto, William Wrede, Paul Althaus, Karl Barth, Emanuel Hirsch, Carl Stange, Friedrich Gogarten, Walther Zimmerli and Joachim Jeremias. But this history may mislead, obscuring from us the fact that in a wider context the fame of Göttingen rests largely on its huge reputation in the field of the natural sciences. Apart from its considerable reputation as a twentieth-century centre for research in theoretical physics and chemistry, academic historians concur that the golden age of Göttingen as a centre of scientific research and writing coincides with the second half of the nineteenth century, when the fame of the university was extended by the labours of the mathematician Gauss (a joint founder, with W. Weber the physicist, of the electric telegraph) and the chemist F. Wöhler (the discoverer of aluminium and the founder of modern organic chemistry).[14] These facts must be recorded to help us keep in mind that the most important and productive 25 years of Ritschl's life were spent within a great *scientific* university, where the fruitfulness and precision of scientific method were most highly regarded, and where the fashionable philosophies of evolutionary naturalism and materialism were not merely examined by scientists but fully discussed by workers in the humanities. These facts ought to remind us of the obligation not to do injustice to Ritschl (as it has so often been done in the past) by wrenching his work from that philosophical and scientific matrix which helped to determine it.

We have already alluded briefly to Ritschl's main life's work, *Die christliche Lehre von der Rechtfertigung u. Versöhnung*, published between 1870 and 1874. A brief word about his choice of title is appropriate. By naming his three-volumed systematic theology *The Christian Doctrine of Justification and Reconciliation* he intended to convey his conviction that there can be no material knowledge of God, of Christ, of redemption, of providence, of man's true nature and destiny, apart from the genuinely Christian experience within the justified community to which has been committed the tasks of reconciliation. There can, in short, be no such thing as a genuine or normative 'natural' theology. Moreover, by selecting the terms 'justification' and 'reconciliation' he intended to convey the Pauline, Lutheran and Calvinist orientation of his work. The first volume, devoted to the history of the doctrine from Anselm until the first half of the nineteenth century, was published in Bonn in 1870. (An English translation, made in the Manse of Kirkcaldy by a former pupil of Ritschl, appeared rather swiftly in Edinburgh in 1872.)[15] The second, devoted to Ritschl's researches into the biblical foundations of the doctrine, appeared in Bonn in 1874, and until the present day has not found an English translator. The third volume, by far, from the standpoint of systematic theology, the most important, appeared also in 1874, and was brought out in English in 1900.[16] In the same year there appeared also his *Die christliche Vollkommenheit*,[17] a little essay on the notion of Christian perfection.[18] In the following year his *Unterricht in der christlichen Religion* was brought out, a little compendium of his system which was in the first instance intended by him as an advanced *Gymnasium* textbook, but which later functioned in a more advanced manner, being used as a university set text and also as a succinct introduction to his system for more mature students. More than one distinguished Ritschlian had his interest in the master's system wakened by reading the text of the *Unterricht*.[19] It has long been recognized that Mrs Alice Swing's turn-of-the-century rendering of the title as *Instruction in the Christian Religion* rather fails to convey Ritschl's intended meaning, which was *Institutes of Christian Religion*, since he wished the reader to recognize that the little treatise stood in the same line of succession as Calvin's classic. (The German *Unterricht*, commonly and correctly translated as 'instruction', carries the connotation of instruction in the basics or fundamentals of a subject; hence 'fundamental principles' or 'institutes' would in no way violate the meaning of the German word.)

By 1875 the most important of Ritschl's works had been published, and it was during the period 1874–80, as Dr Garvie records, that he attracted to himself the first group of significant disciples, including Harnack, Herrmann and Adolf Schürer.[20] It has often been remarked of Ritschl that on the whole he did not attract disciples from his university students but by his writings which, because of their appeal (to be examined in a later chapter) to 'solid historical fact', and their remarkably systematic nature, exercised a considerable spell over his contemporaries. (A significant exception was Ernst Troeltsch, who was a pupil of both Ritschl and Lagarde at Göttingen.) It was during the same period that opposition to Ritschl, which had been growing in the Hanover-Braunschweig ecclesiastical district since not long after his translation to Göttingen, became not merely outspoken but even harsh and potentially violent. Conservative Lutherans objected to his attempts to mediate with modernity, confessional Lutherans objected vehemently to his advocacy of Lutheran-Reformed union on the Prussian model, pietists were stung into counter-attack by his excessively insensitive remarks about their religious experiences, and Lutherans of all shades of opinion were provoked into opposition by his assertion that 'the real meaning of the Reformation is more concealed than revealed in the writings of Luther and Melancthon', and his claim that the Reformation's authentic message was at long last being unfolded in his own writings. Further, certain academic critics vigorously counter-attacked his attempt to exclude all metaphysics from theology. It can hardly be denied though that Ritschl cannot be totally absolved from blame in the creation of the violent controversy which marred the closing decade or so of his life; he could frequently be singularly insensitive to the deeply-entertained convictions of others and simultaneously hyper-sensitive to criticism of his own positions, and it is hard to resist the conclusion that he exaggerated the odium which, he alleged, others directed against him.[21] Be that as it may, much 'Ritschlian' theology saw the light of day as a result of his disciples and sympathizers springing to his defence, making his real meaning clear, reinterpreting his words in order to strengthen his position, or, in certain cases, conceding that his critics had a point, leading to a modification or abandonment of his position.

Of the final decade of his life, only a few points need to be made. The main production of the 1880s was the massive *Geschichte des Pietismus*, of which the first volume was published in Bonn in 1880, the second in 1884 and the third in 1886. Between the publication of the first and second volumes Ritschl twice withdrew temporarily from his researches on pietism: first, as noted above, in order to compose the *Theologie u. Metaphysik* in 1881 (whose teaching will be examined in detail in the next chapter); second, in order to work on his festival address on the occasion

of the four-hundredth anniversary of Luther's birth, which he
delivered before the University of Göttingen in November 1883.[22]
The 1880s are also significant for the acquisition of two more
distinguished disciples, his successor at Göttingen Th. v. Haering
and Julius Kaftan of Berlin. He died in Göttingen on 20 March
1889, just before his 67th birthday – amongst those who cared
for him during his final illness was his son-in-law, Johannes Weiss,
at that time a *Privat-Dozent* in the Göttingen faculty. His
successor, Haering, continued a strongly 'Ritschlian' tradition in
the faculty until his transference to Tübingen in 1895.

It is now time to survey briefly two things, the development of
the Ritschlian school after Ritschl's death, and some of the main
literature that sprang up around his theology, in order that we
may fully understand not only the demise that befell it but also
the Ritschl Renaissance that has been a feature of recent theology.
Not much needs to be said of the first of these. We have already
noted the adherence of Harnack, Herrmann, Schürer, Kaftan
and Haering. For the others we may rely on Dr Orr, whose
factual scholarship on Ritschl is quite impeccable.[23] Orr's list
includes Schultz in Göttingen, Wendt in Jena, Lobstein in
Strassburg, Kattenbusch and Stade in Giessen, Bornemann in
Magdeburg, Loofs, Kähler and Reischle in Halle, Gottschick (a
colleague of Haering) in Tübingen, Troeltsch in Heidelberg, Sell
in Bonn. Orr further mentions the 'party' literary organs, the
Theologische Literaturzeitung, the *Zeitschrift für Theologie u.
Kirche*, and the semi-popular weekly *Die christliche Welt* (of
which the younger Karl Barth was an editorial employee in the
first decade of the present century). As early as 1879, Philip
Hefner reminds us, Ritschl had been able to write that '. . . his
dogmatic position was expounded by disciples on every theological faculty in western Germany except for Heidelberg'.[24]
Dr Orr, commenting on this not without disapproval, advises us
perhaps to discount as excessive the charges brought by Ritschl's
critic Nippold and others, that Ritschl had used unworthy
means to 'capture' the theological faculties for his disciples,
though his zeal in the promotion of their candidature is undeniable.[25] Now when one contemplates these facts (and keeps in
mind the tremendous American and European prestige not only

of Ritschl himself but of Herrmann, Harnack and Kaftan), it becomes very difficult to understand and quite impossible to accept the polemical judgement of Karl Barth (to be discussed below at a later stage) that 'Ritschl has the significance of an episode and not, indeed not, that of an epoch'.[26]

And our impression of Ritschl's very great significance for modern systematic theology may be strengthened if we turn to survey briefly a cross-section of the literature which his movement brought into being (with special reference, here, to books published in these islands and in the United States). In 1888, the year preceding Ritschl's death, there appeared L. Stählin's influential *Kant, Lotze und Ritschl*, translated into English the following year under the title *Kant, Lotze and Ritschl*. Here, significantly and archetypally, we have one of the first works trying to damn and stereotype Ritschl simply as a reductionistic neo-Kantian child of the Enlightenment, and, reading it, we are hard put to dissent from Dr Garvie's judgement, that the work, however acute it may sometimes be, is so disfigured by its violent polemical tone that it is an altogether untrustworthy guide to the study of its subject; even more telling is Garvie's conclusion that one cannot but regret that Ritschlianism should have had so unfriendly a herald in English theological literature.[27] In 1892, Ritschl's son-in-law, Johannes Weiss, brought out his *Die Predigt Jesu vom Reich Gottes*, in which he examined and criticized his father-in-law's fundamental conception of the Kingdom of God (to be examined below in Chapter VII).[28] In 1894 there appeared in English the Ritschlian Kaftan's *The Truth of the Christian Religion* (with a very cautious prefatory note by Professor Flint of Edinburgh), followed in 1895 by Herrmann's *The Communion of the Christian with God*.[29] But in 1894 there had already appeared one of the first 'evangelical' Scottish works to deal with Ritschl, Dr James Denney's *Studies in Theology* (a set of lectures delivered in Chicago Theological Seminary),[30] which were uncompromisingly hostile in tone and content to the German theologian and his disciples. Holding up Ritschl's views (frequently out of context) to comparison with what Denney described as 'the older evangelical faith of the Church', Denney castigated him with great severity. An example of Denney's excessive language is found in his discussion of Ritschl's treatment of the biblical miracle narratives, which he accuses of being brusque, peremptory and possibly insolent![31] No wonder that the eminently fair and reasonable Dr Garvie refused in his study to follow any of the lines taken by Denney on the grounds that the latter's criticisms in *Studies in Theology* are unduly severe. In 1896 there appeared in Germany Herrmann's *Der evangelische Glaube u. die Theologie Albrecht Ritschls*,[32] followed in 1897 in Scotland by Dr Orr's influential *The Ritschlian Theology and the Evangelical Faith*,[33] (Orr had already dealt perfunctorily with Ritschl in his Kerr Lectures, *The Christian View of God and the World*). Of Orr's book two comments must be made: on the one hand, one cannot but admire the fine scholarship, the wide and deep reading of the German literature, the impeccable loyalty to fact, and the evident desire to be fair; on the other hand, the title of the work and the tone of the concluding chapter convinces that, in a much less severe and belligerent way than that of Dr Denney, Orr's initial purpose was also to exhibit the alarming discrepancy between Ritschl's work and 'the older evangelical faith of the Church'. In 1899, the 29-year-old H. R. Mackintosh published a widely-read paper in *The American Journal of Theology*, 'The Philosophical Presuppositions of Ritschlianism',[34] in which he took the unfortunate Ritschl to task in a polemical, even unscholarly way. In discussing Ritschl's account of the origin of religion as related to man's experience of *pleasure* and *pain*, Mackintosh quite fantastically accuses Ritschl of Hedonism, ignoring the Lotzean connotation which he had given to the words! It is hard adequately to account for this widespread anti-Ritschl hostility of the 1890s, but the truth is that probably too many here were introduced to Ritschl by the very hostile accounts of his work given not only by Stählin and Denney, but also by Otto Pfleiderer in his immensely influential *The Development of Theology in Germany Since Kant*, published here in the year after Ritschl's death.[35]

In 1899 the balance began to be redressed by the publication of the eminently fair, just, judicious and scholarly work by Dr Garvie, *The Ritschlian Theology*, who consciously and deliberately tried to get Rischl a fair hearing, rebuking the excesses and the injudiciousness of Dr Denney, Dr Orr and Dr Pfleiderer. As noted earlier, Ritschl-interpretation in English-speaking circles was much assisted by the Mackintosh-Macaulay translation of the third volume of *Justification and Reconciliation* in 1900. If we now cross swiftly to the United States, we find a very different state of affairs, where, after the turn of the century, a deliberate attempt was made to redress the balance and to do something more like justice to Ritschl. Thus, in 1901, Professor Albert T. Swing brought out his *The Theology of Albrecht Ritschl* which incorporated, as noted earlier, the first English rendering of Ritschl's *Unterricht* by Swing's wife.[36] Not only did Swing sternly rebuke Ritschl's British critics (including the scholarly Dr Orr) for their injustices, but rightly protested at the mindless caricature of Ritschl as a 'neo-Kantian' reductionist which, in his view, overlaid and obscured the more authentic picture of Ritschl as *the* pivotal German theologian, wrestling with the message of the New Testament and that of the Reformation, against the background of nineteenth-century thought-forms. After the turn of the century, one centre of Ritschl scholarship was Union Theological Seminary in New York City, where two redoubtable adherents of Ritschl strove valiantly for the cause, Professors A. C. McGiffert and William Adams Brown. In the latter's *The Essence of Christianity*,[37] an enthusiastic and valiant attempt is made to interpret Ritschl against the wider background of post-Reformation German theology, and the narrower background of nineteenth-century science and philosophy. Another staunch defender of Ritschl's system in America was Dr H. C. King, a former graduate-student of the Ritschlians in German universities, who was first a professor in and later President of Oberlin College, Ohio. Not many would quarrel with the widely-accepted generalization that Ritschlianism, because of the pragmatic involvement of Christianity in American social and political life, had a wider and deeper appeal in North America than in Europe, and, indeed, the demise of Ritschlian theology was far more complete in Europe than it ever was on the other side of the Atlantic. As late as 1963, the late President Henry Pitney van Dusen of Union Theological Seminary, one of the last of the so-called American 'Ritschlians', published his *The Vindication of Liberal Theology*,[38] in which he made an impassioned but still scholarly plea for a balanced post-Barthian assessment of that nineteenth-century German systematic theology of which

Ritschl's was so significant a constituent.

Brief mention might finally be made of two further works. First, in 1909, John Kenneth Mozley, a Fellow of Pembroke College, Cambridge, brought out his *Ritschlianism: An Essay*,[39] in which he pleaded with his fellow-Anglicans for a fair hearing for Ritschl and his colleagues. From today's standpoint, one cannot but be slightly amused by the way in which Mozley reiterated his apology for the fact that in the main Ritschl and his sympathizers were Germans![40] And just before the outbreak of the First World War a maturer H. R. Mackintosh published his paper, 'The Development of the Ritschlian School',[41] in which Mackintosh more than bent over backwards towards the Ritschlians in order to compensate for his rather uninstructed hostility of 1899. According to Gerhard Ruhbach's bibliography of works by and on Ritschl up until 1965,[42] nothing at all of note was published in the difficult circumstances of the First World War. This brings us to the post-war years after 1919, a very changed theological climate, and the beginnings of the *demise*.

When we speak of the *demise*, as we must, of Ritschl's theology, there are not many in theological circles who would confess complete ignorance of it and its causes. But some of the causes put forward are very superficial. There is, for example, the alleged *unreadability* of Ritschl's writings.[43] His writings, it is alleged, are heavy, ponderous and circuitous; his magnetic attraction to polemic prevented him from sustaining a continuous argument for more than a few consecutive pages. There is confessedly much truth in this, but it does little to explain the awful and sudden *demise* which occurred just before and after 1925. Much nearer to the truth are those who point to the abrupt change in theological fashion which occurred after 1920, when so-called liberal Protestantism gave way quite quickly to Barthian neo-orthodoxy. For so-called Barthian theology cannot be understood at all unless it is seen, *partly at any rate*, as the deliberate, patient and eventually monumental attempt to terminate and reverse that thrust of nineteenth-century German theology which began with Schleiermacher and ended with Ritschl and school. From the publication of his 1919 *Römerbrief* onwards, therefore, Barth could accurately and almost literally describe his theological enterprise as 'Against the Stream'. For Barthian neo-orthodoxy to prevail, the century which ended with Ritschl had to go! But there is more to it than that.

In order to understand the allegedly complete *demise* which overtook Ritschl after 1925 and the awful oblivion to which he was thereafter consigned, one is forced, however reluctantly, to invoke an explanation in terms of *some mysterious, but very potent, quasi-personal dislike entertained by Barth for Ritschl and all that he (allegedly) stood for.* This is a melancholy business of which one hesitates to speak, but some account of it must be attempted.[44] It is likely that Barth's antipathy became concentrated in the following manner. In 1921, the 35-year-old Barth, then the pastor of Safenwil in Switzerland, and the much-discussed author of the explosive *Römerbrief* of two years previously, was called to Göttingen as the occupant of the new (and first) Chair of Reformed Dogmatics in that hitherto staunchly Lutheran city. It must be conceded that the circumstances surrounding the establishment and filling of the new chair were, to say the least, fraught with unforeseen frictional elements! Göttingen had long been the cultural and academic centre of the solidly *Lutheran* Lower Saxony, and the chair had been offered to the province by the Reformed Church Alliance, which was in this instance being financed by funds contributed by American Presbyterians. The appropriate ministry had indeed consulted the Göttingen theological faculty, which had agreed to the establishment of the chair at Göttingen, but only on formal conditions whose actual operation turned out to be impossibly irritating for its first incumbent. For example, in the published faculty lists Barth was deliberately included in the section of *Honorarprofessoren* (honorary professors). For the first three years of his incumbency (1921–24) the faculty appended to his name the qualifying description *ausserhalb der Fakultät* (outside the faculty). So that his position was highly anomalous from the first day of his occupancy of his new post.[45] Moreover, from the beginning of his first semester he was involved in a running dispute with the faculty over how his lectures were to be announced in the twice-yearly university *Vorlesungsverzeichnis* (lecture-timetable). The faculty insisted that each announcement under Barth's name *must* be qualified by the adjective *Reformed* (i.e. in contrast to the Lutheran confessional stance of all other faculty members).

Barth's not unreasonable reply to this was that it in effect, in an undesirable and odious confessional manner, *warned off* from his lectures Lutheran students prosecuting their studies in preparation for the ministry of one of the Lutheran *Landeskirchen*! Whether or no this was the faculty's intention, a frustrated Barth resolved to take legal action with the ministry in Berlin in order to have this insistence of the faculty overruled, and also to rid himself, if possible, of the misleading title *Honorarprofessor*. After three difficult and quarrelsome years, in 1924, he failed in his first object but succeeded in his second (although it was resolved to remove the qualifying pejorative description *ausserhalb der Fakultät*). (After all, it was argued, a professor paid exclusively by an extra-mural agency is from the university's point of view an *Honorarprofessor*!)[46] But by the time these vexatious legal proceedings were over in Berlin, a disillusioned and chastened Barth was seeking a move from what appeared to him as a wretched university, which he obtained the next year on his appointment as an *ordentlicher Professor* at Münster.

Apart from these very real legal and administrative difficulties, there were other more intellectual and theological frictions which were probably in the long run more damaging for Barth's relationships with the German orthodoxy of the day. On his arrival in Göttingen in 1921, he found amongst his colleagues three formidable representatives of the high Lutheran-Ritschlian orthodoxy – Carl Stange, Georg Wobbermin, and his own near-contemporary Emanuel Hirsch. The first two of these were much senior to the young and inexperienced Barth, Wobbermin being 52 years old and Stange 51. There can be no doubt that the relations between Barth and Stange swiftly became quite odious, and that Barth's antipathy was soon, and cumulatively, extended to that theologian regarded by Stange as Göttingen's shining light – Ritschl himself, at this time dead for a mere 30 years. It was Stange (always described by Barth as 'Ritschl's third successor'!) who in 1922 on behalf of the university organized and acted as host for the anniversary of Ritschl's birth, an occasion attended not merely by distinguished academic disciples of Ritschl, but by members of the not undistinguished Ritschl family (a celebration about which Barth wrote scathingly to Thurneysen on 9 May),[47] a year which also saw the publication of Stange's own book expressing gratitude to the Göttingen master, *Albrecht Ritschl*,[48] as well as Harnack's appreciative monograph, *Albrecht Ritschl 1846–64*.[49] Clearly, Barth was enraged by all of this, when one recalls that what had occasioned his own final break with the century ending with Ritschl was the signing, by several members of the Ritschlian school, of the notorious public manifesto of 1914, expressing approval of and even enthusiasm for the war policies of Wilhelm II. It could only be *rage* – or, as described above, a quasi-personal dislike – which gave expression to one rather tasteless and unpleasant paragraph about the dead Ritschl in a circular letter from Barth in Göttingen, dated 26 March 1922: 'To be a proper professor of theology one must be a sturdy, tough, insensitive lump who notices absolutely nothing, much like the blessed Ritschl at whose grave we celebrated yesterday the centennial of his birth, standing there in top hats to dedicate a wreath to him "the founder of the fame of our Göttingen theological faculty". I reread some chapters in his biography in the afternoon, shuddering as I did so. Or will I perhaps in time myself become such a blockhead?'[50] Not, we must hasten to notice, that all the unpleasantness was on the side of the younger Barth! How he must have been stung by Stange's notorious taunt, echoing a charge made by Harnack, and recalling Barth's pre-war period of employment with *Die Christliche Welt*, that he (Barth) was but a theological *Zeitungs-schreiber* (journalist), and that his work, in the light of the rather rollicking, rumbustious language of the first edition of the *Römerbrief*, was essentially *unwissenschaftlich* (unscientific)! For had not, was Stange's insinuation, the great Ritschl valued in theology above all else 'scientific precision'?

Doubtless the final truth in these unhappy matters is now concealed from us. But, and this is our principal concern here, for whatever reason, thereafter the writings of Barth are marked by *an uncompromising hostility towards and harsh criticism of Ritschl, his achievement, and all that these are held to stand for*. In order to be convinced of this, one must only work through the indices of a few volumes of Barth's *Church Dogmatics*. It is anything but a historical accident that Ritschl's disappearance into near-oblivion coincides with the heyday of Barthian orthodoxy, around 1935. Ruhbach's bibliography lists only two works in Europe from 1935 until 1950, the Swede Gösta Hök's book,[51] and Barth's own hostile, not to say contemptuous eight-page dismissal in his *Die Protestantische Theologie im 19ten Jahrhundert*, published in 1947.[52] Barth's hostility never really waned as he mellowed; in the late 1950s, he contributed a monograph to the demythologizing controversy, in which he attacked Bultmann by suggesting that behind Bultmann stands Herrmann, and behind Herrmann 'Ritschl, dry-as-dust'![53] Mention has just been made, and by no means for the last time here, of Barth's classic history of nineteenth-century Protestant theology. The book was in the post-war period significantly influential on both sides of the Atlantic. The present author can recall, as a student of Barth, the conditions prevailing in the theological faculty at Basel around 1955–6. Many students were baffled by Barth's many detailed references, in his dogmatic lectures, to the classic theologians of the nineteenth-century German tradition; consequently, most of them tried to remedy the situation by obtaining a copy of Barth's book. The disturbing consequence was that far too many of them *began* to study the nineteenth century from the pages of Barth, even though many were disturbed by a cruel joke invented, as it was believed, by an opponent in the theological faculty – that to study Ritschl and his disciples by reading Barth was not entirely unlike studying Judaism by reading *Mein Kampf*! On one occasion, after a seminar on Schleiermacher's shorter writings, an argument broke out about Ritschl's class as a theologian in comparison to Schleiermacher's. In response to a suggestion that compared to the first-class Schleiermacher Ritschl might be graded as second or even third class, Barth's grimly humorous contribution was that this was hardly possible, since Ritschl was in his judgement not a theologian at all!

But such attitudes and assessments were bound to pass, and pass they did with the post-war decline in enthusiasm for Barthian theology and the emergence of new theological emphases, paramount amongst which was Bultmann's stress on anthropological theology, which helped to generate the suspicion that just as Barthian orthodoxy had been found dissatisfying theologically, so consequently historical studies prosecuted under the aegis of Barth's viewpoint might have to be re-assessed with critical eyes. Possibly, one of the earliest references in the post-war period to the term 'Ritschl Renaissance' is to be found in the introduction to the re-issue of Ritschl's *Unterricht* by Gerhard Ruhbach in 1966.[54] Ruhbach connects this Renaissance with 'a thorough-going reconsideration of the nineteenth century' (*im Zusammenhang einer Weitgehenden Rückbesinnung auf das 19. Jahrhundert*), which had been going on since after World War II. Ruhbach was, of course writing of Germany where indeed from the early 1950s re-examinations and re-evaluations of Ritschl's thought had begun to appear as items interconnected within a more general reconsideration *of nineteenth-century German theology as a whole.*[55] We have already noted above the successful scholarly attempt to rehabilitate the reputation of F. C. Baur, and in this connection it is interesting to note the attempts being made within German universities to re-examine the texts of Hegel with a view to ascertaining their 'original' meaning, which involve, significantly for our study of Ritschl here, setting aside the meaning they have come to have for us through the interposition of the views of Hegel's subsequent disciples, interpreters and detractors, a scholarly process which has been found unavoidable for workers within the contemporary renaissance of nineteenth-century studies as a whole.

But the same happy state of affairs did not obtain in the post-war period within English-speaking circles. Writing, around 1964, a work on the thought of Schleiermacher,[56] Richard R. Niebuhr was still compelled to bewail the grip of Barth upon nineteenth-century studies. Niebuhr rightly and generously concedes that students of nineteenth-century theology do owe gratitude to Barth in the case of Schleiermacher: Barth's 1947 book on the century, Niebuhr wrote, has done much to stimulate reading on the original materials, more than has any other secondary source, and Barth's work served to intrigue many readers with the period. And through his work on Schleiermacher, 'Barth enjoys the larger part of the credit . . . for having kept Schleiermacher in the eye of the public'. (It goes without saying that in the case of Ritschl he has done exactly the opposite.) Nevertheless, Niebuhr goes on to complain of the dominance that Barth's interpretation of the history of theology has exercised and still exerts today. He complains further that 'a Barthian captivity of the history of modern Christian thought' reigns in theology outside ultra-orthodox theological circles. Having indicated how this captivity manifests itself, Niebuhr puts forward the following (now fulfilled) prophecy: 'I suspect the time to be not far away, when the Barthian reading of the history of Christian thought will be corrected in a fashion comparable to that in which the last generation veered away from the theological presuppositions of Adolf von Harnack's history of dogma.'

The truth of Niebuhr's prediction is demonstrated by, among other things, the appearance in English of works devoted to the re-assessment of Ritschl's thought in the contemporary situation. In 1966 there appeared Philip Hefner's *Faith and the Vitalities of History: A Theological Study Based on the Work of Albrecht Ritschl.*[57] In 1969 there appeared David L. Mueller's *An Introduction to the Theology of Albrecht Ritschl.*[58] Students interested in the Ritschl Renaissance were greatly assisted by the translation of Ritschl's '*Prolegomena*' *to the History of Pietism*, his *Theology and Metaphysics*, and his *Instruction in the Christian Religion* by Philip Hefner in his *Albrecht Ritschl: Three Essays* (1972). And in 1974 David W. Lotz's *Ritschl and Luther: A Fresh Perspective on Albrecht Ritschl's Theology in the Light of His Luther Study* was brought out. Moreover, the bibliographies of these books demonstrate incontrovertibly the quite tremendous resurgence of interest in Ritschl which has occurred in the last couple of decades. And amongst nineteenth-century classics which have reappeared in recent years which presuppose a sound grasp of Ritschl are Herrmann's *The Communion of the Christian With God* and Johannes Weiss's *Jesus' Proclamation of the Kingdom of God.*

Finally, we must note briefly certain of the common characteristics of the work that has gone into the Ritschl Renaissance. First, and very predictably, the attempt is made to throw off neo-orthodox preconceptions and prejudices, and to persuade others of their fundamental inadequacy. Mueller, for example, makes the quite crucial point (to be examined in great detail in our concluding chapter) that the Barthian attack upon Ritschl conveniently ignores the thesis that there may well be more continuity between the thought of Ritschl and that of Barth than the latter knew or cared to admit.[59] Hefner deplores the ruthless and even condescending remarks of Karl Barth.[60] Elsewhere, Hefner remarks, ironically and paradoxically, that whereas post-1920 dialectical theology branded Ritschl as an arch-heretic it nevertheless used the framework of Ritschl's theology for the incorporation of its own ideas.[61] David Lotz also deplores the overtly hostile attitude of Barth to Ritschl, and the harsh, cursory treatment meted out to him by Barth in his nineteenth-century history book.[62] In Lotz's view, Ritschl and his nineteenth-century colleagues grappled with certain inescapable issues which are still very much with us (the relation of Christ to culture, faith to history, and Christianity to the world religions), perennially pressing issues which, he notes, were conveniently ignored by that neo-orthodoxy which is now appropriately accused, by Jürgen Moltmann and others, of acosmic and ahistorical tendencies.[63] Lotz announces therefore his programmatic intention to disengage himself from the still widespread neo-orthodox critique and to return to the 'original' Ritschl.

Second, a determined attempt is made to throw off the restricting and disfiguring shackles of conventional, glib, hastily-applied and distorting *stereotypes*. But Ritschl is by no means the only nineteenth-century theologian who has been relegated to undeserved obscurity by means of crude stereotypes. R. R. Niebuhr in a penetrating analysis shows clearly how the great Schleiermacher has suffered terribly from the same kind of thing. Schleiermacher was 'the theologian of Romanticism', and as the term is now one of reprobation, Schleiermacher has suffered accordingly; after all, were the German Romantics not partially responsible for the Third Reich? Schleiermacher believed in a positive link between Christianity and contemporary culture, and during the Prussian struggle against Napoleon became a German nationalist of sorts: *ergo*, did he not produce a 'culturally conditioned Protestantism' and the German *Volkgeist*? Again, did not Schleiermacher dally with philosophical idealism, which has become the scapegoat for so many European misfortunes in the modern world? Those who are interested in the destructive power of conventional stereotypes, as we must be here, could do worse than read Niebuhr's analysis.[64] That Ritschl's reputation has suffered disgracefully from this kind of thing lies beyond all doubt. Hefner complains bitterly that modern 'scholarship' has emphasized Ritschl as a Kantian, a Lotzean, a defender of value-judgements in theology, an ethical interpreter of Christianity, to the detriment of Ritschl as 'a theologian of the Christian tradition'.[65] By far the most vehement protest against distorting stereotypes has come from David Lotz, who deplores, for example, the distortingly onesided picture of Ritschl as 'the great betrayer of Protestantism to Enlightenment rationalism', the heuristic labels 'neo-Kantian' and 'Ritschl and Idealism'. In place of these rather derogatory and threadbare labels, Lotz pleads for broader and heuristically more illuminating themes such as 'Ritschl and Luther' or 'Ritschl and the Reformation'.[66] And in one important section of his book, David Mueller re-opens the question of the *key* (once held universally but glibly to be the epistemology of value-judgements) to Ritschl-interpretation: is it, he asks, epistemology, Redemption and/or the Kingdom of God, Anthropological (i.e. Existential) Theology, the doctrine of God, Christology, or the teleological notion of Christian perfection?[67]

Third, answers must be furnished to questions quite reasonably put about the nature of the Ritschl Renaissance. Even if there is such a contemporary Renaissance, it might be asked, does it matter? Does it really have anything to do with more recent and contemporary theology? What is the point of it all – to turn us into neo-Ritschlians, or whatever? These are reasonable questions that must be answered. One type of answer that might reasonably be given is that defended by Lotz, who demonstrates that those questions with which Ritschl's century grappled are still very much with us (now that their peremptory dismissal by Barthian theology has been overcome). But I think that the most promising answers are rooted in the notion of Ritschl as a 'bridge-figure'. If it is true that the theology of today and the theological interpretation of today's extremely complex situation can only be understood in the light of those factors which have helped to produce them, then to ignore the central figure of a 45-year period (1875–1920) since the European Enlightenment is intellectually suicidal. Professor Claude Welch has recently argued that it is at least a defensible thesis that the theological situation of the twentieth century is peculiarly dependent on the development of the nineteenth century. Welch continues, 'not only do the same problems continue to bedevil and to fascinate, but the shapes which those questions still bear are essentially derivative from the forms they were given in the nineteenth century'. His conclusion is as follows: 'This is one of the reasons why in the present generation we see an impressive renewal of study of nineteenth-century theology, not only of the few giants whose names have always been familiar, *though whose work may actually have been as much hidden as disclosed by well worn clichés*, but also of many other thinkers whose significance has been less well attended to.'[68] To put all of this slightly differently, the attempt will be made here to show that in the period from the Enlightenment (say, from 1780 until 1970) there is much more direct and unbroken *continuity* and development than has hitherto been supposed – very much more, indeed, than we have been informed by those historical studies composed from the standpoint of the Barthian school. Accordingly, the attempt will be made to show that (at least) two major movements in twentieth-century systematic theology must remain partly unintelligible unless read in the light of the thought of Ritschl. The first of these is *Barthianism*, however shocking and unthinkable that may now seem to some! The Barthian claim that Barth's 'new beginning' in theology involved a massive abandonment and reversal of central theological trends from Schleiermacher to Ritschl will, hopefully, be shown to be not merely false, but intellectually arrogant. Rather, the thesis will be defended that Barth and his colleagues stood more on the shoulders of Ritschl than they knew or admitted, that we can now see clearly (when the dust of the battles of the 1920s, 1930s and 1940s has cleared away) that there are more significant *overlaps* between Ritschlianism and Barthianism than has hitherto been recognized. The second movement is theological *existentialism* (especially but not exclusively in its Bultmannian form). The thesis will be defended that the conventional interpretation of theological existentialism as having been largely or wholly informed by thinkers such as Kierkegaard or Heidegger is intolerably onesided, and quite overlooks the important impulses received by Bultmann and his theological sympathizers from their having been nurtured, like Barth, in *Ritschlian* theological schools early in this century. If so, it is plausibly arguable that the so-called *demise* of Ritschlian theological thinking was nothing like so complete as we have been taught to believe; that in the abandonment of Barth by Bultmann in the late 1920s we have the beginnings of a certain kind of 'underground Ritschlianism', informed indeed by Kierkegaard-Heidegger, and in new, if rather misleading, terminology; that the strong objections entertained by Barth against Bultmann are rooted mainly, if not wholly, in the not unjustified suspicions of Barth that Bultmann's new theological programme of the 1930s and 1940s represents some kind of refurbishing of that Ritschlian style of systematic theology which Barth had tried (unsuccessfully, as it now appears!) to overthrow after 1920. But such hypotheses can only be considered after we have learned a little of the *content* of Ritschl's theology. To that we now turn.

NOTES TO CHAPTER I

1 See Karl Löwith, *From Hegel to Nietzsche*, London 1964.
2 Ritschl, *Theology and Metaphysics*, in *Albrecht Ritschl: Three Essays*, translated and with an introduction by Philip Hefner, Philadelphia 1972, p. 165; hereafter referred to as *Three Essays*.
3 J. B. Bury, *A History of Freedom of Thought*, 2nd ed., London 1952, p. 158. For nineteenth-century positivistic and naturalistic interpretaions see Robert Flint, *Anti-Theistic Theories*, Edinburgh 1879, chs. IV and V, and F. Copleston, SJ, *A History of Philosophy*, vol. vii, London 1963, ch. XVIII.
4 See, for example, Paul Tillich, *Perspectives on 19th and 20th century Protestant Theology*, London 1967, ch. V, D, 'The "Back to Kant" Movement', pp. 215 f.; Otto W. Heick, *A History of Christian Thought*, vol. ii, Philadelphia 1966, ch. VI, 'Neo-Kantian and Ritschlian Theology', pp. 234–45; Karl Barth, *Protestant Theology in the Nineteenth Century*, London 1972, ch. 29, 'Ritschl', pp. 654–61.
5 See below, pp. 23–4 and 46–8.
6 See Haering's interesting and informative paper, 'In welchen Sinn dürfen wir uns immer noch "Göttinger" heissen? Albrecht Ritschls Bedeutung für die Gegenwart', in *Zeitschrift für Theologie und Kirche*, Heft 20, 1910.
7 See Wilhelm Ebel, *Catalogus Professorum Gottingensium, 1734–1962*, Göttingen 1962: for the remainder of the chapter I am immensely indebted to Professor Ebel's work. In what follows, I am equally indebted to Johannes Meyer, *Geschichte der Göttinger theologischen Fakultät 1737–1937*, in *Zeitschrift der Gesellschaft für niedersächsische Kirchengeschichte*, 42 (1937), pp. 7–107.
8 For Ritschl's relations with Lagarde, see Robert W. Lougee, *Paul de*

Lagarde 1827–1891: A Study of Radical Conservatism in Germany, Cambridge, Mass. 1962, ch. III, 'The Göttingen Period', pp. 88 f.; also pp. 161, 223.

9 In the English translation of 1872, this is to be found in ch. VIII, pp. 387–439.

10 C. W. Valentine, *The Philosophy of Lotze in its Theological Aspects*, Glasgow 1911, p. 41.

11 *Albrecht Ritschls Leben*, vol. ii, 1864–89, Freiburg 1896.

12 *Die philosophischen Wurzeln der Theologie Albrecht Ritschls: Beitrag zum Problem des Verhältnisses von Theologie u. Philosophie im 19ten. Jahrhundert*, Berlin 1964.

13 See Ebel, op. cit.

14 For information on the nineteenth-century university of Göttingen I am deeply grateful for a private discussion with Professor Dr Wilhelm Grunwald, Director of the Lower Saxony State and University Library in Göttingen; Dr Grunwald is an honorary Professor of the History of the Exact Sciences in the Mathematics and Natural Sciences Faculty at Göttingen. Cf. again Ebel, op. cit.

15 *A Critical History of the Christian Doctrine of Justification and Reconciliation*, translated by John S. Black, Edinburgh 1872. To date this has never been republished and is quite rare.

16 *The Christian Doctrine of Justification and Reconciliation: the Positive Development of the Doctrine*, translated from the third German edition by H. R. Mackintosh and A. B. Macaulay, Edinburgh 1900.

17 Göttingen 1874.

18 For an English discussion see R. Newton Flew's *The Idea of Perfection in Christian Theology*, Oxford 1934, pp. 374–93.

19 Bonn 1875. First translated by Alice Mead Swing and published as an appendix to Albert T. Swing, *The Theology of Albrecht Ritschl*, New York 1901. A revised version of the Swing translation has recently appeared in Hefner's *Three Essays*, pp. 219–91. A new edition of the text of the first German edition has recently appeared in the series *Texte zur Kirchen- u. Theologiegeschichte*, edited by Gerhard Ruhbach, Gütersloh 1966.

20 A. E. Garvie, *The Ritschlian Theology*, Edinburgh 1899, pp. 386 f.

21 See the preface of the second edition of *Justification and Reconciliation* III, where Ritschl, writing in 1883, tells us that 'for the past two years the question has been raised of using force against me'!

22 The first English translation of this has appeared recently. Executed by David W. Lotz, it is included as an appendix of Lotz's important *Ritschl and Luther*, Nashville, Tenn. 1974, pp. 187–202.

23 James Orr, *The Ritschlian Theology and the Evangelical Faith*, London 1897, pp. 27–8.

24 Hefner, in his introduction to *Three Essays*, p. 15.

25 Orr, ibid.; see Otto Ritschl, *Albrecht Ritschls Leben*, ii, pp. 303 and 331.

26 *Protestant Theology in the Nineteenth Century*, p. 654.

27 Garvie, op. cit., p. 26.

28 The first Göttingen edition has recently (1971) been translated and published with introduction and notes by SCM in London and Fortress Press in Philadelphia, as *Jesus' Proclamation of the Kingdom of God*.

29 Kaftan's work was published in Edinburgh in 1894; Herrmann's book

has recently (1972) been re-issued by SCM and Fortress Press, edited and introduced by Robert T. Voelkel, *The Communion of the Christian With God.*

30 London 1894.

31 *Studies in Theology*, p. 11.

32 Marburg 1896.

33 London 1897.

34 Republished in Mackintosh's *Some Aspects of Christian Belief*, London 1923. In the republished paper, Mackintosh nervously explains that he has changed his mind about Ritschl, and that 'the perspective of the subject as a whole has changed', op. cit., p. 121.

35 London 1890; for Ritschl, see pp. 183–95.

36 New York 1901.

37 Edinburgh 1904; for Ritschl and school, see ch. VII, pp. 223–87

38 New York 1963.

39 London 1909.

40 Mozley, *Ritschlianism*, pp. viii and 5 f.

41 *London Quarterly Review*, January 1914; republished in his *Some Aspects of Christian Belief*, pp. 156–76.

42 Printed in Ruhbach's recent edition of Ritschl's *Unterricht*, pp. 7–9.

43 Several years ago, I contemplated the notion of producing a *Ritschl Reader*; the comment on this by a colleague was that this title would be a contradiction in terms!

44 For what follows I am greatly indebted to the work *Revolutionary Theology in the Making: Barth–Thurneysen Correspondence, 1914–25*, translated by James D. Smart, London 1964.

45 See the theological faculty section of Ebel, op. cit., p. 39; for Barth's own complaints about the situation, see *Revolutionary Theology*, pp. 162 f., 166–7, 175, 177, 182.

46 op. cit., p. 177.

47 ibid., p. 100.

48 Leipzig 1922.

49 Bonn 1922.

50 *Revolutionary Theology*, pp. 92–3.

51 *Die elliptische Theologie Albrecht Ritschls*, Uppsala/Leipzig 1942.

52 Zürich 1947.

53 From 'Rudolf Bultmann – An Attempt to Understand him', *Kerygma and Myth*, II, edited by H.-W. Bartsch, translated by R. H. Fuller, London 1962, p. 123.

54 *Unterricht*, p. 6.

55 See Ruhbach's chronological bibliography in the *Unterricht*, p. 8: significant from this list are P. Wrzecionko, *Der Einfluss der Philosophie Kants auf die Theologie Albrecht Ritschls*, D. Theol. dissertation, Münster 1953; pp. 557–9 of vol. 5 of E. Hirsch's *Geschichte der neueren evangelischen Theologie*, Gütersloh 1954; Walter Klaas, *Ritschls 'Unterricht in der christlichen Religion' und Karl Barths Abrisse der Dogmatik*, in *Antwort: Festschrift für Karl Barth*, Zürich 1956, pp. 388–98; Christian Walther, *Der Reich-Gottes-Begriff in der Theologie Richard Rothes u. Albrecht Ritschls*, *Kerygma u. Dogma*, 2, Göttingen 1956, pp. 115–38; Paul Wrzecionko's *Die philosophischen Wurzeln* . . . (see above, n. 12); Ernst Haenchen, *Albrecht Ritschl als Systematiker*, in

Gott u. Mensch, Tübingen 1965, pp. 409–75.
56 *Schleiermacher on Christ and Religion*, London 1965, pp. 10 f.
57 New York 1966.
58 Philadelphia 1969.
59 *An Introduction to the Theology of Albrecht Ritschl*, 'The Neo-Orthodox Critique of Ritschl', pp. 145–9.
60 *Faith and the Vitalities of History*, p. 4.
61 Introduction to *Three Essays*, p. 40.
62 *Ritschl and Luther*, pp. 15–16.
63 ibid., p. 15.
64 *Schleiermacher on Christ and Religion*, pp. 12 f.
65 *Faith and the Vitalities of History*, pp. 108–9.
66 *Ritschl and Luther*, pp. 151–3; amongst those taken to task by Lotz is myself, because of certain remarks about Ritschl in my *Faith and Philosophy* (1966), pp. 84 f. In a recent correspondence with Lotz, a former colleague, I was glad to acknowledge that 'were I writing about Ritschl today (1974) I could not write of him in the same way (i.e. so harshly) as I did in 1965'.
67 *An Introduction to the Theology of Albrecht Ritschl*, pp. 151–9.
68 *Protestant Theology in the Nineteenth Century*, vol. i, 1799–1870, New Haven, Conn. 1972, pp. 1 f., italics mine.

CHAPTER II

Religious Epistemology

By commencing a modern appraisal of Ritschl's theology with a treatment of his epistemology we might, it could be argued by those involved in the Renaissance, be perpetrating that injustice to which he was subjected from very early days; namely, encouraging the labelling of him as a 'neo-Kantian' or 'Lotzean' epistemologist who was interested only or mainly in 'value-judgements in theology'. It must be conceded right away that this danger is a real one that must ever be kept in mind. On the other hand, it can hardly be denied that there are certain kinds of epistemological factors of a regulative kind operative in Ritschl's theology which it would be disastrous to ignore. But it should not be beyond the wit of man to reconsider, in the light of the latest researches on his work, the nature of these factors, with a view to ascertaining the proper place and scope of his epistemology, at the same time avoiding the notorious danger of labelling and stereotyping in a destructive way. In point of fact the anxiety expressed in the Renaissance that Ritschl be not stereotyped in this way has quite a long history. When, in 1909, J. K. Mozley pleaded for a balanced interpretation of Ritschl's system, he quoted the opinions of Pfleiderer and Garvie that Ritschl did not make his theory of cognition the basis of his theology from the first, but propounded it afterwards in its defence. In so doing, he was forced by hostile critics to reply to them 'on ground that was not his own and with weapons in whose use he was not skilled'.[1] This is perfectly true. As mentioned earlier, the only work composed by Ritschl on epistemology (his *Theology and Metaphysics*) was hastily written in 1881, eight years before his death, in response to criticism of his system published by Professors Luthardt and Frank. In so doing, he reviewed his system from its end back to its beginning, so to speak, extrapolating from it those epistemological factors which he judged had been functioning within it. (This goes a long way to explain the alleged confusion and incompleteness of the little treatise – as Ritschl's thought developed, he changed his mind about cognitive issues, and so we can never be quite sure when he is appealing to Kant, or Lotze, or Luther, on nineteenth-century positivism.) This ought to be enough in itself to help us avoid the caricature of Ritschl as some technically sophisticated epistemological theoretician, constructing a rigid and reductionistic theory of knowledge, which he then grimly, not to say aggressively, applied to the theological data. Another insight of the Ritschl Renaissance is that Ritschl, like his master Luther before him, had as his dominating motive *the practical, everyday, mundane, life of the Christian in Church and world*, and that all *apparent* conceptual, logical and epistemological interests were well and truly subordinated to and utilized by this. But this, too, was well recognized long before the twentieth-century onslaught on Ritschl was commenced several generations ago. It was also Mozley who, in discussing Ritschl's alleged 'empiricism', argued that the Ritschlian dislike of metaphysics and the attempt of Ritschl's school to bring reality down into the phenomena of the world, where it can be more certainly known by man, *is due in very large measure to pure theological interest*.[2] He continued to argue that it was the motives of Ritschlianism to recover the original gospel of God's revelation in Christ, and to peel away from this all obscurantist and disfiguring dogmatic, metaphysical and mystical veils that left the movement with no choice but to adapt their principles in metaphysics and epistemology to the needs of *both their positive and negative theological position*. But ten years before, the fair and sympathetic Dr Garvie had said much the same thing. In discussing the Ritschlian attack on metaphysics, speculative theism and mysticism in theology, the adherents of the movement had removed, Garvie argued, a great deal that had hitherto been judged significant for Christian thought and life, only that it may offer what it deems to be very much more valuable. Garvie puts this another way when he argues that the Ritschlian onslaught against much traditional Christianity was carried on on the principle that the good is the enemy of the better.[3] Indeed, Garvie goes so far as to argue that Ritschl would have served his purposes better by omitting from his work his epistemological discussion altogether: Ritschl only had himself to blame for introducing confusion into his own thinking, and his attempt to

expound and defend a particular 'theory' of cognition attracted
to his theology quite unnecessary condemnation![4] And H. R.
Mackintosh, writing in 1936 (and doubtless remembering his own
disastrous attempt to interpret Ritschl purely philosophically in
1899), remarked that Ritschl's desire to exclude metaphysics
from theology has attracted a somewhat false importance. The
truth of the matter is *that we inevitably go wrong when we approach
his system from the side of philosophy.*[5] 'We *inevitably* go wrong,'
wrote Mackintosh in the heyday of Barthianism, when to stereotype or caricature Ritschl was no great sin. We could do worse
than remember these words when we come to estimate the
significance of epistemology in Ritschl's system as a whole.

We turn now to a brief consideration of Ritschl's 'theory' of
religious cognition. It is a matter of historical fact that his
epistemological position has attracted the titles 'empiricism' and
'phenomenalism', from which all sorts of unfortunate conclusions have been drawn. Nevertheless, if these be understood
rightly, there is no reason why they should not be used without
distorting his meaning. The fundamental qualification is that in
trying to base knowledge upon 'experience' he was using this
term in a much broader and flexible sense than that in which it
has been understood in much British empiricism from Hume to
Wittgenstein, where it has been progressively narrowed down to
'sense experience'. As an 'empiricist', Ritschl holds that knowledge is based upon all kinds of sensations within man's environment, of all kinds of phenomena, moral, religious, historical and
social. Included with these are, of course, the reports of the
senses. The corollary of modern empiricism has almost invariably
been the rejection of metaphysics, and this is also what we find in
Ritschl. Before therefore we enquire further into Ritschl's epistemological position, we must indicate exactly what is involved
in his attempt to exclude metaphysics from theology.

When we try to do so, we encounter what was indicated above
– that his attack upon metaphysics was motivated hardly, if at
all, by purely philosophical considerations. His motives are
almost entirely religious, deriving from concern for the positive
life of the Christian in Church and world. His first reason for
opposing metaphysics in theology is that, in his view, classical

metaphysics only too often *ignores the distinction between nature and spirit*, and for Ritschl the Christian theologian this is intolerable and unacceptable. Clearly, he is here defining metaphysics, as he admits,[6] either as a general *ontology* which aims at setting out the most general characteristics of being with the most economical set of concepts (thus failing to distinguish sharply between 'natural' and 'spiritual' things), or a general *cosmology*, which aims at setting forth an account of the unity of the world as constituted by the interrelatedness of 'things'. It would be easy, and tempting, to demonstrate that here he is using the term 'metaphysics' in an impossibly and arbitrarily narrow sense, but this would be to misunderstand the point he is aiming at, which is that the vital distinction (between nature and spirit) is not arrived at by detached observation and description, but by introspection and ethical reflection. And even the metaphysician, Ritschl contends, can only reach this distinction when he 'as spirit, knows himself to be set off from all nature and feels superior to it'. His fundamental point is that all genuine religion is rooted in that experience where 'the human spirit differentiates itself . . . in value from the phenomena within its environment and from the workings of nature that press in upon it'.[7] We shall, in the next chapter, return to this description of the origins of religion, but at the moment several things must be observed about it. First, it is not hard to indicate part of the root of Ritschl's anti-metaphysical aversion here – it is clearly his aversion, already noted, to the alleged impersonalism of Hegelian philosophy in general and of the Hegelian Absolute in particular. Hence, in *Theology and Metaphysics* he rejects the notion of the Absolute as 'a metaphysical concept which is entirely foreign to the Christian'; the Absolute, he contends, exists 'only for itself, outside all relationships to others', and this is incompatible with the irreducibly personal nature of the Christian religion.[8] Second, at later points an attempt will be made to show that Ritschl's theology is (despite certain superficial appearances to the contrary) one of the richest sources of twentieth-century theology. Now clearly one of the leading characteristics of much recent theology has been the fruitful use made of phenomenological analyses of personal selfhood in order to disclose the basic structure of Christianity as a religion. For example, modern scholarship has made much of themes such as Kierkegaard's analysis of *Angst* and finitude, and of Heidegger's analysis of *Angst*, and of basic affective states such as *Geworfenheit* (thrownness) and *Jemeinigkeit* (mineness), in order to articulate theologies of human existence. But one of the insistences of the Ritschl Renaissance has been that to ignore the pioneering thrust of the Ritschlian school in this context would be onesidedly unscholarly. Long before modern theologies of existence entered the field Ritschl's understanding of religion and Christianity took as its starting-point an analysis of *consciousness*, of man's cognitive feeling (or awareness) of himself as a being who, though part of nature, is nevertheless superior in value to nature, and called to be master over nature. If this analysis of consciousness were erased Ritschl's account of the Christian religion would not even begin to leave the ground. Third, quite crucial significance attaches to Ritschl's *distinction between nature and spirit* in the context of recent existentialist theology. Within the latter much has been made of, for example, the Heideggerian terms *Dasein* and *Vorhandenheit*, denoting 'human' and 'non-human' being respectively, and roughly equivalent to the Ritschlian terms 'spirit' and 'nature'. In exploring the thought of Bultmann, John Macquarrie brings out the difference between these two by saying that human being (*Dasein*) is to be contrasted with the being of a thing (*Vorhandenheit*), '. . . for to say that man exists means that in some way he stands outside (*existere*) the world of things'.[9] And when he goes on to characterize Heidegger's understanding of *Dasein* as having a unique relation to himself, as possibility and as individual (*Jemeinig*), he reveals how intensely personal such thinking is.[10] Mention has just been made of Kierkegaard, another many-sided source of much recent theology. It is worth recalling here Kierkegaard's basic anti-Hegelian point (which has influenced moderns such as Heidegger and Bultmann), that a metaphysical system like Hegel's, insofar as it aims at comprehending reality under a set of *universals*, and insofar as it commends detachment and objectivity in doing so, is unacceptably defective insofar as it is unable to comprehend the concretely existing individual, determined by time and history, who must begin from the stance of subjectively existing in the world. In terms borrowed from Ritschl, the Hegelian philosophical system does not distinguish nearly sharply enough *between spirit and* nature, and does not testify clearly enough to the tension between the two. To these matters in greater detail we must return at a later point. For the moment it is sufficient to stress again the way in which Ritschl's system may have been overlooked as a significant source of modern theology.

His second reason for resisting the intrusion of metaphysics into theology has to do with a quite *religious*, rather than *philosophical*, antipathy towards natural theology, understood as a set of logical demonstrations or proofs. Ritschl's treatment of the ancient proofs need not detain us long, since it adds hardly anything of note to Enlightenment and post-Enlightenment criticism. His *religious* interests oblige him, he tells us, to resist any theological thought which '. . . commingles the divine essence with the material world'. The two *a posteriori* proofs for the existence of God are rejected as metaphysical 'because they disregard the difference between nature and spirit, since they regard the content of the world as a chain of effects and causes'.[11] For Ritschl, the world is nothing of the kind; it is a complex structure of nature and spirit. The weakness of the teleological proof is precisely that 'it is by no means a proof for the existence of the *supramundane* God that we believe in *as Christians*'.[12] Such statements establish beyond doubt that his objections to the *a posteriori* proofs are overwhelmingly religious, in the sense that even if they were logically valid (and on broadly Kantian grounds he thinks that they are not), the 'God' whose existence they would establish would not sufficiently coincide with the God of Christianity to give them Christian significance. This is brought out sharply when in *Justification and Reconciliation* III he gives a religious appraisal of the two *a posteriori* proofs.[13] 'Now it is true,' he writes, 'that the Christian idea of God, our Father in Christ, includes in itself the idea of First Cause and Final End, as subordinate characteristics.' 'But,' he continues, 'posited as independent things, the conceptions of first cause and final end fail to transcend the conception of the world, and therefore fall short of the Christian idea of God.' Ritschl's purely religious aversion to the proofs comes out strongly again, when he contrasts most sharply the God of Aristotelianism with the God of Christianity, in which he follows very closely in the footsteps of his master Luther. The contrast comes out most clearly in the fact that 'the compassion for men in the midst of the difficulties of life . . . is excluded in the unmoved *actus purus* which the philosopher conceives of as the destiny and ordering ground of the world in general'.[14] Similarly, the God conceived of as Fate by Hellenic religion stands in the sharpest possible contrast to the God of Christianity. 'Fate,' says Ritschl, 'can no more be venerated as the true God than the entity in the world, which Aristotle calls God, can attract religious veneration to itself, because fate leaves men caught in their misery.' Briefly, what is wrong with all these conceptions of God is that 'the specific differentiation between the world and God has not yet arisen'.[15] (As will be explained in the following chapter, Ritschl's conception of God is exclusively *soteriological*.) As already suggested, Ritschl's attitude to the ancient proofs need not detain us long; he takes his stand firmly in that long tradition which includes Tertullian, Occam, Pascal, Luther, Kierkegaard and Barth, which emphasizes the gulf which yawns between the God of Christianity and that God referred to in the profane reasonings of philosophers and men of science. So far as logical validity is concerned, he depends at after point on the criticisms of Kant which were re-affirmed by nineteenth-century neo-Kantians. That is, he points again and again at the ambiguity of the evidence used, and relies heavily upon the broadly Kantian principle that the attempt to move from empirical evidences to transempirical conclusions involves a logical jump that has never been satisfactorily explained.[16] Predictably, his brief consideration of the ontological argument adds nothing whatever to the Kantian critique, his main criticism of the inference made by the argument being that it 'is true only for our ideas, not for the reality which stands opposed to our thought'.[17]

The matter is somewhat and significantly different in the case of the so-called moral argument of Kant. 'Kant's moral argument,' says Ritschl, '. . . stands under the unmistakable influence of the Christian world view.'[18] This is so because it satisfies the following condition: '. . . no proof of God's existence starts properly save that which accepts a given man's self-distinction from nature, and his endeavours to maintain himself against or over it'.[19] Kant's notion of God agrees broadly with the Christian one, since for him God '. . . denotes the ethical Power Who assures to man the position above the world befitting his ethical worth, and this, too, as the final end of the world'.[20] Ritschl, wanting to underscore the *antimetaphysical* thrust of Kant's argument, highlights how in Kant's thought it is only the practical (as distinct from the theoretical) reason which can grasp the thought of God, that this thought possesses 'only subjectivo-practical reality', and that the notion of God as guaranteeing the final end of the world is 'a matter of faith' (rather than theoretical knowledge).[21] So far Ritschl follows Kant fairly closely, and for doing so he has been loosely and carelessly labelled a 'Kantian'. But this can only be done if we choose to turn a blind eye to his criticisms of Kant and the extent to which he deliberately and sharply diverged from Kant. The quite crucial point seized upon by Ritschl here is the way in which Kant's conviction that our awareness of the reality of God (as Moral Legislator and Creator) is limited to 'the merely practical use of our reason' is closely bound up with Kant's complete and tragic separation of the spheres of the theoretical and practical reason.[22] For Ritschl the theologian this was tragic because Kant in his view gravely undervalued the practical reason. He failed to perceive, that is, the aspect under which the practical reason can be regarded as *a function of theoretical cognition.* In view of the attempt to stereotype Ritschl as a Kantian reductionist, it is instructive to note how he deplores Kant's sceptical conclusion that since a notion of God is theoretically impossible, theology must be *abandoned* to the practical reason.[23] In answer to the question why Kant has done so, Ritschl interestingly suggests that the reason is Kant's equation of *sensibility* (i.e. sense-data) with *reality.* Ritschl forthwith affirms his rejection of empiricism as dependent exclusively upon sense-experience and proceeds to explore how an experiential approach to the question of God can be formulated in terms of a broader, more flexible and tolerant empiricism. This he does by expanding the concept of 'reality' to include the moral and spiritual life of man, an area in his view just as 'real' as that of nature, possessing, like nature, its own autonomous principles and laws. Despite repeated criticisms that he had capitulated to nineteenth-century naturalism, it is clear that Ritschl strove valiantly, within his historical limitations, to overcome the powerful tendency of late nineteenth-century 'scientism' to subsume the uniquely valuable *human* under the categories of the *natural* or the *material*. Broadly speaking, his response to the all-consuming demands of philosophical naturalism is that man's exploration of his ethical vocation and the laws which operate in it (the impulses of knowledge, of feeling, of aesthetic intuition, of will in general and of its social application, of religion) brings him firmly to the conclusion that man's chief end is the spiritual life to which nature is the means. The failure to realize this and to conclude that spirit is subject to the 'laws of mechanism' (i.e. materialism) is closely related to Kant's fallacy of opposing 'practical Reason as one species of Reason to theoretical Reason as another'. The misleading distinction between *practical* and *theoretical* has at this point obscured the insight that '. . . knowledge of the practical laws . . . falls under theoretical cognition no less than natural science does'. The contribution which the declarations of the practical reason may make to theoretical understanding comes about thus. Human cognition is faced with a vast problem in explaining the 'coexistence of two heterogeneous orders of reality'. These two are spirit and nature, and they are heterogeneous because of a discrepancy between the declarations of spirit on the one hand and the apparent impersonal apathy of nature on the other. The declarations of spirit point towards a final blessedness for man through a practical faith in God as bringing man into that kingdom which is God's final end for the world. On the other hand, 'nature is subject to quite other laws than those which spirit obeys, . . . is independent of spirit, and forms a restraint on spirit, and so far keeps it in a certain way in dependence on itself'. There emerges from this *impasse* an either/or for theoretical cognition. *Either* it must concede that the declarations of spirit – that man is ordained for a life of blessedness in a moral and spiritual kingdom which is not only his chief end but God's – are unattainable moonshine, *or* that spirit's view that nature is but a means towards this end is grounded in a divine will which has not only ordained man's final end but created the world as a means towards it. Accordingly, Ritschl does not shrink from drawing the conclusion that in a sense the Christian notion of God is *rationally satisfying*. His argument claims, he shows, that 'the Christian religion is . . . proved to be in harmony with reason' because 'the Christian view of God and the world enables us comprehensively to unify our knowledge of nature and the spiritual life of man in a way which otherwise is impossible'.[24] His final view here is that an exploration of man's moral structure, beginning from the principles of Kant's moral philosophy, serves as 'the *ratio cognoscendi* of the validity of the Christian idea of God when employed as the solution of the enigma of the world'. Ritschl does not use this language, but can this be anything other than a *natural theology*, in the classical sense of being a rational construction which removes a mystery, which 'solves a problem', which relieves an intellectual anxiety, which, in his own words, 'solves the enigma of the world'?

It is hard to deny that it is just that. Indeed, on his own admission, by radically modifying Kant's moral argument he has become more of a rational theologian than the sceptical Kant himself. If so, Ritschl's own claim that he was eliminating all speculative philosophy from theology, a claim rather too unreflectively accepted by critical interpreters, must be highly qualified. He was not, to be sure, allowing his account of Christianity to be determined or distorted by the intrusion of some metaphysical scheme (such as Hegelian idealism); but he was without question allowing what has in recent decades been dubbed a philosophical *Vorverständnis* (pre-understanding) to influence both the form and content of his systematic theology. This term is used deliberately to remind us once again of Bultmann, who has used a philosophical anthropology to formulate a hermeneutical *Vorverständnis* which he has used as a key to uncover the fundamental structure and content of the Christian faith. And just as Barth's fundamental objection to Bultmann's theological procedure has been the extent to which the latter has allowed anthropological analysis, obtained from contemporary philosophical sources rather than Scripture, to determine his exegetical and systematic theology, so Barth's fundamental objection to Ritschl has run along parallel lines. David Mueller has put the matter very neatly: Ritschl's procedure at this point accounts for the frequent charge that his theology is strongly anthropological rather than theocentric or Christocentric,[25] charges identical to those which Barth has brought against the school of Bultmann. Indeed, Mueller rather sides with Barth in alleging that Ritschl is vulnerable to the charge that his use of a Kantian natural theology in the description of the human problem predetermines the kind of answer that God's historical revelation must provide.[26] Of course, at this point we cannot assume that this rather neo-orthodox criticism of Ritschl is valid, and this is an issue which must be opened up at a later point. Nevertheless, the committed defender of Ritschl cannot argue that his opening the door to a certain natural theology is not significant for the structure and content of his theology or that the broadly Kantian analysis of the human predicament plays a merely peripheral role in Ritschl's system as a whole. Even a cursory examination of Ritschl's texts swiftly convinces the enquirer that the spirit/nature dichotomy and all that derives from it (the doctrine of God, sin, redemption, the kingdom of God, human perfection, etc.) is to be found on almost every page of the main works. Still, in the spirit of the Ritschl Renaissance, to be as fair to Ritschl as possible, the centrality of the spirit/ nature dichotomy in itself does not imply distortion or disloyalty to the tradition, for it begs the interesting question of how far the spirit/nature (or man/world, man/society) split may reflect the teaching of the New Testament itself, as well as that of late nineteenth-century intellectual movements.

Ritschl's third reason for resisting the intrusion of metaphysics into theology reinforces our conviction that his motives were overwhelmingly *religious* or *theological*, rather than philosophical. He entertained the most intense suspicion that so-called neoplatonic metaphysics, and the 'neo-platonic' psychology and anthropology inseparably connected to this, had a most distorting effect upon genuine Reformation Christianity. It is impossible for the reader of Ritschl to resist the conclusion that it was to the second of these that he took the greatest exception, and that on strictly *theological* grounds, derived from a lifetime's scholarship upon (and, it must be admitted, antipathy towards) mystical and pietistic understandings of Lutheran Christianity. Not many serious students of Ritschl today would deny that the basic root of his (philosophically expressed) aversion was his almost totally *theological* objections to the seventeenth-century Lutheran doctrine of the *Unio Mystica* between Christ and the believer, a doctrine which, in his view, was imported into Lutheran

Christianity from alien sources, and which not merely obscured but also undermined that understanding of Christianity transmitted to the modern world by the Lutheran Reformation.[27] It lies beyond the scope of this work to investigate and evaluate Ritschl's vast historical work on mysticism, pietism and Christianity. But it may be worth pointing out that this was ground with which he was probably more familiar than any other Western scholar. Philip Hefner, writing of the decade 1876–86, when Ritschl wrote the three-volumed *History of Pietism*, reminds us that he literally read every primary source for Dutch, German and Swiss pietism that the libraries of his time could provide.[28] Clearly no modern research on the subject could do other than begin with Ritschl's monumental work. Ritschl's views here, as elsewhere, have been productive of considerable controversy, generating a bewildering array of estimates from the warmly sympathetic to the implacably hostile. The fair and judicious Garvie, for example, while deploring Ritschl's immoderate language leading to unnecessary polemic, nevertheless warmly welcomes his onslaught upon unhealthy pietism, including familiar irreverence involved in the intercourse with Christ as the bridegroom of the soul, the over-imaginative picturing of the exalted Christ, immodest curiosity concerning the last things, and the over-familiarity of demanding prayer.[29] On the other hand, the late H. R. Mackintosh reminds us that a bitter accusation thrown against Ritschl was to the effect that those who wished to discover how little real religion there was in the man ought to read his *Geschichte des Pietismus*![30] But, laying polemic to one side, and without condoning Ritschl's sometimes unforgivable insensitivity to the religious claims of those in different religious traditions from his own, it is not impossible to summarize the most serious and thoughtful objections to a mysticopietistic version of the Christian faith.

At this point it would be disastrous to forget that Ritschl was paramountly a *Lutheran* theologian, attempting in the light of modern intellectual factors to return to the New Testament message *via* the teaching of Luther and the sixteenth-century Reformers. Or, as we have been arguing throughout, his dominating motives were overwhelmingly theological. In the light of these motives, it can be stated that Ritschl considered Christian mystico-pietism to be theologically objectionable because it was *ahistorical, amoral, individualistic*, and *otherworldly*. First, it was *ahistorical* because in his view there could be no such thing as an *unmediated* encounter between God and the believer, in the sense of bypassing or dispensing with the interposition of God's word in Christ. In other words, the Christian religion, as understood by him and his followers, was incompatible with all talk of an *immediate* contact between the soul and its God, or of the soul's being absorbed by the ultimate divine reality. To quote Ritschl: '. . . without the means of the word of God as law and gospel and without the precise recollection of this personal revelation of God in Christ, there is no personal relation between a Christian and God'.[31] Second, it was for him *amoral* because there was not 'built into' the mystical experience (so to speak) a powerful inclination towards ethical transformation or moral perfection. Traditionally, at this point, that anti-Ritschl polemic which has produced stereotypes has branded him as an insensitive and unsubtle Prussian Kantian moralist. But this is difficult to sustain. The theologian Hermann Weiss of Tübingen accused Ritschl of this during his lifetime. In his reply to Weiss he made quite clear where his loyalties in the matter lay: 'Did Luther base his reformation on the doctrine of justification by faith or on the doctrine of the *unio mystica*?'[32] And he proceeds to expound for Weiss's benefit the relation between Luther's experience of justification by faith and a Christian *Lebensführung* (lifestyle) based upon belief in providence, and marked by humility, patience and prayer. Having done so, he remarks: 'I hope that I have answered Professor Weiss's insinuation that it is not a Kantian moralist antipathy which leads me to this position.' Even though we may not be totally unconvinced of the operation of some kind of 'Kantianism' in this matter, it is nevertheless incontrovertible that one of the dominating themes of his *magnum opus* was that fundamental to Reformed Christianity is the doctrine of God's free gift of justification in Christ *inseparably linked to* the tasks of reconciliation laid upon the justified sinner in his concrete, historical life in the world (hence his carefully chosen title *Justification and Reconciliation*, in that precise order). Third, it was in his view *individualistic*, and that in two directions. In the first place, the mystical experience can be and usually is enjoyed in isolation from one's fellows, and this is incompatible with Ritschl's view of Christianity as essentially a communal phenomenon. There are several notable fundamental statements of Ritschl here worth recalling. There is his celebrated claim, central to his entire programme, that systematic theology as a whole can only properly be attempted when 'every part of theological knowledge is construed from the standpoint of the Christian community'.[33] There is also his opinion that a construction of the Christian view of the world and of life 'can hope for success only when it is attempted from the standpoint of the community of believers'.[34] In brief, Ritschl's theology was a classical type of *Gemeindetheologie* (community theology), and his defenders have always rightly stressed its community basis in their attempts to make his work invulnerable to the charge of subjectivism brought against the nineteenth century. In the second place, mystical individualism was quite incompatible with Ritschl's fundamentally *teleological* and social understanding of the Christian faith as a whole. It is hard to underscore too heavily this characteristic of his thinking. For what is God, in his thinking if not that eternally loving will who in creating man and the world has ordained from all eternity that final end of mankind and the world in the supramundane interhuman state of affairs called the Kingdom of God? If so, it is no wonder that he looked askance at pietistic Christianity understood as a normative or ideal representation of the historic Christian faith. It was, finally, *otherwordly* for Ritschl in several important senses. In the first place, it was so metaphysically (a view to be examined below); that is, the alleged intercourse between the soul and its heavenly bridegroom is alleged to occur in a plane or dimension 'behind' or 'beyond' that in which the observable human person lives his mundane life in Church, vocation and market-place. Literally, such a mystical relation is 'not of this world', a notion incompatible with the Lutheran-Ritschlian doctrine of worldly vocation. This leads us to say that mystical otherworldliness was incompatible with Ritschl's unprecedentedly heavy emphasis on the Christian's concrete, historical, temporal and above all *observable Lebensführung* as one of the principal normative criteria of having been justified by God in Christ. But, in the second place, the term 'otherworldliness' has another grave disadvantage attached to it: God's free word of justification in Christ is extended quite literally 'to the world', and the Kingdom of God is intended eventually to comprehend mankind, not just a select élite, favoured by 'religious' gifts, or predisposed by temperament or character towards ineffable experiences of a rarified kind.

At this point it is comprehensible if the modern student of mysticism holds up his hands in horror at this partial, onesided, 'partisan' portrayal of 'mysticism'. This reaction is unwarranted. It is so because it overlooks that Ritschl was no objective, disinterested phenomenologist of religion, exploring with sterilized categories the phenomenon of mysticism as such, in a world-wide range of manifestations. As insisted above, he was pre-eminently a Christian theologian attempting to demonstrate the incompatibility between what he regarded as authentic Christianity on the one hand and, on the other, quite specific quasi-mystical approaches which had in a quite empirical way in quite specific historical periods, attempted to alter the nature of biblically-oriented Christianity. There are several other points about Ritschl's discussion of mysticism that must be noted before we move on to deal with his attempt to exclude 'neo-Platonic' metaphysics from theology. These points derive their significance from the attempt, already initiated in these pages, to demonstrate that it is impossible any longer to overlook Ritschl's thought as one of the major sources of twentieth-century theological work. In this context, there are two aspects of Ritschl's work on pietism worth underscoring. First, it is impossible to read what he has to say about the encounter between God and the believer being *exclusively* determined and conditioned by the word of God in Christ, without being persuaded that this emphasis of his operates as a significant link between the nineteenth century and the twentieth, during which were initiated the so-called *theologies of the Word of God*. Probably the truth of the matter is this: Ritschl, grateful though he was for Schleiermacher's post-Enlightenment emphasis, over against the Deism of the eighteenth century, upon the person and work of Christ within the divine-human encounter, was nevertheless uneasy over Schleiermacher's alleged 'subjectivism', construed as an unjustified stress on the content of the religious consciousness of redeemed Christians *at the expense of* the contents of the objective, historical pole of God's self-disclosure in Christ. Hence his stress on 'God's word' spoken to us in Christ. And since truth is not uncommonly obtained from hostile critics, it is worth recalling that one of the first systematic German anti-Ritschlian movements was that initiated by his former pupil, Ernst Troeltsch, who took strong exception to what he regarded as the excessively narrow and exclusive *christocentrism* and *bibliocentrism* which lay at the heart of his teacher's thinking. In brief, at yet another point, post-1920 dialectical theology borrowed more from Ritschl's thought than it knew or cared to admit! Indeed, it is instructive to recall that more than twenty years before Barth initiated his revolution, the luminous Dr Garvie, in summarizing what he regarded as the 'distinctive merits' of Ritschl's system, applied certain descriptive terms to various aspects of it, two of which were *biblio-spheric* and *christocentric*.[35] He defines the first of these thus: The *formal* principle of Christian dogmatics is not the Holy Scriptures in their entirety, but the confession of the first Christian community as recorded in the New Testament Scriptures. And, evaluating this principle with an eye to the future, Garvie adds: 'Ritschlianism stands on the path of necessary and desirable Christian progress.' Believers in second sight might well suspect that Garvie had prescience of early dialectical theology! But, from the standpoint of the beginnings of dialectical theology, even more disconcerting are Garvie's remarks upon the second of these, which he defines thus: The *regulative* principle (of Christian dogmatics) is the Person and Work of Christ as Founder of the Kingdom of God. Admittedly Garvie is critical of Ritschl's christocentrism, wishing that it had received a more thorough application and a fuller development at his hands. But once again, with an eye on the future development of theology, he cautiously judges that the importance which Ritschl's system does certainly attach to the Person and Work of Christ proves that it is already moving along the lines of *a sound and healthy development*, and is, therefore, not incapable of such correction as seems desirable. What gives Garvie's words pointed significance is the well-known astonishment and disappointment entertained by some members of the Ritschlian school after World War I at Barth's unwillingness to acknowledge his debt to Ritschl and his Ritschlian training. We cannot but be reminded of the remark of the Ritschlian Ferdinand

Kattenbusch, quoted by David Mueller, that Barth's early theology can be interpreted as bringing the best of Ritschl to fulfilment.[36] The second aspect of Ritschl's work on pietism worth mentioning here need not detain us long, since it is really so evident as hardly to need comment. It concerns Ritschl as one of modern theology's pioneers of *Gemeindetheologie*. At this point Ritschl is clearly dependent upon his great predecessor, Schleiermacher, whose *Glaubenslehre* was, in marked contrast to the excessive individualism of the *Aufklärung*, very much the systematic articulation of the beliefs and convictions of the Christian community. But it could be argued, because of his knowledge of and researches into the Christian tradition *as a whole*, that Ritschl's system gives an even more central place to the Church and to its witness than did Schleiermacher's. And here, once again, it is impossible to contemplate Barth's *Church Dogmatics*, with its claim that dogmatics is a science done *in*, *bv* and *for* the Christian community, without being compelled to the view that Barth and his colleagues were standing firmly on the shoulders of the previous generation of workers in systematic theology. In other words, Barth's theology was not, we note once again, nearly so discontinuous with what immediately preceded it as we have been taught to believe by the last generation.

We are perhaps now in a position to say a few words about Ritschl's attack on so-called 'neo-Platonic' metaphysics and its alleged effects on Christian theology. Clearly, Ritschl's aversion was religious rather than philosophical, being rooted in the conviction that such metaphysics supplied the defenders of the *Unio Mystica* doctrine with a conceptual scheme within which the doctrine could be given meaning and justification. Hence, he attacks the Pietists' presupposition that man's authentic being lies somehow 'behind' or 'beyond' the observable, ethical and social life of the individual in a realm, designated 'God', where the concrete, differentiated, individual being may be swallowed up. He comments: 'The only conceptual scheme in which this process is intelligible is the neoplatonic with its deprecation of all particular, determinate being and life in favour of universal being.'[37] At the same time, it is hard to overlook a residue of anti-Hegelianism when he characterizes the 'neoplatonic' God as 'the universal, colourless scheme in which all particularities and inter-relations of things are eliminated'. Hence, he can say: 'mysticism is the practice of the neoplatonic metaphysics'. But it would be mistaken to regard Ritschl as some kind of philosophically motivated anti-Platonist: he was a religiously motivated theologian whose concrete researches into seventeenth-century Lutheran pietism obliged him to link closely together a certain type of what he called 'neoplatonic metaphysical thinking' with a specific type of psychology which, in his view, obscured and marred that type of Christianity which the Lutheran Reformation claimed to have recovered from the original biblical witness to Christ. That psychology was, in other words, incompatible with Ritschl's stress on man's dynamic, active, observable, social, interpersonal, decision-making, willing development in the historico-temporal world, determined by God's word in Scripture and in Church, and directed towards the supramundane end of the Kingdom of God.

Mention has just been made of Ritschl's use of the epistemological terms 'behind' and 'beyond' in his dispute with mystical pietism. His use of such terms is highly important, for it is this above all else which has attracted to him, in a pejorative sense, terms such as 'phenomenalist' and 'empiricist'. But it is impossible to condemn his critics for describing him so, in the light of his plain and reiterated statements that we come to know things only in their *effects* or *appearances*, or (following Lotze) in their *relationships*.[38] Of course, when one considers the high estimate that has been accorded to empiricism in the post-Enlightenment West, one might arguably evaluate Ritschl highly as a theologian who has come to terms with philosophical modernity in a positive way, by using only those epistemological insights which have meaning for modern man. Perhaps therefore he deserves high respect and warm praise here. But, on the other hand, we cannot ignore the fact that the main criticism brought against Ritschl until recent decades has been that by committing himself consistently to a form of empiricism he has committed himself to a form of theological *reductionism* which has gravely impoverished his account of Christianity. It is a notoriously difficult matter to make up one's mind about where the truth lies between these two types of estimate. But what does the charge of *reductionism* mean? In Ritschl's case, it implies that there is no room in his thought for the transcendent, conceived of as lying somehow 'beyond' or 'behind' or 'after' the stream of spatio-temporal history and experience; that he exhaustively identifies 'God' with the so-called 'appearances' or 'effects' or 'phenomena' of God; that there is no room in his thought for the contrast between what God has disclosed of himself to us in the 'here and now' and what he will reveal of himself 'hereafter and then' (1 Corinthians 13:12); in brief, that he has, because of his philosophical commitments, committed himself to an intramundane, immanentist, humanistic account of Christianity which serves merely personal and social needs and aspirations. If this could be conclusively demonstrated, it would indeed cast grave doubt upon Ritschl's claim to be reinterpreting Christianity for modernity – even to be reinterpreting Christianity at all!

But can it be conclusively proved? Or, on the other hand, is there room in his work for some kind of *transcendental* or *ontological* reference which would allay the fears which his theology has created in many breasts? Naturally, these questions are so large that they can only be answered in the light of a thorough and wide-ranging examination of Ritschl's system as a whole, with special reference to his treatments of, say, the doctrine of God and of christology. At the same time, the question is an epistemological one, and a very important one at that, and so some attempt at answering it must be outlined here. First of all, it must be conceded to his critics right away that if he has been accused of producing a merely humanistic Christianity, then he has only himself to blame. He has foolishly supplied much ammunition to his critics, and we cannot but be forcibly reminded of Dr Garvie's suggestion that he erred in committing himself to any explicit statement of epistemological principles, and that his theology is not always consistent with his philosophical commitment.[39] The matter is a quite crucial one, for around it cluster all those damning accusations from Leonhard Stählin to Karl Barth, that Ritschl reduced theology to anthropology, that his theology was hopelessly and irredeemably anthropocentric, that he was a moral reductionist who was in theological matters essentially agnostic, and the like. Unless these accusations are blunted, there is little that can be done to rebut the charges of hostile critics that the 'stereotypes' applied to Ritschl are largely or wholly

justified. But before we begin to look for some kind of transcendental or ontological reference in his work, we must in all fairness survey the counter-evidence traditionally seized on by his
detractors. For example, in discussing one subject in which he
was clearly not at home, perception, he falls back upon an analogy
taken from Lotze's *Metaphysik*: repeated and fairly constant
perceptions of the same object are followed by a concentration of
thought 'so that we conceive of the unity of the thing in analogy
to the perceiving soul, which feels and remembers itself to be an
enduring unity in the midst of the alterations which correspond
to its sensibilities'.[40] This leads to the isolated object being
'thought of as existing through and for itself'. Now in objecting
to this procedure Ritschl unfortunately uses language which may
mislead us into believing that he is following in the empiricistic
footsteps of Hume or Mach, as when he describes the procedure
as nonsensical, 'because an object in and of itself would be in-
accessible to our perception and representation'. But, here again,
we must beware of concluding that Ritschl was moved by mainly
logical or epistemological considerations! His motivation is
purely *theological*, for he at once strongly objects that the 'thing-
in-itself' strongly and objectionably resembles the Hegelian
Absolute (defended in the theology of his day by Frank of the
Erlangen school), and that to predicate 'personhood and love'
of a 'thing-in-itself' is contradictory since both of these 'express
relationships to another'. So anxious, indeed, is Ritschl to avoid
confusion of the Hegelian Absolute with the God of Christianity,
that he goes so far as to urge against Frank and his colleagues
that there can be no correlation of 'the loving will of God' and
man's metaphysical 'thrust towards the Absolute'.[41] Doubtless at
this point Ritschl was writing as a typical son of the century of
Schleiermacher, whose equally experiential view of Christianity
led him to say in the *Reden* that 'religion cannot and will not
originate *in the pure impulse to know*', and that 'what we feel and
are conscious of in religious emotions is *not the nature of things*
but their operation on us'.[42] And equally doubtless Ritschl, like
Schleiermacher before him, cannot be absolved from blame for
producing that divorce of speculative reason from faith which the
early twentieth century inherited from the nineteenth. But his
motives here, as elsewhere, were based on religious zeal and not

pure philosophical interest, of which he possessed very little. It is also arguable that it was anti-Hegelian aversion that involved him in the highly misleading terminology of 'before' and 'behind', and to that of the 'front realm' and the 'back realm', which has led to the suspicion that he was some kind of radical empiricist in a purely philosophical sense. There is a notable example of this in his discussion of christology, where he sternly forbids his critics to penetrate 'behind' the public and historical life-work of Christ, to some shadowy and nebulous dimension of 'being' which Christ allegedly shares with God. Clearly, we might suspect that this is mainly or merely the working-out of Ritschl's 'philosophy'. But this conclusion would be prematurely misleading. For, as we shall see in a later chapter, it was largely, if not wholly, the result of his christological attempt to follow Luther and Melancthon in their christological attempt 'to begin with Christ from below and move upwards'. There is, indeed, one remarkable passage in *Theology and Metaphysics* where he argues so vehemently, apparently, on behalf of a radical empiricism that one cannot wonder that he attracted so many stereotypes to himself.[43] Here, Ritschl identifies and attacks two errors in perception. The first of these has to do with the relationship between actually receiving sense-impressions and recollecting them in memory. In working over a set of impressions we may easily, Ritschl avers, fall into the error of fabricating the concept of a thing as it is *in itself*, in isolation from those impressions in which we first grasped it. For the idea of 'thing-in-itself' may involve grave distortion. First, it may overlook that a thing originally perceived exists within a network of other things, an insight negated by the predicate 'in itself'. Second, this predicate obscures the unique relatedness of a thing to us as subjects of experience and perception. He goes on to argue that the reason for the flight to the 'thing-in-itself' is an unjustified fear of 'false, deceiving appearances', unjustified because it ignores a certain limited reliability based upon 'the consensus of many persons' perceptions'. Hence his well-known conclusion that our knowledge must be firmly linked to actual appearances and relations, and his fierce polemic against the 'thing-in-itself'. Clearly, one can have much sympathy with those who react to Ritschl's teaching on purely philosophical grounds, but, once again, this is really to attribute to him motives and interests which he did not in fact possess. For at once he discloses his genuine motivation, once more a purely *theological* one, when he articulates his fear that the concept of '*Ding-an-sich*', *allowed to impinge upon theology*, produces the theologically intolerable 'claim that one can teach something about God *in himself*, something that is allegedly knowable for us *apart from his revelation* which, however it is fashioned, is sensed and perceived by us', or the unthinkable claim of Luthardt that there are predicates of God's nature *in itself* which 'can be known prior to those attributes of God that are efficacious for us'.[44] Alternatively, in the same place, he objects to such epistemology on the grounds that it might admit Frank's insistence that we must 'think of God as the Absolute'. This makes our point very neatly: although, on the surface, Ritschl uses the language of critical epistemology, his motivation and meaning are both thoroughly religious. To put this another way: in reality (as distinct from appearances) the Lutheran Ritschl was urging against his fellow-Lutherans Frank and Luthardt the pristine early Lutheran doctrine of God as revealed exclusively *pro nobis* in Christ as incompatible with the late-medieval rationalist claim that reason can attain to a certain knowledge of God as he is *in himself* independent of or prior to his soteriologically decisive self-revelation in Christ. If so, it should make us sceptical of the glib assumption that Ritschl was some kind of neo-Kantian sceptic philosophically disinclined towards the ontological side of Christianity. At the same time, the other side of the coin cannot be ignored – Ritschl's flagrant and rather uncircumspect use of vigorous empiricistic language readily gave rise to misinterpretation and misunderstanding, from which it is hard to absolve him completely. Historically speaking, Wolfhart Pannenberg is right when he says that behind the dangerous twentieth-century 'dichotomization of religion and metaphysics' stands Ritschl and school, and that even Karl Barth's critical reservations about all programmatic apologetics, as well as his fight against everything he calls 'natural theology', is likewise in many respects an extension and radicalization of the battle position set up by Ritschl. And in the context of discussing Ritschl's christological position, Pannenberg speaks of 'the antispeculative reaction of the second half of the nineteenth century, which today appears in many respects as intellectual superficiality'.[45] And contemporary theologians, interested in the theological possibilities of descriptive and revisionary metaphysics, conceived of as the structuring and restructuring of one's past experience in a religious direction, would be certain to find highly restrictive Ritschl's dubious ban on 'subsequent precise recollection and representation'.[46]

Ritschl's discussion of the second perceptual error which he claims to have identified is a splendid example of how, in attacking opponents, he quite unnecessarily commits himself to the use of excessively strong empiricistic (and hence, anti-ontological) language. This error is rooted, in his view, in the formation of *Errinerungsbilder* (memory-images). He argues that the memory-image we form to encapsulate 'the repeated perceptions of a thing' ignores 'certain alterations which we have subsequently perceived from time to time in that very thing'.[47] This need not detain us too long, because it exhibits clearly that Ritschlian pattern to which we must now be accustomed. He draws the sharpest possible contrast between perceptual *experience* itself and the *memory-image* subsequently built up on its foundation. To the former he applies the following predicates: changeable (by which he means 'elusive'), individual, original, actual, real, authentic, immediate, mobile, active, dynamic, efficacious and direct. Of the latter he predicates (pejoratively) the following: placid (that is, inert), recollected, non-immediate, unreal, indifferent, 'without relationship', and powerless. To be sure, Ritschl recognizes clearly the epistemological attraction of the memory-image; in contrast to the changing and altering flux involved in the realm of immediate experience, the memory-image appears, seductively, to possess solidity, clarity, essentiality and value, because of the way in which it directs and facilitates future experience of the thing. Yet, epistemological seduction is involved: for our cognitive instinct mistakenly comes to place the memory-image in what he calls the 'back-realm' position, behind the 'front-realm' dimension of immediate (and authentic) experience. The intolerable contradiction he finds in this is that a placid, pallid, indifferent, unrelated, inert thing is *supposed simultaneously* to be dynamic, mobile, fluctuating, active, and efficacious. Now in the case of man's knowledge of God this is a singularly interesting account of its history. The crux of the matter is, however, Ritschl's proposed treatment of the epistemological contradiction. If it could be demonstrated that Ritschl proposed the complete abandonment of the latter, metaphysical, recollected-image dimension to the former phenomenal, experiential dimension, the discussion could be closed – he, it might be argued, is left floundering in the area of appearances, the flux of phenomena, completely bereft of any ontological anchorage, and deserving of those philosophical stereotypes which his name has attracted. But, significantly, he does not go nearly so far. To be sure, as his critics have pointed out, he never ceased to be suspicious of all talk of enduring memory-images. Indeed, he goes so far as to suggest that it is derived, not from the authentic Christian tradition at all, but from 'Platonic idealism', although he does not bring forward a single shred of evidence for the suggestion. Within such idealism, he argues, recollected images or ideas are held to be 'more real' than actual experienced entities, since the latter are held only to 'participate' in the former, so that 'individual things are only the shadow-images of the ideas'.[48] His criticism of the doctrine of ideas is that the 'images become more and more dim and imprecise and even . . . uncertain', and the doctrine itself hopelessly imprecise and even . . . uncertain'. At this point, it is clear that Ritschl is almost inviting hostile attention from the philosopher, who would be entirely within his rights in asking if he is not guilty of perpetrating a most serious confusion. Particularly, the philosopher would be justified in enquiring if Ritschl culpably fails to distinguish between a Lotzean *Errinerungsbild* and a Platonic Form or Idea. And he would be equally justified in suspecting that lying behind the confusion is Ritschl's unreasonable prejudice against Greek philosophy within a Christian context, and his rudimentary plans for that dehellenization of the Christian tradition later put into effect by his disciple Harnack. At the same time, it must once more be urged that to tackle Ritschl on purely philosophical grounds is to attribute to him an interest which he did not possess. Since, as has been maintained throughout these pages, his interest was overwhelmingly theological, he was neutral towards metaphysics as such but *parti pris* with regard to its allegedly distorting effect when allowed to intrude upon Christian theology as he saw it.

Although lacking interest in metaphysics as such, he was passion-
ately interested in what we might call the psychologically misleading characteristics of metaphysics in theology. For example,
the notion that we can know 'things-in-themselves', 'spatially
"behind" and temporally "before" their appearance, is nothing
but a deceptive distortion of the recollected image which one ac-
quires "behind" the first observations and which he carries with
him "before" subsequent observations'. Exactly – he has no objection to metaphysical thinking as such, but only to certain distortions which it perpetrates in theology. Hence, he has no intrinsic
objection to our formation of an *Errinerungsbild* because, he
argues, we can 'rightly treasure it because it serves to simplify and
stabilize our cognition'; but he objects vehemently when 'the
recollected image is overvalued or improperly cherished when a
person *substitutes it* for the actual reality of a thing'. In other
words, Ritschl's so-called aversion to metaphysics is rooted in
the fear that it might negate or obscure the experiential, experimental, active and dynamic characteristics of man's knowledge
of God.

So far we have been probing the question of whether it can be
proved that Ritschl, through a commitment to some form of
philosophical empiricism, was guilty of a form of theological
reductionism in identifying God exhaustively with the operations
or effects of God, thus ruling out of court the possibility of some
transcendent or ontological referent which we have characterized
as 'beyondness'. We have seen, by a careful examination of
Ritschl's language, that it is very hard to prove anything of the
kind. At the same time, no attempt has been made to conceal
Ritschl's part in evoking the accusations made against him.
Perhaps now it is possible to go a little further and say something
a little more positive on his behalf. There are, indeed, various
notable instances, very much neglected by hostile interpreters,
where he took steps to ensure that he was not regarded in this
way. There is the instance in *Justification and Reconciliation* III
where he, while summarizing various optional theological epi-
stemologies, *explicitly* rejects that of Kant, because Kant
'declares unknowable the thing or things in themselves'. Alternatively, he affirms his agreement with that of Lotze, who holds that
'in the phenomena which in a definite space exhibit changes to a

limited extent and in a determinate order we cognise the thing as
the cause of its qualities operating upon us, as the end which
these serve as means, as the law of their constant changes'.[49] We
know the thing *in* the phenomena. But, the critics retort, why not
say that we know it not merely *in* but *through* the phenomena?
The clear answer to this is that Ritschl throughout his writings
exhibits desperate fear that he is interpreted as recommending
some attempt to penetrate *through* or *beyond* or *beneath* the
phenomena, what is immediately experienced, to an order of
images, described by him as placid and inert, which comes to
weaken or detract from a vigorously exercised Christian faith in
man's everyday existence. At the same time, his prohibitions of
this penetration are quite bland. Of the attempt to distinguish
between, on the one hand, the experienced characteristics 'in a
front plane' and, on the other, the thing itself 'in a rear plane', he
says that at the elementary level of the formation of the concept
of 'thing', there is no reason for us to do it. Of the assertion that
one can know the 'thing "behind" its characteristics or "before"
the naming of those characteristics' he states quite mildly that
it is not necessary. Of the attempt to state that 'a law can be conjectured from the perceived history of a thing', he says reasonably
and unargumentatively that there is no occasion for it.[50] And in
his celebrated argument with Frank of Erlangen about construing
God as the Absolute, Ritschl reveals that he has no *philosophical*
antipathy whatever towards the notion that *behind* the love of
God the Christian must posit God as the subject of that love.
Most certainly, he concedes, from the point of view of Christian
theology *but not of metaphysics*, the Father of Christ who through
Jesus' sacrificial death reveals his love for us and promises us
through him all good gifts, must be believed in as the 'all-
powerful One'. 'We would,' Ritschl freely admits, 'have to believe
that *behind his love* God *stands* as the subject of all-powerfulness',
although he proceeds to reformulate the notion in a way which,
he feels, approximates more closely to the central teaching of the
New Testament.[51] Passages such as these ought, in all fairness to
the unfortunate Ritschl, to render us very sceptical of any glib
accusation that he transformed Christianity into a completely
humanistic or intramundane phenomenon by a rigid, quasi-
philosophical attempt to identify divine realities with their effects

or operations, so eliminating from his work all possibility of a transcendent or ontological referent.

We are now in a position to make several supplementary comments, in order to clarify further this matter of the ontological reference in Ritschl's theological construction. First, it is worth at this point recalling Garvie's pregnant comment that Ritschl's theology is not always consistent with his philosophical principles, leading him to argue that in an important sense his so-called epistemology is a 'foreign element' in his work.[52] Garvie supplies several interesting examples of how this worked out in practice. For instance, there is the well-known, and contentious, teaching of Ritschl that 'the Church, and not the individual members . . . is . . . the subject of justification'. Garvie plausibly argues that from the standpoint of a consistent empiricism it cannot be said that the permanent (or underlying) unity of the Church is given in experience – at the grass roots, we experience only those individual, discrete units who comprise the Church. Garvie argues that the notion is a 'speculative inference' which is thoroughly metaphysical in nature. His wry conclusion on this point is that Ritschl's practice is sometimes better than his theory![53] Even more telling is Garvie's demonstration of how Ritschl's commitment to metaphysical speculation has been productive of great difficulty at a central point in his doctrine of God. He construes God, as is well known, as love expressed in an eternal will directed towards the final reconciliation of mankind in the Kingdom of God. This, says Garvie persuasively, is a '*speculative construction* of the idea of God's eternity' from which Ritschl refused to budge, *notwithstanding overwhelming Christian experience to the contrary*. Quite incredibly, for a Lutheran (and, much more to the point in this context, for someone alleged to be a narrow empiricist), he refused to give weight to the universal Christian experience of being under the wrath of God, which led Luther typically and paradoxically to construe God as simultaneously love and wrath. No, says Ritschl, the consciousness of being under God as wrath is false, rooted in human ignorance and illusion – God is eternally and immutably love! Garvie's very apt comment is that Ritschl here sacrifices the truth of the religious consciousness on the altar of a speculative idea![54] We really ought once more to feel distinctly uneasy about the application of the stereotype 'antimetaphysical empiricist' as applied to Ritschl. Second, there is the question of a certain *reverent agnosticism* in Ritschl. One of the most famous (or infamous) statements in his work is the following: 'I, too, recognize mysteries in the religious life, but . . . when anything is and remains a mystery, I say nothing about it.'[55] This remark is made in the context of a discussion of the justification and regeneration of the individual, brought about by the continuous action of Christ in his community which evokes trust and faith through the Holy Spirit. Having given a general description of the process, he remarks: 'How this state is brought about eludes all observation, like the development of the individual spiritual life in general.' Discussing this sentence, John Macquarrie has recently linked it with the 'positivist trend in Ritschl's theology', and with Wittgenstein's remarks in the *Tractatus* about the identity of the 'mystical' and the 'inexpressible'.[56] There is some truth in Macquarrie's charge of positivism, and we cannot but be reminded of one of the charges of the luminous Garvie, to the effect that Ritschl fixes his regard on what may be called the phenomenal aspects of reality, and averts his gaze from what we may in contrast call its ontological bases.[57] It is perfectly true that the interpreter cannot help feeling irked by Ritschl's stubborn reluctance to press through beyond the phenomenal towards its ontological anchorage, even though this means the stretching to breaking-point of parabolic, symbolic and analogical language. Indubitably, his 'reverent agnosticism' was somewhat restrictive and inhibiting. There is the famous instance where he refuses to allow us to *go beyond the datum* of Christ's revealed solidarity with God, expressed in an identity of will to the point of death, because the attempt to determine in detail Christ's relationship with God, 'how it has come into being and empirically how it has come to be what it is', is superfluous because ineffectual, and 'it is dangerous to give oneself to these attempts since they are superfluous'.[58] It is quite distressing and frustrating to observe him approaching the very core of the Christian faith, Christ's identity from all eternity with God, and then allowing an inhibiting agnosticism to stop him in his tracks and make him fall into silence! But the conclusion to draw from this is not that Ritschl was some kind of philosophical phenomenalist trying to eliminate all mystery from Christian existence, but a hesitantly agnostic theologian, vividly aware, indeed, of those points in Christian existence where phenomena point beyond themselves to areas of mystery which appeared to him to elude the grasp of language, and before which therefore the only appropriate response is a reverent reserve which calls for silence. He is not beyond criticism for adopting such a stance. But his position does not warrant the coarse charge that there is no room for talk of the 'beyond' in his work, or that his theology is incapable of being supplemented or corrected (as it eventually was by his disciple Julius Kaftan of Berlin) by talk of the ontological. Third, at various points in our exposition we have been obliged to interpret Ritschl as having been motivated by a 'nervous fear'. Now it is hard to read the epistemological sections of his work without being strongly impressed by the disillusionment he expressed at the collapse of the Hegelian idealism of his youth and the supplanting of it by scientifically oriented forms of materialism and positivism. Philip Hefner, commenting on Volume 1 of Otto Ritschl's biography of his father, makes the point that from the beginning of his university days Ritschl lived in the atmosphere in which a supernatural approach to Christian belief was fighting for its life, partly over against a scientific, materialistic world view that rejected both.[59] But Professor Claude Welch uses stronger language. Speaking of the period 1835 to 1870 in European intellectual history, Welch remarks that 'the collapse of idealism, which had been born out of the Protestant spirit, *was experienced as a collapse of Christianity itself*; and the influence of the mixture of Christianity with *Aufklärung* was weakened'.[60] It is almost superfluous to point how these words cast light on Ritschl's nervousness lest he be interpreted as making the Christian faith rest upon an outmoded and discredited idealism.

If so, it is not particularly hard to sketch in broad strokes Ritschl's theological vision and the motivation behind it in their *Sitz im Leben*. He visualized two types of Christianity, the first of which in his view needed to be supplanted in his time by the second. The first of these we conveniently label *Christianity A* and the second *Christianity B*. The crucial differences between them may without difficulty be spelled out under the four

categories of God, Man, christology and sin. Taking *Christianity
A* first, we may summarize and say that so far as its doctrine of
God was concerned it over-emphasized God's hiddenness, un-
observability and elusiveness, leading him to predicate of its
God-image the attributes of placidity, indifference, inertia, pallor
and unrelatedness. Of its doctrine of man his view was that the
dominant trend was to stress man's genuine or authentic nature
as hidden, imperceptible, located somehow 'behind' or 'beyond'
man's public, observable, historico-temporal behaviour, so that
the locus of the divine-human encounter was regarded as in the
otherworldly depths of the soul. Christologically, *Christianity A*
stresses the union between God and Christ as essentially one of
metempirical, unobservable being or substance, *inferred* in some
way *from* the data of Christ's public, historical life. Under the
category of sin, attention is focused upon 'sinfulness' rather than
upon 'sins', the comprehension of which involves us in inferring
to a mysterious, hidden, metaphysical corruption or dislocation
whose location is posited within an elusive, hereditary substratum identified as substantial human nature, a doctrine which
within Catholic scholasticism and Protestant orthodoxy alike had
become the subject of fruitless and tedious metaphysical hair-
splitting – a doctrine which had played a not insignificant role in
alienating modern post-seventeenth-century man from the
Christian faith as a compelling interpretation of his existence in
the world.[61] Turning to *Christianity B*, we find that in its doctrine
of God emphasis is placed upon God's *purpose* as displayed in the
revelation of Christ in history, and perpetuated in the consciousness and work of the Christian community, in which attention is
focused upon the observable effects of encounter with Christ.
Christianity B's anthropology understands man first and fore-
most as a spatio-temporal, empirical, historical, social creature,
impelled by moral awareness towards fellowship with others in a
community grounded on brotherly love, but gravely impeded
from so doing by his worldly environment interpreted in both
material and social terms; this anthropology understands man in
an 'existential' way, as resolving, decision-making will aiming at
observable fruits of Christian character organized into a concrete
worldly vocation and *Lebensführung*. Christologically, *Christianity B* is grounded firmly on the historical witness to Christ's

observable effort to conform his will, in the teeth of hideous opposition from the world, to God's will understood as an eternal ordination to found the Kingdom of God, into which men are drawn simply on account of their redemption wrought by Christ, understood as Lord of the world and source of all supramundane lordship. Within this context, sin is seen as the empirical, behavioural result of a quite empirical corruption of man, in which he tragically fails to realize himself as more than a natural creature and in which he becomes trapped within a network of interacting evil relations and influences. In the case of *Christianity A* the following predicates suggest themselves: idealistic, otherworldly, unempirical, mystico-pietistic, metaphysical (i.e. overconcerned with essentiality and substantiality), static, individualistic, and epistemologically elusive. In sharp contrast, *Christianity B* attracts the following: experiential, empirical, observable, social, communal, historical, ethical, dynamic, existential (because concerned paramountly with a concrete lifestyle). Ritschl's claim would undoubtedly have been that *Christianity A* was rooted in outmoded philosophical idealism and quietistic pietism, complacently insensitive to new, important scientific and philosophical convictions, unhealthily linked to Christian traditions cherishing the static and the unchanging, sitting far too lightly to that rediscovery of original worldly Christianity whose exposition and transmission was the principal aim of the sixteenth-century reformers. And he would have claimed, likewise, that *Christianity B* in sharp contrast was sensitive to all that was best in the post-*Aufklärung* stress on experience which issued in the demands of the practical reason, in critical touch with the best in modern philosophy and science, which gave prominence to the observable, the ethically valuable, and the socially transforming, and rooted firmly in that dynamic Christianity which Luther and his colleagues strove to bequeath to the modern world. In articulating this vision, Ritschl was, as we have indicated, dependent upon epistemological tools, insights and terminology, but only in a subsidiary or peripheral or utilitarian way – certainly not in any way which has justified the unreflective, damaging application to him of stereotyping labels which restrictively confine him to the narrow viewpoint of any philosophical school. In what follows, no attempt will be made to overlook the extent to which Ritschl's reaction from *Christianity A* to *Christianity B* may have been an unfortunate over-reaction, or that *Christianity B* involved its adherents in certain long-term problems. But it seems only just to attempt a fair-minded interpretation of Ritschl's visionary aim or purpose taken as a whole.

NOTES TO CHAPTER II

1 J. K. Mozley, *Ritschlianism*, p. 24.
2 op. cit., p. 27, italics mine.
3 *The Ritschlian Theology*, p. 161, italics mine.
4 op. cit., p. 375.
5 *Types of Modern Theology*, London 1937, p. 143, italics mine.
6 *Theology and Metaphysics*, in *Albrecht Ritschl: Three Essays*, p. 155; hereafter, this will be referred to as *T. & M.* in the pagination of *Three Essays*.
7 *T. & M.*, p. 157.
8 ibid., p. 165.
9 *An Existentialist Theology*, London 1955, p. 32.
10 ibid., pp. 32–4.
11 *T. & M.*, p. 158.
12 ibid., p. 160.
13 *J. & R.* III, pp. 215 f.
14 *T. & M.*, p. 156.
15 ibid., p. 157.
16 J. Macquarrie, *Principles of Christian Theology*, London 1966, p. 43.
17 *J. & R.* III, pp. 216–17.
18 *T. & M.*, p. 161.
19 *J. & R.* III, p. 219.
20 ibid., p. 220.
21 ibid.; Kant's *Critique of Judgement*, para. 88.
22 For what follows, see *J. & R.* III, pp. 221 f.
23 *Critique of Judgement*, para 90.
24 *J. & R.* III, p. 226.
25 *An Introduction to the Theology of Albert Ritschl*, p. 168.
26 ibid., p. 169.
27 See *T. & M.*, pp. 195 f.
28 Introduction to *Three Essays*, p. 16; see also Hefner's translation of Ritschl's *Prolegomena to the History of Pietism*, pp. 51–147.
29 *The Ritschlian Theology*, p. 385.
30 *Types*, p. 140.
31 *T. & M.*, p. 196; cf. *J. & R.* III, pp. 108–14.
32 *T. & M.*, p. 198.
33 *J. & R.* III, p. 6.
34 ibid., p. 8.
35 For what follows, see *The Ritschlian Theology*, pp. 379 f.

36 *An Introduction to the Theology of Albrecht Ritschl*, p. 149.
37 *T. & M.*, p. 174.
38 See, e.g., *T. & M.*, p. 166; cf. ibid., p. 184: 'A thing "exists" in its relationships and it is only in them that we can know the thing and only by them that we can name it.'
39 See *The Ritschlian Theology*, pp. 375 f.
40 *T. & M.*, p. 166.
41 ibid., pp. 169–70.
42 *On Religion: Speeches to Its Cultured Despisers*, ET by John Oman, New York 1958, p. 48, italics mine.
43 For what follows, see *T. & M.*, pp. 178–84.
44 ibid., p. 180.
45 Wolfhart Pannenberg, *Basic Questions in Theology*, vol. ii, London 1971, p. 121, italics mine: Pannenberg's entire essay, 'The Appropriation of the Philosophical Concept of God as a Dogmatic Problem of Early Christian Theology', pp. 119–83, is a remarkable attempt to explore the extent to which contemporary theology might bridge the gap between theology and metaphysics introduced by Ritschl; *Jesus – God and Man*, London 1968, p. 389, n. 53.
46 See, e.g., my *Theology and Metaphysics*, London 1970, ch. III.
47 *T. & M.*, p. 181.
48 ibid., pp. 183 f.
49 *J. & R.* III, pp. 19–20.
50 *T. & M.*, pp. 184–5.
51 ibid., pp. 163–5.
52 *The Ritschlian Theology*, pp. 375–6.
53 ibid., p. 63.
54 ibid., pp. 376–7.
55 *J. & R.* III, p. 607 n.
56 *Thinking About God*, London 1975, p. 30; Macquarrie's paper 'Mystery and Truth', pp. 28–43, is a suggestive attempt to show how mystery may be tentatively probed in order that the truth 'behind it' may be grasped.
57 *The Ritschlian Theology*, p. 62.
58 *T. & M.*, p. 178.
59 Introduction to *Three Essays*, p. 6.
60 *Protestant Thought in the Nineteenth Century*, vol. i, 1799–1870, New Haven, Conn. 1972, p. 3, italics mine. It is interesting that here the matrix of Ritschl's theology is considered to be the *weakening* of the mixture 'Christianity and Idealism'. Much nonsense has been talked of 'nineteenth-century idealism' without precise definition. Hence Lotz (*Ritschl and Luther*, p. 153) is critical of the heuristic scheme 'Ritschl and Idealism'.
61 See the brief discussion in *T. & M.*, pp. 200–6, and Ch. IV below.

CHAPTER III

Religion and God

Since Ritschl prefaces his doctrine of God with a discussion of the nature and characteristics of religion in general, it is a commonplace that we must first have some grasp of the latter before we can appreciate the former. Thus stated, the issue seems clear – but in fact the relation between these two, religion and God, is not merely complex but also extremely polemical, as even a superficial acquaintance with twentieth-century theological discussion informs us. But more of this polemic presently. In approaching the question of religion, Ritschl draws another sharp distinction between purely philosophical and truly religious knowledge by asserting (and here he would have been supported by Aquinas) that the latter transcends the former in that its content includes reference to 'blessedness', to what Catholic theology denotes as 'man's supernatural end'.[1] But Ritschl hastens to distinguish his position from that of St Thomas by abandoning any rational or speculative substructure (in any metaphysical sense) for his own soteriological interpretation of Christianity. Indeed, *all religion* for him is exclusively soteriological in nature, a fact which leads him to define religion as 'an interpretation of man's relation to God and the world, guided by the thought of the sublime power of God to realize the end of this blessedness of man'.[2] The immediate objection to this is that it arbitrarily excludes, for example, the nontheistic religions, such as Theravada Buddhism, and he willingly concedes that this is so. His formula, he admits, employs terms with such a definite Christian connotation (God, world, blessedness) that it cannot function as a definition proper. It could not possibly comprehend phenomena such as dualism, pluralism, ancestor worship, animism and the like. Nevertheless, he argues, 'advancing insight into the history of religions has forced on us the task of formulating a universal *conception of religion*, under which all the particular species of religion might find their peculiar features determined'. But for the moment all he claims to need is 'a general conception of religion more or less distinct in outline' enabling him to 'determine the chief characteristics of the various species of religion'.[3] Now clearly his contribution to the history of religions here is not only a little imprecise but also rather slight. But we learned in the previous chapter that, *ex hypothesi*, it is always worth while considering Ritschl's motives to be overwhelmingly *theological* rather than scientific, and we find, indeed, that this is as true of his flirtation with the history of religions as his treatment of epistemology. In the first place, his general 'conception of religion' enables him to make an antiphilosophical point of some importance, namely, that a slight acquaintance with other faiths teaches us that 'the secular knowledge they involve is not disinterestedly theoretical, but guided by practical ends'.[4] The *theological* converse of this is that the secular knowledge (he means Greek metaphysics, Hegelian idealism, and the like) which has made its way into the Christian Church 'should be expelled, as something accidental, from the idea of the Christian religion'.[5] In the second place, he insists that the 'general conception of religion' should be used *regulatively* but not *constitutively*. He means by this that the general conception informs us in a broad way of what is authentically and what is inauthentically religious (e.g., the desire for salvation contrasted with the desire for metaphysical understanding), but not the specific *content* and *meaning* of the Christian religion itself. In illustrating the illegitimate *constitutive* use of the general conception, he points to the theological method which involves adopting a stance of neutrality towards Christianity, so that its meaning may be deduced from the general conception. The only effect of this, he writes, 'is to undermine the Christian conviction', and this, as a theologian, he will not have! In all probability he has in mind the typically *Aufklärung* notion of Christianity being but one Western instantiation of the pure, universal religion of reason. In the third place, the general conception allows him to argue for the science of religion as an attempt to view the various religions 'as elements in the spiritual history of humanity', rather than as a 'comparison of the historical religions as species of this genus'. If this former method were pursued, and he admits that so far it has not, in a scientific (i.e, impartial and unprejudiced) way, religions would be viewed as *stages* rather than as *phenomena*. The great virtue of this, and here we have Ritschl the Christian theologian speaking at his clearest, is that Christians would be able to judge the religions 'by the principle that Christianity transcends them all, and that in Christianity the tendency of all the others finds its perfect consummation', and that it would then be 'impossible for us when arranging religions in a series of stages, to shut our eyes to the claim of Christianity to occupy the highest place'.[6] That he made no claim whatever to be a disinterested, scientific phenomenologist of religion is demonstrated incontrovertibly by his statement that 'those qualities in other religions by which they *are* religions are intelligible to us chiefly as measured by the perfection which they assume in Christianity'; it follows that, for Ritschl, the study of religion 'amounts to no more than a scientific attempt to promote mutual understanding *among Christians*'! After all, he remarks, Buddhists and Hindus have become acquainted with Christianity only to argue that their faiths are superior to the Christian, and our experience should lead us to abandon the attempt, *by scientific scholarship*, to demonstrate to Mohammedans or Buddhists the superiority of Christianity.

It is beyond the scope of this work to investigate the problems in what has been described as Ritschl's not altogether clear and rather insignificant contribution to the science of religion. But we must not overlook the considerable historical significance of his views for religious thought in the early twentieth century. Curiously, his views here have evoked two diametrically opposed and mutually incompatible judgements, which makes it difficult for us to reach a clear estimate of his teaching on the relation of Christianity to religion as such. For, on the one hand, when, early in the twentieth century, members of the so-called *Religionsgeschichtlicheschule* (Bousset, Heitmüller, Gunkel and Troeltsch) criticized prevailing Christian theology as provincial, limited, narrow minded, emphasizing Christianity as a unique and isolated phenomenon, exclusively absolute in its decisive christocentrism and bibliocentrist, *they had Ritschl's theology explicitly in mind*! Indeed, some of them, like Troeltsch, had begun their careers as his pupils and disciples. But Troeltsch came to deplore, above all else, the fact that in the work of Ritschl the broader, more tolerant, more universal and flexible view of Schleiermacher on religion had been abandoned in favour of an incredibly narrowly-based and exclusively christocentric view of the relation between man and God, which led him to abandon his earlier Ritschlian claim to Christianity's exclusive monopoly of universal truth. To be sure, Ritschl's view did not go as far as Barth's later claim that 'Christianity is the abolition of all religion', but it could be interpreted, as it undoubtedly was interpreted by those of Troeltsch's persuasion, as *a definite stage on the way to Barth's position*. But, on the other hand, a completely opposing and incompatible judgement has been put forward and defended. In 1927, the dialectical theologian, Emil Brunner, published his christological book, *Der Mittler*,[7] which contains important, if harshly critical, discussions of the main theologians of the nineteenth-century German tradition.[8] (In this connection, it is only fair to remember that Barth did not altogether approve of the violence of some of Brunner's strictures – hence his rejection of Brunner's 1924 book on Schleiermacher, *Die Mystik u. das Wort*.)[9] Brunner praises Ritschl for having openly condemned Schleiermacher's dependence on the idea of a universal religion, conceived in the spirit of the Enlightenment, although, tragically, Ritschl did not perceive that he had built his own theology upon a similar conception of religion. Brunner concurs with the harsh judgement of Ritschl that 'he adorned a building constructed wholly in the Rationalistic style with a supernatural gateway', with the proviso that this refers to Ritschl's accomplishment rather than to his actual intention. Despite his laudable attempt to exclude metaphysics from theology, he erred in identifying metaphysics exclusively with Hegelian ontology, forgetting that there is also an ethical metaphysic. Hence Ritschl's theological system is simply 'a well-constructed system of ethical metaphysics developed along logical lines'. Brunner is here implying that Ritschl, right from the outset, allowed a 'general conception' of religion to intrude itself and become determinative for his system, giving his account of Christianity a shape and slant and perspective derived from profane philosophy, a procedure anathema to that theological school of which Brunner was a distinguished founder. It is not easy to appraise simultaneously these two violently diverging reactions to Ritschl's teaching on religion, but there are good grounds for suggesting the following. It is hard to dissent from the judgement of Troeltsch and his colleagues that the overall tendency of *Ritschl's theology as a whole* was to steer twentieth-century theological endeavour into rather exclusively christocentric and bibliocentric channels in which it could insulate itself from wider cultural, philosophical and religious currents of thought, an insulation which they all came to regard as stultifying and sterile. Ritschl's *over-all* christocentrism and bibliocentrism, which we have tried to bring out by reiterating his overwhelmingly theological motivation at point after point, is plain upon every page that he wrote on Christian theology. If this is so, we can plainly appeal to the support of Troeltsch and his colleagues for our claim that in yet another way Barth and his colleagues stood more upon Ritschl's shoulders (theologically speaking) than they knew or admitted. On the other hand, there is the neo-orthodox critique of Brunner which, despite the fact that Brunner was notoriously prejudiced, must be reckoned with. For it was criticism like Brunner's, that the determining factor of Ritschl's system was a rationalistic and ethical 'general conception' of religion, which produced the vexatious stereotypes of Ritschl as a 'neo-Kantian' or 'Lotzean' or 'moralistic' distorter of Christianity. Whether Brunner's criticisms of Ritschl can be substantiated or not depends upon a careful examination of exactly what is involved in his 'general conception' and its relation to the structure and content of his system as a whole, to which we now turn.

First, it is necessary to set down and examine several celebrated expressions of Ritschl's 'general conception'. The following is probably the most famous of them all:

> In every religion what is sought, with the help of the super-human spiritual power reverenced by man, is a solution of the contradiction in which man finds himself, as both a part of the world of nature and a spiritual personality claiming to dominate nature. For in the former role he is a part of nature, dependent upon her, subject to and confined by other things; but as spirit he is moved by the impulse to maintain his independence against them. In this juncture, religion springs up as faith in superhuman spiritual powers, by whose help the power man possesses of himself is in some way supplemented, and elevated into a unity of its own kind which is a match for

the pressure of the natural world. The idea of gods, or Divine powers, everywhere includes belief in their spiritual personality, for the support to be received from above can only be reckoned on in virtue of an affinity between God and men.[10]

Beside this may be placed the following:

> ... In heathen and even in polytheistic religions there is always a tendency at work towards belief in the unity of the Divine power, and in the measure in which this is the case the supplement to his own resources which man seeks in religion becomes more clear and more worthy.[11]

Finally, we may consider the following:

> In every religion, not only is some sort of communion with God (or the gods) sought after and attained, but there is also a search at the same time for such a position of the individual vis-à-vis the world as will correspond with the idea of God which guides that religion.[12]

Self-evidently the nerve of such definitions is what Ritschl means by terms such as 'world', 'world of nature', and so on, but before analysing these there are several other factors worth careful note at this point. The first is that the general conception at one stroke rules out of court any subsequent doctrine in Ritschl's system of *the total depravity or corruption of human nature*. For Ritschl, God is that condescending being 'by whose help the *power man possesses of himself* is in some way supplemented'; grace is regarded as 'the supplement to *his own resources* which man seeks in religion'. For hostile critics, this has led to outright condemnation. 'The Ritschlian doctrine of sin,' writes the implacably hostile Brunner, 'comes very close to that of Pelagius.'[13] But these are the words of a critic and need to be handled with extreme caution. For, as we shall see in the next chapter, there were powerful motives for Ritschl to be punctiliously careful in handling potentially 'explosive' doctrines such as original sin and total depravity. Having to consider these at a later point, it is enough to say now that one of the elements in Ritschl's *Zeitgeist* was the highly articulated accusation that Protestantism, with its 'objectionable doctrines' of original sin and total depravity, justification by faith at the expense of works, was morally ennervating and irresponsibly antisocial. As an apologetic theologian this was a charge of which he was vividly conscious (it was brought against him personally, as a Lutheran theologian, by his academic colleague, Paul de Lagarde) and which he felt, as a life-or-death matter, must be definitively answered in his lifetime.[14] (But of this attempt to understand Ritschl's thought in its *Sitz im Leben* there is, in the harshly critical Brunner, not a word.) There is more to it than that. The issue of human responsibility, the place of works in the Christian life alongside faith, lies right at the heart of Ritschl's life-work, of his researches on pietism, of his Reformation studies, of his systematic theology, with their stress on the Christian's concrete ethical lifestyle in the secular world. He tried to bring this out by the choice of title for his main work *Justification and Reconciliation*, which reflects intentionally the complementary pairs 'faith' and 'works', 'gift' and 'task', God's gracious *gift* of salvation in Christ coupled with the *task* inescapably laid upon man of responding by actively involving himself in God's work of reconciliation. But it is most precisely brought out by Ritschl's celebrated statement that 'Christianity, so to speak, resembles not a circle described from a single centre, but an ellipse which is determined by two *foci*'.[15] The first *focus* refers to 'redemption through Christ' and the second to 'the ethical interpretation of Christianity through the idea of the Kingdom of God'.

It was Ritschl's conviction, as a historian, that n the entire history of Christianity very unequal emphasis had been laid on these two defining characteristics. Indeed, he seems untypically to favour Catholicism at this point because there at least an attempt has been made to give fair treatment to both poles, an attempt duplicated for modern Protestantism by Kant in his doctrine of the Kingdom, while the main sixteenth-century reformers (Calvin, Luther, Melancthon, Zwingli) are held responsible for having transmitted to the modern world either a Christianity overwhelmingly centred on the former pole (to the detriment of the latter), or one in which the Kingdom of God has been disastrously spiritualized or internalized. In contradistinction to all of this, he wanted to expound a Christianity in which faith and ethical works would be presented in the closest possible unity, as the coherent systematization of these diverse theological thrusts which had been rather ill-married partners in the West since the late Middle Ages. At this point, hopefully enough has been said to refute the insinuation that Ritschl was some kind of 'liberal-protestant', superficial nineteenth-century rationalist who lacked insight into the orthodox 'profundities' of original sin and total depravity. On the contrary, his alleged 'Pelagianism' has, as we shall see in the next chapter, broad and deep theological, historical and ethical roots.

The second is that the 'general conception' of religion demonstrates that for Ritschl religion originates in the *human predicament* and that the 'postulate' of God arises in the attempt to resolve this. Man experiences his existence, so to speak, in intolerable tension; he is 'torn asunder' by the downward pull of the 'world of nature', which is agonizingly counteracted upon by the upward pull of his ethical and spiritual consciousness which informs him that, as spirit, 'he is worth more than the entire natural world'. The point not to be overlooked here is that once more the picture of the unfortunate Ritschl mediated to modernity is onesidedly hostile. Hence the late H. R. Mackintosh, writing in the heyday of neo-orthodoxy (1936) of Ritschl's general conception, informs us that his (Ritschl's) view of religion as such is utilitarian and intramundane.[16] Ritschl argues 'that religion has emerged as a product of the struggle for existence'. This means, in Mackintosh's view, that on Ritschl's terms the attitude of man to the cosmos is made central and all-determining, not his attitude to God. But an element of caricature intrudes itself when Mackintosh summarizes Ritschl thus: 'God is the needed prop of ethical aspiration, the trustee of our moral interests.' Significantly, and here we see with great clarity the actual formation of one of the principal neo-orthodox stereotypes, the long-term damning criticism of Ritschl reproduced by Mackintosh is that to speak, even incidentally, as if the function of God were to stand surety for the attainment of human purposes, even though these purposes at their highest are moral, was to invite the graver error of *Kulturprotestantismus* in the next generation (a specific criticism to be explored in Chapter VI). All of this, in Mackintosh's judgement, could only end in 'this-worldly' religion. And, as the stereotypes proliferated, we have the application to Ritschl of the pejorative labels 'anthropological', 'anthropocentric', 'humanistic', and the like. These criticisms must be spelled out in some detail if only, by a process of scholarly catharsis, to rid our minds of those stereotyping filters through which, in the last few decades, we have been encouraged to regard the unhappy Ritschl! Not that it should be too difficult, from today's theological standpoint, to rid our minds of these. For we live in a generation which has become as impatient with the preconceptions of neo-orthodoxy as the interwar generation became with those of the Ritschlian school. That is, we have become sceptical of a theological system in which the place of the concretely human has been reduced almost to vanishing-point, a scepticism nurtured by criticisms like those of John Baillie that neo-orthodoxy has been guilty of the progressive *dehumanization* of man,[17] or of Paul Tillich that man simply cannot receive answers to questions that he has never asked.[18] In other words, in his quest for God, man must begin *from within his finitude in the world* – there is just no other starting-point.

No one knew this better than Ritschl. In his lifetime he was accused by critics of 'moralizing' Christianity through his adherence to Kant's analysis of the moral structure of human nature and of man's moral predicament in the world. In his answer to this, Ritschl remarks tartly that such critics 'would do better to acquire a thorough knowledge of the elementary distinction between the *ratio essendi* and the *ratio cognoscendi*, instead of sitting in judgement on me'.[19] In an interesting discussion of Ritschl's statement, John Baillie relates it to the teaching of Christian orthodoxy, remarking that there it has long been taught that God comes first in the *ordo essendi* but not in the *ordo cognoscendi*; that he is therefore *notior per se* but not *notior nobis*; or again that he is *prior simpliciter* but not *prior quoad nos*. Baillie rightly adds that Christian orthodoxy has taken no exception to a theology which makes our *knowledge* of God derivative, so long as it is made clear that God's *being* is not derivative; this, it has long been held, 'is in accordance with the facts of the spiritual life'. Hence, according to orthodoxy, God is the first reality to exist but the last to be known. Baillie rightly remarks that this distinction has been maintained in modern times by Kant, Ritschl and Herrmann, but also long before them by medieval rational theologians, paramountly St Thomas Aquinas, so that it is now regarded as a necessary part of Roman ortho-doxy.[20] Ironically, and amusingly, if Baillie is right, it is the 'liberal-protestant' arch-heretic Ritschl, rather than his extreme neo-orthodox critics, who stands in the mainstream of the Christian tradition! In other words, Ritschl is aware that it is only from the finitude of our human situation that we can approach God, although our finitude does not necessarily con-struct and determine him, make him what he is. As Tillich puts it, arguing against Barth's claim that any kind of divine-human correlation makes God partly dependent upon man: 'Although God in his abysmal nature (Calvin: "In his essence") is in no way dependent upon man, God in his self-manifestation to man is dependent on the way man receives his manifestation . . . There is a mutual interdependence between "God for us" and "we for God".'[21]

But actually, the changed theological climate which now enables us to give Ritschl a fair and unbiased hearing has been brought about by, above all others, Herrmann's greatest pupil, Rudolf Bultmann. We have previously argued that Ritschl's system must now be seen as a significant source of the recent theology of existence, and nowhere is this more apparent than in the uncanny parallels between Ritschl's general conception and Bultmann's 'hermeneutical framework' for interpreting the Christian faith. For Bultmann, too, the human predicament consists in being 'torn asunder' by, on the one hand, the downward drag of man's empirical, here-and-now self, rooted in inauthenticity of life, and, on the other, by the claims, deriving from man's self-conscious-ness, of man's future, but as yet unrealized authentic self. It is this interpretation of man-in-the-world which supplies man with that pre-understanding (*Vorverständnis*) which alone enables him to approach the Christian sources with any hope of receiving an answer. It must be noted also that for Bultmann, too, man's life (whether within the situation of faith or without it) is inalienably rooted in a certain *relationship to the world*. Hence Bultmann can describe the Christian faith thus: 'Belief means, as the anticipa-tion of every possible future, *the taking of man out of the world*, and his ingrafting into eschatological existence. In this way it gives to the man of faith a peculiar detachment from the world (1 Corinthians 7: 29–31).'[22] The outcome of this, in Bultmann's view, is that with this eschatological reservation, the world has again become perceptible as creation (or, as Ritschl puts it, in faith the world comes to be seen, not as an end or good in itself, but as God's created means to God's and man's *Summum Bonum*, the Kingdom of God). Throughout his writings, Bultmann makes it clear, by his reiterated quotation of the Pauline passage 1 Corinthians 7: 29–31, that in Christian faith man is liberated *from the world* so that henceforward the Christian lives *vis-à-vis* the world in a dialectical way – although *not of* the world (i.e., constrained, determined, confined, motivated by the purely worldly) he goes on living *in* the world, freed by God to serve God and his neighbour in a new, fresh way, but *never* (cf. Ritschl!) in a mystical mode.[23] Bultmann summarized it all neatly in a 1926 paper: 'According to Paul, the Christian stands in a peculiarly broken relation to the world. The existence of the Christian is in the world, but does not belong to the world. It belongs to the future which is God's (1 Corinthians 7: 29–31).'[24] Naturally, in all this we must be careful not to read an affinity with Ritschl *into* Bultmann, and so it is necessary to enquire if Bultmann himself has ever noticed such an affinity. The answer to this is in the affirmative. While it is true that Bultmann mentions Ritschl's name only infrequently, he does so in a passage which contains a crucial judgement.[25] One of Bultmann's main preoccupations has always been the problem of *hermeneutics* – the problem of how a historical text cannot be properly understood unless the hermeneute approaches it with an appropriate *Begrifflichkeit* (system of concepts) which possesses a close affinity or sympathy with the intentions and preconceptions of the text's author. An inappropriate *Begrifflichkeit* violates these intentions and may issue in a calamitous misunderstanding of the historical work. As long ago as 1928 Bultmann was wrestling with such problems in the context of New Testament exegesis, as a prolegomenon to his more recent existential interpretation of it. In pleading for the programmatic application of an existential or anthropological *Begrifflichkeit* to the New Testament text, he rightly warns us that our conventional understanding of human existence has been determined by the development of modern thought, into which has been woven all kinds of elements (e.g., from rationalism, Greek metaphysics, the natural sciences and modern psychology), possessing little if any affinity with, for example, the *Begrifflichkeit* of St Paul. Hence Bultmann is fairly unsympathetic to much biblical interpretation of the past, due to lack of appreciation of and interest in these difficulties. He comments therefore: 'Hence – with a few exceptions *such as the interpretations of Albrecht Ritschl* and Adolf Schlatter – the concepts of Pauline anthropology are interpreted on the basis of a conception of existence wholly different from that out of which they came.' In other words, Bultmann is claiming that Ritschl's hermeneutical principles are, like his own, *existential* ones, possessing an affinity with St Paul's as a theological author! There is, though, one apparent difficulty in Bultmann's claim. How can there be a fundamental affinity between Ritschl's exegetical approach and that of Bultmann if, according to the 'historians', the former was overwhelmingly ethical (even 'moralistic') in his intentions and methods, while the latter is overwhelmingly 'existential' in his? But having had reason to be sceptical of the verdicts of the 'historians' at point after point, perhaps we should question their judgement at this point. Perhaps Bultmann has perceived something of great moment: namely, that when Ritschl spoke, as he did so often, of 'ethical' and 'moral', he did not intend by these terms a dry as dust,[26] legalistic, puritanical, conformist, 'duty for duty's sake' business, but (like Schleiermacher before him) of ethics as the science of concrete, historical, practical, existential, lifestyle-forming action, which would more than indicate an affinity between his approach and that of Bultmann (an issue to which we shall return in Chapter VI). Our conclusion therefore on this point is that, in the light of a changed theological climate there is no longer any compelling reason to judge that Ritschl, by using regulatively a general conception of religion in his systematic theology, 'distorted' or 'humanized' the Christian faith. To the contrary, it can be argued (as we shall do presently) that by doing so Ritschl made available to his contemporaries a restatement of Christianity which possessed striking relevance for their life-situation, leading to the formation of the Ritschlian school and the dominance of his name for over forty years.

To return to his general conception of religion, we now investigate critically what is clearly its key-term, 'world' ('natural world', 'world of nature', and so on). To do so leads to a fascinating discovery. By making 'world' his key term, he significantly correlated the life-situation of late nineteenth-century man on the one hand with on the other at least one significant strand in the soteriological and christological material of the Christian tradition. We are reminded of Mackintosh's hostile judgement: 'On Ritschl's terms the attitude of man to the cosmos is made central and all-determining, not his attitude to God. The point is one at which the theologian wholly loses touch with Scripture.'[27] Apart from the ignoring here of the crucial distinction between the *ratio essendi* and the *ratio cognoscendi*, this statement can be demonstrated to be factually untrue. Ritschl, as a mediating theologian, in making 'world' a key concept, was mediating between the Christian tradition and the situation of nineteenth-century man. The term 'world', so used, has two roots: the understanding of the world in nineteenth-century materialism and naturalism, and its connotation in the Christian tradition rooted in the New Testament itself. To deal with the first of these, both the early and the most recent research on Ritschl insist that here he must be interpreted in his *Sitz im Leben*, which means reading him against the background of the rise of philosophical naturalism in the second half of the nineteenth century. (It is disconcerting that the interwar neo-orthodox literature is entirely devoid of any such attempt.) Predictably, the fair Dr Garvie gives careful attention to Ritschl's naturalistic background,[28] quoting Schoen's judgement of his theology (in his *Origines Historiques de la Théologie de Ritschl*): 'To scholars trembling to see theology fall before the attacks of the positive sciences, it shows a way by which all collision with the natural sciences becomes impossible.'[29] But the relatively unsympathetic Dr Orr also draws attention to it, if briefly and immaterially: of Ritschl's era in Germany, he says that following the breakdown of speculative Hegelianism 'a bold materialism, pressing in like a flood, threatened the foundations of moral life'.[30] And very much more recently Philip Hefner has, as noted above, clarified the materialistic aspect of Ritschl's intellectual background.[31] It follows that for Ritschl and his time *the relation of man to the world was quite crucial*. For if reality is equated with the natural world, and if this can only be studied by the natural sciences, then Ritschl saw clearly that man might well be reduced to the stature of one tiny, and perhaps negligible item amongst the myriad items of which nature is composed. If nature is ultimate reality, and man simply a part of nature, it is a short step to the conclusion that man is but one interesting little organism in a world of organisms.[32] It can hardly be stressed too heavily that for reflective Europeans of Ritschl's day the 'world' was experienced as a 'threat', as an impersonal, even hostile, mechanical dimension of causal law within which human personality and its creative uniqueness were doomed. It is only partly against such a background that we can find meaning in the Ritschlian key terms such as 'the threat of nature', the 'threat of the natural world', the 'pressure of the natural world', and, it must be added, correlative ones such as 'lordship over the world', 'supremacy over the world', 'elevation over nature', and the like. Ritschl rightly remarks that what is involved in all this is not so much a straight fight between science and religion, but between philosophico-religious 'scientism' (to borrow a term from C. F. von Weizsäcker)[33] on the one hand, and authentic religion on the other: 'Thus the opposition which professedly exists between natural science and Christianity, really exists between an impulse derived from natural religion blended with the scientific investigation of nature, and the validity of the Christian view of the world, which assures to spirit its pre-eminence over the entire world of nature.'[34] By combating scientific materialism and naturalism, Ritschl was not unsuccessfully attempting to anchor his theology in the life-situation of nineteenth-century man. Had he been so unsuccessful as we have been led to believe, it would be hard to account for the wide and deep influence his theology exercised over several generations. It might, of course, be argued at this point that the implication is that Ritschl's theology, tied as it appears to be to a nineteenth-century culture dominated by these 'scientisms', is hopelessly dated and therefore of antiquarian interest only. But this might be a superficial, not to say dangerous argument. For it has in recent decades been argued that in the light of the insights put forward by twentieth-century logical positivism and empiricism some form of anti-transcendental naturalism has an excellent right to be considered the basic, orthodox philosophical outlook of our contemporary North

Atlantic culture. Those who wish to disagree with this argument might do well to ponder the following recent words of John Hick:

> The more general legacy of the long history of interlocking scientific advance and theological retreat is the assumption, which is part of the characteristic climate of thought in our twentieth-century Western world, that even though the sciences have not specifically disproved the claims of religion, they have thrown such a flood of light upon the world (without at any point encountering that of which theology speaks) that faith can now be regarded only as a harmless private phantasy.[35]

But that is not to expound exhaustively the content of the key term 'world' in Ritschl's system. For it has also an unmistakably *social* connotation. He indicates this neatly when he says that all religion has to do with that sublime power which holds sway in or over the world, 'which sustains or confirms for the personal spirit its own value over against the limitations imposed by nature or by *the natural workings of human society*'.[36] And in explaining that sense in which God's chief end, the Kingdom, is *supramundane*, he says that it is so 'insofar as we understand as "mundane" the nexus of all natural, naturally conditioned and organized existence'.[37] The meaning is that the world of natural society, organized as it is for its own ends, is, like the world of nature, not merely *apathetic* but even *hostile* to the attainment of those moral and spiritual ends encompassed in the divine and human end of the creation, the Kingdom of God. It is not hard to seek out the roots of his teaching here. For (as we shall see in the next chapter) when he comes to investigate the doctrine of sin, he looks, *under the guidance of Scripture*, for the origins of sin in an encounter between individuals and human society viewed under the aspect of a 'kingdom of sin'. And, complementarily, when he undertakes christology, he sees the work of Christ, again *under the guidance of Scripture*, as consisting in the faithfulness of Christ to the point of death to his divine vocation in the teeth of *the most hideous opposition from natural society* – hence, his doctrine of Christ's work can be summed up in the words put into the mouth of Christ by the fourth evangelist, 'I have overcome the world.' It might be helpful if at this point we reminded ourselves of some of the Johannine teaching on the Christian view of the 'world'. An excellent source of this is G. H. C. Macgregor's commentary *The Gospel of John*.[38] Dealing with John 1: 10, Macgregor makes the point that in this verse we have the first hint of that tragic opposition of the world to the Christian community which is everywhere presupposed in the Gospel. The correlative Johannine conception of Christ's work is to draw to himself certain disciples out of the unbelieving mass and to consecrate them as a people apart, within the world and yet 'his own' and no part of it (13: 1; 14: 19, 22; 17: 9, etc.).[39] In commenting upon John 7: 7, he describes the Johannine conception of the 'world' as the sum total of forces ranged against Jesus and his cause (1: 10; 14: 17; 15: 18–19; 16: 20 and 33; 17: 9, 14).[40] And in his treatment of John 8: 23, he quotes with approval Godet's verdict that for the Johannine Gospel the term 'this world' 'signifies human life as constituted independently of, and consequently in opposition to, the will of God'.[41] And in the introduction to his discussion of John 15: 18–16, 33, he speaks of the Johannine distinction everywhere presupposed between 'Christ's own' and that 'world' in which they dwell and which represents the sum total of the forces opposed to Christ.[42] And finally, commenting upon John 17: 9–10, Macgregor makes this point: 'The line of separation between the Christian community and the "world" (i.e. the section of society deliberately hostile to the Church) could not be more strongly stressed than by putting on our Lord's lips the words, "I pray not for the world".' Macgregor explains: 'Let it be remembered that for the Evangelist and his contemporaries the barrier between the Church and the world was in fact a very solid one.'[43] To summarize then, the key term 'world' in Ritschl is rooted not only in nineteenth-century materialistic and naturalistic pessimism, but also in the teaching of the Christian tradition rooted in the New Testament; it refers also to man's social and organizational environment in so far as this is not merely apathetic but even hostile towards man's spiritual and ethical becoming. If so, then Mackintosh's judgement about the centrality of man's attitude to the cosmos rather than God in Ritschl's thinking must be rejected. And his statement that at this point Ritschl 'wholly loses touch with Scripture' is demonstrably false. But his emphasis on 'transcendence over the world', 'independence from the world', 'lordship over the world', and the rest, anticipates also some of the most important theological themes of our own century. Dietrich Bonhoeffer, we recall, in his famous 'Outline for a Book', points out that whereas Western religion's goal was formerly 'to be independent of nature', '. . . our immediate environment (is) not nature, as formerly, but organization'. Hence he asks: 'What protection is there against the danger of organization? Man is once more faced with the problem of himself.'[44] And one of the central themes of the modern philosophy (and theology) of existence concerns the possibility of man losing his authentic being by identifying himself only with those possibilities forced upon him by contemporary society (the 'world'), rather than moulding his own existence upon possibilities placed before him by conscience and by that authentic self which he is not, but which he ought to become.[45] This has been described by saying that man belongs to history rather than nature. This is very much the language of Heidegger (which has been adopted by Bultmann), but behind these, and all existentialists, stands the figure of Kierkegaard, the Christian existentialist, who had more than a century previously brilliantly analysed those ways in which man, in his quest for authenticity of life, was opposed most formidably in so doing by organized society which, in its lust for conformity, anonymity, uniformity and mediocrity, levels a lethal challenge to the genuine ethical and spiritual becoming of the self.[46] In other words, it is hard to agree that Ritschl's teaching on the 'world' is hopelessly dated or possesses merely antiquarian interest. His thought at this point could be described as both pioneering and anticipatory.

The merit of these analyses is that when in their light we turn back to reconsider Ritschl's 'general conception' of religion,[47] we find that, far from being an arbitrary, eccentric or uninformed one, it is one that illumines and is illumined by the post-medieval history of doctrine, 'existentialist' thought, modern hermeneutical problems, modern scientific philosophies, together with elements from the Pauline, Johannine and Synoptic strata of the New Testament. And conversely, we see that a neo-orthodox dismissal such as Brunner's – that Ritschl adorned a building constructed wholly in the Rationalistic style with a supernatural gateway or that his theology is based entirely on a post-Kantian 'ethical

metaphysic' – simply will not hold water. A greater merit of the
analyses is that they enable us at once to make some sense of the
celebrated (or notorious) Ritschlian doctrine of *value-judgements*
which he applied in the first instance to his doctrine of God.
Before doing that, a few preliminary comments might be helpful.
We have already alluded to the fair-minded comment of H. R.
Mackintosh that in Ritschl-interpretation a somewhat false importance has been attached to value-judgements, and it is much
to Mackintosh's credit that he rebutted criticisms of Ritschl here
as 'perverse' and 'childish'.[48] One of the main causes of this was
the publication in the year of Ritschl's death of Leonhard
Stählin's violently hostile *Ritschl, Kant u. Lotze* which, translated
into English in the following year, served to introduce a whole
generation of English-speaking students to the system of Ritschl.
Thanks to Stählin and those who thought like him, by the turn
of the century the battle was raging about the propriety or
impropriety of 'value-judgements in theology'. In this conflict we
can see beginning what has been called the 'terrible vilification' of
Ritschl's name. He, alleged Stählin, had 'subjectified' and
'psychologized' the Christian faith; more valuable to him than
God was the uplifting thought or intramentally entertained
postulate of God. This was shameful, because so easily avoidable.
Actually, it is quite impossible to appreciate Ritschl's value-
judgement theory except *against the background of the history of
the relationship between modern theology and modern science*. To
this subject we now briefly turn. The confusing commingling of
theological, scientific and metaphysical concepts had already
become a frightful problem for theologians by the beginning of
the seventeenth century, when the Christian Pascal, who saw the
problem with great clarity, tried vigorously to cut Christianity
free from scientific and metaphysical entanglements by distinguishing sharply between 'the God of Abraham, of Isaac and
of Jacob, the God and Father of our Lord Jesus Christ' and 'the
God of the philosophers and men of science'. Despite Pascal's
unheeded protest against the Cartesian school, the thinkers of the
Age of Reason, through their subordination of faith to speculative reason, produced a philosophico-theological amalgam which
presented 'the Christian faith' as a not overly difficult target for
the hostile philosophers of the Enlightenment. Despite his ex-

pressed hostility for traditional theology and organized religion, Hume, in his *Dialogues Concerning Natural Religion*, may quite properly be interpreted as sorting out in a neutral but rigorous way that in religion which belongs to faith and that which belongs to reason and *the natural sciences*. And Kant, in a more positive way, was doing much the same thing when he described his attack on metaphysical theology as 'the abolition of reason' which would 'make room for faith'. (By 'faith' Kant meant naturally a purely moral faith. It is worth remarking in passing that when Ritschl's contemporary and neo-orthodox critics accused Ritschl of 'moralizing' Christianity after the fashion of Kant, they were able to do so only by ignoring his important discussions in which he deplored, in his own words, the way in which Kant 'has presented religion as a kind of appendix to morals'.)[49] And Schleiermacher, in his *Reden*, knowing that the 'cultured despisers' of religion cared as little as he did for Kant's ethically based Christianity, sought to make religion completely autonomous by distinguishing it not merely from metaphysics and *natural science*, but also from ethics. Hence, he writes: 'Piety cannot be an instinct craving for a mess of metaphysical and ethical crumbs'; 'Though you pass from the laws to a Universal Lawgiver, in whom is the unity of all things, though you allege that nature cannot be comprehended without God, I would still maintain that religion has nothing to do with this knowledge'; 'Religion is not knowledge and science, either of the world or of God.'[50] The Kant-Schleiermacher thrust of philosophical theology had therefore the aim of distinguishing, as a matter of life-or-death urgency, Christianity from *scientific* and metaphysical themes (and, in Schleiermacher's case, from ethical ones also). In the philosophical theology of Hegel we see the return (or, as some would put it, the regress) to a metaphysico-religious amalgam, producing classical nineteenth-century 'Christian idealism', about which two brief points must be made. First, it was Kierkegaard who brilliantly perceived the acute dangers of the marriage between Christianity and Hegelianism, and violently argued for the short- and long-term incompatibility of the two. Second, the collapse of speculative Hegelianism (and, with it, as already noted, the shattering collapse of 'Christian idealism') was brought about largely by *the rapid progress of the nineteenth-century natural sciences*, and was experienced by Europeans as the shaking of the foundations of European culture and Christian civilization themselves. In these historical developments, the most powerful and possibly the most overlooked factor was the unprecedented *progress of the natural sciences*, which turned out to have profound and far-reaching religious, philosophical and social consequences.

It is only against this historical backdrop, it must be insisted, that we can grasp Ritschl's much misunderstood and much maligned theory of value-judgements. For, as noted in chapter I, by the 1860s theologians were again facing a challenge from scientific philosophies, materialism and evolutionary naturalism. It is no wonder then, that we find Ritschl beginning his value-judgement discussion with the attempt *to prevent a religion-science collision* from which religion, to judge by events in the previous 250 years, *would emerge very much the loser*! Hence we have the celebrated sentence: 'The possibility of both kinds of knowledge mingling, or, again, colliding, lies in this, that they (i.e. religion and philosophy) deal with the same object, namely, the world.'[51] It is utterly important to grasp that Ritschl held that Christianity, like philosophy (in his time), is committed to the construction of a *Weltanschauung* (world-view). It is worth noting this, if only to give the lie to the insinuation that he gaily handed over the task of systematic construction to science and philosophy, leaving religion tied to the unsystematized, vague and nebulous realm of values. No, just as philosophy exercises its ambition 'to comprehend the universe under one supreme law', '. . . for Christian knowledge also one supreme law is the form under which the world is comprehensible under God'. (In this context, it is worth remarking that Ritschl, who, we have argued, anticipated in remarkable degree modern 'existentialist' theologies, is *philosophically* very much more conservative than a thinker like Bultmann, who has long denied that Christianity is or has anything to do with a *Weltanschauung*. Thus, writes Bultmann, 'a *Weltanschauung* stands in sharpest contrast to belief in God.)[52] The difference between the two types of *Weltanschauungen* resides not in their subject-matter (the world) but (and here Ritschl is indebted to the epistemology of Lotze) in the manner 'in which

the mind (*Geist*) . . . appropriates the sensations aroused in it'
Ritschl expounds his view in these words:

> They are determined, according to their value (*Werth*) for the
> Ego, by the feeling of pleasure or pain. Feeling is the basal
> function of mind, inasmuch as in it the Ego is originally present
> to itself. In the feeling of pleasure or pain, the Ego decides
> whether a sensation, which touches the feeling of self, serves to
> heighten or depress it. On the other hand, through an idea the
> sensation is judged in respect of its cause, the nature of the
> latter, and its connection with other causes: and by means of
> observation, etc., the knowledge of things thus gained is
> extended until it becomes scientific.[53]

Several explanatory and apologetic comments are in order here.
First, care must be taken against blatantly foolish misinterpretations of Ritschl's terms 'pleasure' and 'pain'. We have already
alluded briefly in passing (in chapter I)[54] to the young H. R.
Mackintosh's disastrous misinterpretation of Ritschl as a *Hedon-
ist*, on account of the 'pleasure–pain' terminology. Mackintosh's
accusation was this: 'If feeling is to be made the norm of the
judgement of faith in this thorough-going fashion, the most
capricious conceptions of God can claim as much truth as the
purest and most ideal, and theology becomes infected throughout
with *the individual subjectivity of Hedonism*.'[55] 'If religious ideas
and sentiments make their appeal to feeling alone, who shall
decide when feelings disagree? *De gustibus disputandum: each
man's capacity for feeling* becomes the measure of the supernatural world.'[56] 'If the norm (for value-judgements) be objective,
it cannot be defined in terms of feeling alone, as is done by
Ritschl.'[57] Such misinterpretations are ludicrously unfair, if only
because they were so easily avoidable. In partial dependence on
Lotze, Ritschl was obviously using terms such as 'pleasure' and
'pain' in a philosophical, generic sense which goes back to Plato
and beyond. Hence by the generic 'pleasure' and 'pain' he was
intending the pairs 'good' and 'evil', 'happiness' and 'unhappiness',
'blessedness' and 'misery', 'fulfilment' and 'unfulfilment', 'freedom' and 'unfreedom', 'salvation' and 'damnation', 'authenticity'
and 'inauthenticity'. And clearly, objectivity is given to these

terms by linking them firmly to Ritschl's *entire soteriological interpretation of the Christian religion*. Indeed, he makes this very point unambiguously, when he affirms that in this experience of pleasure or pain 'man either enjoys the dominion over the world vouchsafed him *by God*, or feels grievously the lack of *God's help* to that end'.[58] Second, the term 'feeling' (*Gefühl*) calls for comment. Today, due to advances in the phenomenology of religion, we are in a much better position than the young Mackintosh to grasp Ritschl's intention. When he used the German *Gefühl* he was consciously taking his stand in the tradition of Schleiermacher, who both in the *Reden* and in the *Glaubenslehre* had given a phenomenological analysis of the religious consciousness under the category of *Gefühl*. Fortunately, due to the researches of Otto, Tillich, Martin Redeker, R. R. Niebuhr and others, we are able to appreciate that for the Schleiermacher tradition of the nineteenth century the term *Gefühl* has a strongly cognitive flavour, denoting something like 'immediate consciousness', 'immediate awareness', 'inner conviction', 'insight', 'intuition', and the like.[59] One recent writer has unified the Schleiermacher-Otto-Tillich thrust of German thought by suggesting that Schleiermacher's 'feeling of absolute dependence' is comparable to the cognitive 'creaturely feeling' of Rudolf Otto, the 'ultimate concern' of Tillich, and the *Grundbefindlichkeit* of Heidegger.[60] That this preoccupation of nineteenth-century German theologians (Ritschl included) with the structure of human self-consciousness finds its culmination in the twentieth-century existentialists is undeniable. Philip Hefner rightly points out that this was mediated to them particularly through Herrmann, and that it provided an antecedent thrust toward their existentialist orientation. Hefner very importantly continues: 'Their (Bultmann's and Gogarten's) reliance upon the philosophies of Heidegger and Buber, for example, can be construed, as Wrzecionko has done, as a direct elaboration of Ritschl's methodological decision *to avoid metaphysics by turning to the self-consciousness of man*.'[61] Finally, Mackintosh's heavily-laden phrase 'the individual subjectivity of Hedonism' as applied to Ritschl is astounding! 'Hedonism' simply will not do. Neither will the terms 'individual' nor 'subjectivity'. Ritschl had actually taken great pains to protect himself against any such accusations when he composed his celebrated sentence: 'If we can rightly know God only if we know him through Christ, then we can know him only if we belong to the community of believers.'[62] It is quite impossible even to leaf through *Justification and Reconciliation* III without noticing on every other page that the *objective* pole of the man-God relation is God's historic self-revelation *in Christ* (it was not for nothing that Ritschl's theological opponents on the left abandoned his system as 'christocentric'), that the alleged subjectivism of Schleiermacher's school should be overcome by greater stress on the *intersubjectivity* of the belief of Christians in the Church, and that systematic theology should be ever on guard against subjectivism by relating itself as firmly as possible to its own history.[63]

To turn to the second type of judgement (theoretical judgements), although Ritschl affirms that this is what is involved when the human mind attempts to structure reality by means of *objectively perceived relations* (causality, scientific process, and the like), he makes the point that even here it is hard to rule out completely the operation of feeling. He states his view thus: 'Value-judgements therefore are determinative in the case of all connected knowledge of the world, even when carried out in the most objective fashion.'[64] When we engage in scientific research with a practical end in view (as in, say, scientific medicine or agriculture) this is clearly so. In such cases, the mind is involved in what he calls 'concomitant value-judgements'. From all such must be distinguished what Ritschl as theologian calls 'independent value-judgements', for him the most significant class. These are to be encountered in their purest form in the higher stages of religion, viz., 'religion combined with the ethical conduct of life'. From this there follows his enormously important definition of religious knowledge:

> Religious knowledge moves in independent value-judgements, which relate to man's attitude to the world, and call forth feelings of pleasure or pain, in which man either enjoys the dominion over the world vouchsafed him by God, or feels grievously the lack of God's help to that end.[65]

This leads in turn to a concrete value-judgement of huge importance for his view of Christianity; namely, 'that our blessedness consists in that elevation above the world in the Kingdom of God which accords with our true destiny'.[66] Life in the Kingdom has two roots: it is certainly that supramundane goal of the creation anchored eternally in the will of God; but in so far also as man by his creation is inclined towards loving union with his fellows, it is only in this Kingdom that he can find that fulfilment for which he was made. From this, Ritschl continues, it is possible to distinguish between two sets of functions in Christianity; 'the religious functions which relate to our attitude towards God and the world', and 'the moral functions which point directly to men, and only indirectly to God, Whose end in the world we fulfil by moral service in the Kingdom of God'. (This distinction reflects the Ritschlian definition of Christianity, already noted, as an 'ellipse with two foci', and, it must be added, his reading of the dominical Golden Rule enjoining not only love for God but also for the neighbour.) It is true that he tirelessly attacks the view that 'faith in God for our salvation, and a dutiful public spirit towards our fellows, have nothing to do with one another', one which tolerates the co-existence of faith with individualistic, arrogant egoism. But his motives for integrating faith and ethics in this way go deeper than a mere human dislike for pious egoists, for, as noted above,[67] he was convinced that past theology had *never* satisfactorily integrated the two. These motives cast light in turn on what is probably the best-known aspect of Ritschl's system – the unprecedented stress on the regulative and normative function of the Kingdom of God within his work as a whole. The point to grasp about the Kingdom is that if it is made dogmatically supreme there can be no question of separating faith from ethics: 'In Christianity precisely faith in God and moral duty within the Kingdom of God are related to one another.' But to this central matter of the relation of faith to ethics we must return at later points, particularly in our penultimate chapter.

There are several other points requiring clarification in this matter of the value-judgements of religion. The first concerns the relationship between judgements of value and judgements of existence. When we survey the very early history of Ritschlianism, we encounter the shameful fact that very early on caricaturing and stereotyping have manifested themselves, and once again much of the blame belongs to the undisciplined attack of Stählin.

This emerges most clearly in the stereotyped distinction between 'judgements of value' and 'judgements of (factual) existence' (*Werthurteile* and *Seinsurteile*), the realm of values as contrasted with the dimension of fact. The insinuation implied by the distinction is that he anchored religion in the rather ethereal and nebulous area of 'values', waving science and philosophy nonchalantly on their way towards the further accumulation and interpretation of 'facts'. Let it be said right away that nothing could be further from Ritschl's intention (although one can only wish that, in practice, as his disciple and interpreter Julius Kaftan insisted, his terminology had been more precise). There is nothing to suggest that Ritschl *intended* to sit more lightly to the objective, factual existence of religious realities than any theologian of the Christian tradition. Misunderstanding might easily have been avoided at the outset if attention had been paid to the logical status of the theories of religion and of value-judgements (and if his interpreters had not been so determined to regard him as an epistemologist rather than a biblical theologian). For he intended both of these as but *analyses of the subjective conditions of religious knowledge*. As such, they represent formal but not material principles. So far as the 'general conception' of religion is concerned, note must be taken of his actual language, 'the *thought* of the sublime power of God',[68] 'the *idea* of gods, or Divine powers',[69] 'the validity of the Christian *idea* of God'.[70] For Ritschl (as for the entire European theological tradition to which he belongs from Schleiermacher to Bultmann) were the religious mind (*Geist*) devoid of such categories or ideas it would be unable to grasp God at all. In the occurrence of religious knowledge, there is a subjective as well as an objective pole. In Kantian language, the source of knowledge is twofold: an extramental element existing objectively, and an intramental, subjective scheme by means of which the former is appropriated. By the whole sweep of his systematic theology Ritschl makes it clear that this extramental element is constituted by the witness to God's revelation in Christ, which represents the *material* (as contrasted with the *formal*) principle of Christian knowledge. Value-judgements may be construed along similar lines. If the religious subject asks about the existence of a God in a detached, theoretical, even metaphysical way, then the history of modern philosophical theology demonstrates that no certain answer can be given – the evidence is either insufficient or impossibly ambiguous. But, on the other hand, as an agent in the world, trapped by merely material and social pressures, beset by sin, yet impelled and goaded by his consciousness of being fallen away from his spiritual and moral destiny, he asks about God's being as his saviour and redeemer, then, in Ritschl's view, this *formal-valuational* question may receive a positive (i.e. *material*) answer in the witness to God's self-revelation in the person and work of Jesus Christ, which is contemporaneously operative in the proclamation, memory and activity of the Christian Church. Again, it was H. R. Mackintosh, writing in 1936 (and probably remembering the dreadful misinterpretations of the turn of the century) who put the matter bluntly: 'The judgement that a thing is good presupposes or includes the judgement that the thing is real. In our living experience, fact and value never exist apart; both are presented together as a complex whole which is indissociable, or dissociable only for thought.'[71] He can put the same thing from a different point of view; our findings in science and our convictions in religion, in short, are reached by different avenues. This point has been elaborated in some detail because caricatures from earlier decades must be discredited. But that is not the same thing as saying that Ritschl's theory of value-judgements is anything like satisfactory as it stands. For he does leave his committed defenders in an unhappy position with regard to the classic problem of faith and reason. There was something of a controversy over this in the 1890s between Orr and Garvie. Orr and others then urged that Ritschl had bequeathed to his followers a *duality of knowledges* (religious and theoretical), each hermetically sealed off from the other and each unable mutually to influence the other. But the cautious Garvie had little difficulty in showing that this was excessively severe, by showing that there was rather a *duality of approaches*, of methods, of modes of knowing, and that to obscure this only leads to confusion.[72] Nevertheless, even the fair-minded Garvie was worried, because even he had to concede that Ritschl's method involves 'a limitation of theology'.[73] Only those aspects are dealt with 'to which a distinct religious interest attaches'. He went on to remark with dismay that there is much affirmed within the New Testament practically ignored by Ritschl's dogmatics! Garvie's final, very important, and singularly modern judgement is that Ritschl so emphasizes what a man can verify in his own experience that there is overlooked all that is verifiable for him in the typical and normative experience that is presented to us in the New Testament. Garvie very pertinently deplores the fact that while certain kinds of scientific research may be enriched by the motive-power of value, he irrationally prohibits the converse; 'why should there not be,' he asks, 'the theoretical impulse in religious knowledge, that is, why should not the objects of faith be investigated as thoroughly as the conditions will allow?' We could put this another way: Ritschl failed to appreciate the profundity of St Anselm's formula, *Fides Quaerens Intellectum*. Given that, not altogether unlike Anselm, he held to the priority of faith over reason, he devalued his own system by failing to follow up the insights and pointers of faith by a rational investigation which could have strengthened his system, protected it from accusations of 'subjectivism' and 'reductionism', and linked it more positively with certain indispensable affirmations of the Christian tradition. Theologians are right to fear stirring up a science-religion conflict from which religion has nothing to gain and everything to lose, but they ought to prevent this fear from producing a form of intellectual paralysis.

The second point needing clarification is linked closely to that criticism of Garvie which we have just described as singularly modern. This has to do with a problem which is possibly not merely the most intractable one in Ritschl's system, but also in modern post-Kantian systematic theology. It concerns the introduction of a theological system with an anthropology which is alleged to have, by its critics, both ancient and modern, a *constitutive* as well as a *regulative* function. In Chapter II it was argued that Ritschl's so-called epistemology did not function in anything like the way in which his critics alleged that it did. But it is by no means so easy to rebut the charge that his general conception of religion blends with his value-judgement theory into a firm anthropology which determines in advance much of what will and will not count as admissible elements in his overall restatement of Christianity. Garvie alleged that Ritschl's method involves a limitation of the range of theology to those themes to which a distinct *religious* interest attaches. His words, published in 1899, point forward with prophetic power to much that was to be said several generations later. We have already noted Wrzecionko's thesis on Ritschl which highlights those ways in which he was a precursor of Bultmann, in that his system, like Bultmann's after him, is founded upon a formal analysis of the religious consciousness which determines much not only of the form and language, but also the content of the system.[74] We can perhaps survey these ways if we set down two passages concerning similarities between Ritschl and Bultmann, which the present author published over ten years ago. The first similarity can be described thus:

> Under Heideggerian influence, Bultmann has emphasized the religious significance of human existence against the sinister dehumanization of man implicit both in Cartesian thinking and in his life in scientific and technological societies.
>
> Under Lotzean influence, Ritschl had stressed the religious significance of man's uniqueness as a creature of moral worth over against the indifferent, impersonal world of nature as portrayed by nineteenth-century naturalism.

The second is this:

> Another obvious similarity between Ritschl and Bultmann is that whereas the former insisted upon confining all theological statements to value-statements, the latter confines them to existential statements. There is clearly a similarity between the unique value God has for one's soul (Ritschl) and the unique significance God has for one's authentic existence (Bultmann).[75]

The former of these similarities refers to Ritschl's general conception of religion, the latter to his value-judgement theory. It is difficult to overemphasize the importance of these similarities. It is these, for instance, which lie behind Barth's charge that *both* Ritschl's and Bultmann's theologies are anthropocentric rather than theocentric, behind Barth's general allegation that nineteenth-century German theologians in speaking of God were in reality speaking of man, behind his declaration that Jesus Christ is the abolition of all religion,[76] behind Bonhoeffer's attempt to reinterpret and extend Barth's theology in order to produce a *religionless* Christianity. From today's standpoint it is easier to perceive that Barthian neo-orthodoxy in its revulsion from the nineteenth century over-reacted away from genuine and serious human and religious interests. The excessively anti-Ritschlian Brunner, for example, in discussing Ritschl's application of value-judgements to Jesus, rebounds so violently as to make the following astounding statement: 'In the Christian conception of revelation the very possibility of (human) judgement is excluded'![77] But it is not necessary to become a disciple of Brunner (and approach the elimination of the human pole from the divine-human correlation) in order to be disquieted with Ritschl's viewpoint. This disquiet is discernible within the Ritschl Renaissance, and that most obviously in the recent, fair-minded contribution of David Mueller. In discussing the anthropological similarity of Ritschl and Bultmann, Mueller remarks that in the theology of both of them only that is of value in the revelation of God which speaks to the dilemma raised by human existence in the world.[78] In adopting an existential hermeneutics, both of them 'are often guilty of making it appear that God is of value only insofar as he answers man's problem. God is forced to fit the mould of man's preunderstanding and therefore His sovereignty and freedom are denied from the start.'[79] The conclusion reached by Mueller is that Ritschl does not guard himself adequately against the charge that his use of a Kantian natural theology in the description of the human problem predetermines the kind of answer that God's historical revelation must provide.[80] Naturally, we cannot take the truth of this criticism for granted; its truth must be tested against Ritschl's texts in the following chapters. But we are about to survey a topic in his work where such a test may appropriately be applied – his conception of God. In doing so, we may be helped if we recall one central criticism brought against Bultmann: that his existential treatment of the Christian materials has led to the 'dedogmatizing' (*entdogmatisierung*) or 'deontologizing' of Christianity.[81] That is, that his approach tends to eliminate the non-existential, ontological, transcendental anchorage of Christian thought and discourse. Does Ritschl's approach, we may ask, exhibit the same tendency? When we turn now, as we must, to Ritschl's doctrine of God, we find two not very compatible things: first, that he could, on occasion, betray his avowed antispeculative and experiential loyalties; second, and nevertheless, when he was faced with the problem of certain of God's attributes (eternity, omnipotence, omniscience) he could 'existentialize' or 'deobjectify' these with a vigour that leaves us in no doubt that he was a significant precursor of the twentieth-century existentialist theologians.

To turn to Ritschl's doctrine of God proper is to encounter, as just remarked, a remarkable theological procedure in which he sits very lightly to his avowed experiential and nonspeculative method, deducing from the notion of God's personality the essential nature of God as loving will, from which there is deduced in turn the desired conclusion of the exercise, the Kingdom of God. To begin with God's *personality*: he holds that the authentically Christian idea of God, to be most sharply contrasted with pantheistic or deistic notions, as also with the not necessarily personal conception of a First Cause, is necessarily that of a personal being, i.e., 'of God as a Person, Who establishes the Kingdom of God as the final end of the world, and in it assures to everyone who trusts in Him supremacy over the world'.[82] Since the conception is derived from Scripture, he claims that 'a theology based upon it, therefore, is not rationalistic'. Nevertheless, and paradoxically, when he proceeds to expound and defend the conception, he is involved not merely to a high degree in speculation but also in what can only be described as metaphysical theology. It is almost inevitable that he begins by attacking the view of D. F. Strauss that 'the predicates of the Absolute and of personality are mutually exclusive'.[83] The passage from Strauss's *Die Christliche Glaubenslehre*[84] to which he takes exception is as follows:

> Personality is that selfhood which shuts itself up against everything else, which it thereby excludes from itself; the Absolute, on the other hand, is the comprehensive, the unlimited, which excludes nothing from itself but just the exclusivity which lies in the conception of personality.

Ritschl vigorously attacks this view, making such points as that Strauss overlooks the extent to which personal uniqueness is due to acquired rather than original self-distinction, and to which the development of mature personality depends upon the progressive assimilation of external material for the building up of spiritual life. Hence, *exclusiveness* in Strauss's sense is not a defining predicate of personality. In order therefore to rebut the kind of criticism which can be derived from conceptions like Strauss's, he outlines his procedure thus:

> The conceivability of the personality of God is to be reached through the study of what is so worthy of esteem among men – independent personality.[85]

In order to spell out what is involved in this, it is impossible not to conclude that Ritschl employs the ancient method of *analogical predication* in order to make statements about God. Hence, he begins by arguing that 'developed personal individuality consists in the power to take up the inexorable stimuli of the environment into one's plan of life'.[86] The most highly esteemed stage of personal culture 'brings with it that specific experience of eternity for which our spiritual constitution is adapted'. But what does *eternity* mean in this context? It is to be perceived, or experienced, he says, 'in the power of the will actively to pursue a single end throughout the ordered succession of intentions and resolves derived from it'.[87] This is because, briefly, 'eternity is in general the power of spirit over time'. Here he is harking back to one of his central religious themes, 'the world-dominating or subjugating power of spirit' which proves spirit to be *supramundane*. So far, Ritschl has been pursuing the *via affirmata* of the threefold way. He then pursues the *via negativa* by identifying restraints and restrictions imposed upon the transcendence of the human self. He affirms that in its development 'the human spirit always remains conditioned by external stimuli even when it has reached the stage of independent personality'. Moreover, the process of the self's acquiring transcendence 'is limited at every moment'. And our experience of life teaches us that 'as persons, we are always in a state of becoming, and that this is what we are created for'. Predictably, at this stage, he now proceeds to think away these finite limitations imposed on *merely human* personality: 'The personality of God is thinkable without contradiction just because it stands contrasted with the restraints which we find by experience imposed upon our personality.'[88] There now follows a remarkable passage in which personality is predicated of God neither *affirmatively* nor *negatively* but *analogically*:

> As the cause of all that happens, God is affected only by such forces of influence as He has conferred upon His creatures, and as He sees transparently to be the effects of His own will. Nothing which affects the Divine Spirit is originally alien to Him; and there is nothing which, in order to be self-dependent, He must first appropriate. Everything, rather, that the world means for Him is at bottom an expression of His own self-activity; and whatever of the movement of things reacts upon Him He recognizes as the reverent sweep of that reality which is possible through Himself alone.

In other words, those of the Middle Ages, God is *eminently* personality. And when he adds that 'our mind can lend no music or colour to this conception' he is expressing that agnostic reserve, already discussed, which is characteristic of so many of the theologians of the High Middle Ages. This remarkable passage, based upon the notion of the *analogia entis*, requires several comments. First, it might be regarded as an astounding passage to have come from the pen of a theologian who was alleged to be an 'empiricist' and a 'phenomenalist'. But we should be reminded here of our argument in the preceding chapter, that it is misleading to apply to Ritschl restrictive philosophical labels. Second, it is impossible to study such a passage and not conclude that Ritschl, notwithstanding his attacks on the 'Absolute' of the Erlangen school, was in effect predicating a form of *absoluteness* of God. It is not possible here to acquit him of a certain amount of inconsistency. But this very inconsistency should warn off those who want to urge the hostile generalization that Ritschl produced a theological system in which there was just no room for reference to God as he is 'in himself', apart from his relations with human beings. (In this very connection, it is not irrelevant to recall how he, in his main life's work, attempted to solve certain christological difficulties by appealing to the notion of God's *aseity* in Catholic tradition!)[89] Third, the notion of the Personality of God, 'which is the form in which the idea of God is given through Revelation', is clarified and refined by that technique of analogical predication just described, and *becomes normative for the life of the Christian*: 'For that we are independent personalities we judge by reference to the conception of that Personality which, inasmuch as it has the whole ground of its activity within itself, is normative.'[90] To summarize briefly: 'Personality is the form in which the idea of God is given through Revelation':[91] to grasp what this means, human personality is contemplated and purified by analogical predication, enabling us to predicate personality *eminently* of God; this conception is then used as the standard by which we judge the becoming of our own personality in its religion direction towards *Herrschaft* over the world, as a supramundane existence.

There now follows another speculative deduction in which from the notion of God's personality there is derived the conception of God primarily and pre-eminently as *love*. In order to do this, Ritschl first rejects as inadequate for Christian theology two models which have been influential in the past – viz., the model, articulated first by Scotus and later by the Socinians, which understands God as sovereign and unintelligible Will and as *dominum absolutum*; and second, the model fashioned on the analogy of the medieval State, within which the God-man relation is understood strictly in terms of law, a law which determines the will of the divine ruler *vis-à-vis* his subjects. Of these two models (which attract lengthy discussions in his work) there is room here only to remark several things. First, he is able to reject them on the prior ground of his abandonment of natural theology; he tries to show that they represent two *foreign* intrusions into Christianity, one philosophical (Scotist) in nature and the other forensic and juristic. Second, his hostility to all *legal* categories expressed here turns out to have huge implications for his understanding of the divine–human relation as a whole, but with special reference (as we shall see) to his doctrines of sin and salvation. His judgement of the fundamental error of traditional and orthodox theories of God's relation to the world 'lies in the neglect of the question, what end God has, or can have, in common with the human race'.[92] Such theories were not, in his view, *teleological* enough, and he is harshly critical of those theories, mainly late-medieval ones, which introduced a gulf between God's personal end and that end built into human nature, the final gathering together of all men with God and with each other in a supramundane Kingdom. But this, he maintains, is plain in the New Testament, where the main apostolic title for God is *Father* ('the God and Father of our Lord Jesus Christ'), implying that 'God manifests Himself, to the Son and to the community as *loving Will*'.[93] The attribute of the divine father-hood implies 'the truth that He has revealed Himself to the Christian community as love. There is no other conception of equal worth beside this which need be taken into account.' What he means by 'no other conception' is immediately disclosed: he has in mind particularly 'the Divine holiness, which, in its Old Testament sense, is for various reasons not valid in Christianity, while its use in the Old Testament is obscure'. But how is this related to his teaching on divine personality? Briefly, we may say that for Ritschl personality is the *form* of which loving will is the *matter*. Hence his conclusion 'that the conception of love is the only adequate conception of God, for it enables us, both to understand the revelation which comes through Christ to his community, and at the same time to solve the problem of the world'. At this point it is once more illuminating to recall another of the notable discussions of the 1890s, available to us in some of the older, pre-Barthian literature, which has the merit of being unmarred by any systematic attempt to discredit Ritschl. With regard to his seemingly orthodox statement that the love of God is oriented primarily to the Son and secondarily to the Christian community, the incisive Dr Orr rightly warns us not to be misled by this ultra-traditional language, on the grounds that there is really no place in Ritschl's system for an eternal Sonship of Christ, or indeed, an 'essential Trinity' of any kind. The father-hood of God, insists Orr, has relevance to the *historic* personality of Christ and to the community of believers constituted through him.[94] And yet one must wonder why not. It is the perceptive Garvie who with justice observes that the fault is Ritschl's own – he does not take with sufficient seriousness his own view that God's love is directed primarily and originally to the Son, and only secondarily and mediately to the community. Had he done so, is Garvie's judgement, he would have had to face up squarely to the significance and value for Christian theology of a symbol not adequately considered in his system – the doctrine of the

Trinity.[95] Garvie adds that Ritschl's deduction from God's love of the existence and destiny of mankind lacks logical rigour in not considering the problem of God's being and activity *before* the creation of man.[96] The points made by Orr and Garvie (which will be explored in greater depth in our christological chapter below) carry conviction, and it will not do for the committed defender of Ritschl to argue that the notion of 'the Father eternally loving the Son in the union of the Holy Spirit' is an excessively metaphysical one impossible to reconcile with Ritschl's experiential and nonspeculative stance, for, as we have seen, he could, when it suited his purposes, transpose his reflections into a highly speculative key which reminds us of some of the discussions of the High Middle Ages. But why did he not do so? It is hard to disagree with his critics that there are two obvious reasons. First, he did not linger over and probe these so-called metaphysical issues because of excessive haste to move to the all-important conclusion of his deductive exercises, the Kingdom of God. Second, and very obviously, he did not linger because he was blinkered by his regulative viewpoint regarding the intrusion of 'foreign' metaphysics into theology and the antithesis, omnipresent in most of his later work, he entertained between Judaic-Christian 'authenticity' and Greek-metaphysical 'inauthenticity'.

Hence, alas, he rushes on in excessive haste in order to arrive at that final point upon which, as most of his critics have not without justification alleged, his eyes were focused *to the virtual exclusion of all else*![97] His attempt to do so, it is interesting to discover, is not untinged by natural theology, because, as he puts it, 'this quality of love serves to discover to us in God the ground of the unity of nature and spirit, and the law of their co-existence'.[98] It follows from this 'that nature is called into being to serve as a means to God's essential purpose in creating the world of spirits'.[99] But, in order to reach his final point, the Kingdom of God, Ritschl formulates doctrines and makes statements in *Justification and Reconciliation* III in which *the terms 'purpose' or 'divine purpose' come virtually to replace all reference to 'God'*! Such a violent change in terminology has attracted to his system, at the best, extremely severe criticism, and, at the worst, flat rejection of his views as incompatible with the Christian faith. At its most extreme, the criticism has been bluntly expressed that his views come within a hairsbreadth, if so much, *of identifying God with the Kingdom of God*! Even if, in the desire to be fair to Ritschl, we follow our customary procedure of glancing back at the less biased criticism of the turn of the century, his interpreters are more or less agreed. J. K. Mozley, for example, even though he tried hard to defend Ritschl from a charge of excessive continuity between the divine love and human ends, nevertheless had to concede with dismay that in Ritschl's exposition God often seems lost in His Kingdom.[100] But predictably the incisive Dr Orr, at this point almost unable to restrain himself, goes much further: in exploring Ritschl's understanding of love expressed in will and purpose, he complains that Ritschl bans us from going *behind* this purpose, or to speak of any nature or disposition in God from which it proceeds.[101] We are reminded of Orr's labelling of Ritschl as a phenomenalist when we read his judgement that for Ritschl God *is* eternally *in* His purpose – is practically identified with it! Hence, for Orr, Ritschl's conception of God's love is *static*, in that it seems to merge into the eternal will of God to realize his world-end (*Weltzweck*).[102] In fact, he proceeds, it becomes little more than an abstraction of the purpose of the universe – to use an Aristotelian phrase, the *entelechy* of the universe. At this point, even the relatively sympathetic Dr Garvie was unable, and did not want, to aid the unfortunate Ritschl, and deplored the view that an ideal for the human race which has a local and temporary existence, and one, also, which is being only progressively realized, can be identified with God's purpose for himself (*Gottes Selbstzweck*).[103] Indeed, Garvie goes so far as to compare the Ritschlian system with the Hegelian [*sic!*], on the grounds that, despite admirable intentions, he expounds a doctrine of God reaching the goal of his own being only in the social organization of finite mankind! Very sternly he rebukes Ritschl for bringing God into dependence on, even subordination to, his creatures. Indeed, it is the not unsympathetic Garvie who concludes abrasively of Ritschl that in his thought *God is identified with the Kingdom of God*. How did Ritschl attract such criticisms from men who were generally not unsympathetic to him? Mainly because of his definition of love and the qualifications he attached to it. 'Love,' he affirms, 'is love aiming either at the appropriation of an object or at the enrichment of its existence, because moved by a feeling of its worth.'[104] The first two qualifications, asserting a similarity of nature between lover and beloved, and love as implying a will constant in aim, call for no special comment here. But his third and fourth qualifications are disconcerting in the extreme. The third is that 'love aims at the promotion of the other's personal end, whether known or conjectured', and the fourth that 'the will of the lover *must* take up the other's personal end and make it part of his own'. What this boils down to is that *God must not only aim at the promotion of man's personal end, whether known or conjectured, but must absorb man's personal end and make it part of his own.* Now this has been widely felt, and not only by his doctrinaire enemies, to involve a quite unwarranted surrender of God's freedom and sovereignty for human purposes, and a disconcerting insensitivity towards God's transcendence over and discontinuity with the merely human order. We have already listened to Orr's complaint that we are not allowed to penetrate 'behind' God's purpose, or to speak of any disposition in God from which it proceeds. But he goes on justifiably to insist that God can only adopt our end as his own *because God has constituted us for it.* 'It was his end,' he writes, '*before* it was ours.' The entire conception of *Gottes Selbstzweck*, he argues uncompromisingly, 'is *not* the adoption of the end *of* another, but the prescribing of an end *to* another'.[105] What we may derive from criticisms like Orr's is this: *Pace* Ritschl, we are, as theologians, obliged to enquire, however tentatively and reverently, about God's nature *as it is in itself*; we must attend to a doctrine of the creation of man in the image of God in order to explore both the continuity and the *discontinuity* between God and man, and we need an adequate doctrine of the command of God.

Considerable space has been devoted to this matter because, from the standpoint of historical understanding, it is of the first importance. The teaching of Ritschl, read in the light of the moderate but uncompromising criticism of pre-Barthian scholars, points forward unmistakably towards *the neo-orthodox movement's breach with Ritschl*, with its stress on the divine-human *discontinuity*, on God's *judgement* on everything human, on God as love *and* wrath (on God's *Yes* and *No* to man), as grace *and* righteousness, and the rejection of all notions of inexorable human progress in favour of an uncompromisingly *eschatological* under-

standing of human existence and history. But what, in all fairness
to Ritschl, was the source of his characteristic emphases here?
Doubtless, like the rest of us, he was a man of his time – the
second half of the nineteenth century. David Mueller, writing
recently, and trying hard to prevent misinterpretation of Ritschl,
nevertheless admits that in this matter Ritschl's argument led him
into proximity to the views of Lessing, Lotze and others in the
nineteenth century who regarded the idea of the progressive
development of humanity as self-evident,[106] although he rightly
insists that Ritschl's views of human betterment are always
qualified by an understanding of divine providence in the light of
the biblical revelation. Be that as it may, we cannot sweep aside
Orr's remarks about God's love as an abstraction of the entelechy
of the universe and Garvie's comparison of Ritschl with Hegel,
which leads Garvie to argue further in this vein: Ritschl represented God as if he had exercised his freedom once and for all in
a single choice of will, in adopting the Kingdom of God as his
own purpose, and was henceforth rigidly bound by that purpose,
*so that he was unable to vary his method of dealing with men
according to their attitude to himself.*[107] These last several words
are of quite fundamental importance, for on their foundation
Garvie proceeds to argue that this extremely narrow conception
of God's eternal purpose affects in an impoverishing way *much
of what follows in the system*: the doctrines of forgiveness,
atonement, guilt, punishment, all of which we have to examine in
depth in the remainder of this work. To express the same point in
briefer form: God does not, indeed cannot, change over against
man, and so all change must be predicated of the manward side.
Finally, we cannot conceal that Ritschl cannot be acquitted from
responsibility for attracting to himself much of the hostility
which was to emanate in the 1920s and 1930s from the Barthian
school. No wonder therefore that the hostile Brunner could in
1927 peremptorily reject his entire system as a Rationalistic
system clad in scriptural garments or as simply a well-constructed
system of ethical metaphysics developed along logical lines. And
speaking of the historical element in Ritschl's thinking, Brunner
wrote that it 'is nothing more than the rational and ethical idea
of progress, only here it is clothed in definite historical garb'.
The Ritschlian God, he concludes, is not mysterious. 'Since God

is "Love" alone, and it is impossible to speak of His holiness or His wrath, forgiveness, in the scriptural sense, cannot exist.'[108] These may seem harsh words, yet we find echoes of them in recent times from one who has little affinity with Barthian neo-orthodoxy. John Macquarrie quotes the view of Guido de Ruggiero that the God of Harnack, like the God of Ritschl, cannot be worshipped, loved or feared, but only criticized as a logical error. A harsh verdict, which Macquarrie explicates by arguing that Ritschl's God lacks those elements of mystery and majesty for which the deeper aspirations of worship seek. He continues: 'The character of Deity which is variously designated as the "numinous" (Otto) . . . or the "wholly other" (Barth) is not indeed explicitly denied by the Ritschlians, but it is excluded from consideration.' And while Macquarrie is unhappy with the verdict that the Ritschlian God cannot be worshipped, he feels that this conception of God is too thin to answer to the deepest needs of the religious consciousness.[109]

Finally, the promise made above[110] must be fulfilled, to glance briefly at the way in which Ritschl could vigorously 'existentialize' or 'deobjectify' certain of the divine attributes in his doctrine of God. This procedure has a twofold significance: first, it exhibits another strand in Ritschl which must be regarded as an anticipation of twentieth-century existentialist theology; second, the procedure extends and reinforces what has just been said of his subordination of God (and much else besides) to the overarching notion of the Kingdom. First, we consider his treatment of God's *eternity*. Now clearly, eternity can be regarded as a necessary attribute of that Deity who alone answers the needs of the worshipping religious consciousness, as a Being who, in contrast to the contingent, local and temporal world, exists, as Anselm put it, necessarily, eternally, and independently. God, as God, is no part of the 'furniture of the world', for, if he were, he could not evoke worship or absolute devotion from his followers. For this reason, it is wrong-headed to distinguish sharply, as did the Ritschlians, between the so-called 'metaphysical' and the 'religious' attributes, implying that the latter on their own meet the profoundest needs of genuine religion.[111] Now Ritschl, while he does not explicitly deny God's eternity as 'existence without beginning or end',[112] nevertheless excludes it from consideration.

Rather, by God's eternity is meant 'that amid all the changes of things, which also indicate variation in his working, he himself remains the same and maintains the same purpose and plan by which he creates and directs the world,'[113] or that it refers 'to the continual and immutable aim with which His will is directed towards His purpose, and towards the Kingdom of God as within that purpose'.[114] About the unmistakable *subordination* of all else to the goal of the Kingdom here, nothing needs to be added. But if we recall that the Kingdom of God may be identified, without violence to Ritschl's thought, as the area or dimension of fulfilled, genuine, completed, *authentic* human existence, then it is seen that a divine attribute has been interpreted as referring exclusively and exhaustively to *human* needs, aims and aspirations. In other words, the category of *eternity* has been existentialized or deobjectified. Other attributes are treated not dissimilarly. For example, the Christian contemplates God's *omnipotence* and *omnipresence* not at all in order 'to explain the continuance of natural things in whole or in part', but rather to emphasize 'that God's care and gracious presence are certain *for the pious man*'. Indeed, 'the thought of the omnipotence of God finds consistent fulfilment in the thought of His wisdom, omniscience and disposition *to meet the needs of men*'.[115] In similar vein, God's *righteousness* is reduced to that criterion 'of the special actions by which the community of Christ is brought into existence and *led on to perfection*'.[116] (Dr Orr remarks, and not without cause, that righteousness is here deprived by Ritschl of its judicial and retributive character[117] – which also turns out to have crucial implications for his notions of sin and atonement.) Once again, subordination to the Kingdom is so evident as hardly to need comment. And equally, the interpretation of his procedure as 'existentializing' Christianity is self-evident. Of course, it is arguable that we owe gratitude to him for bringing the divine attributes into such an intimate connection with the human order. But *such* a close connection cannot be made except at a price. We have already indicated what part of that price would be – the virtual exclusion from consideration of God's metaphysical attributes. The residue of the price must now be assessed. To do so involves us in a consideration of what is implied by *any* demythologizing process which is carried to its furthest extent. Ian Henderson has done this in the case of Helmut Thielicke's examination of the *creatio ex nihilo* doctrine.[118] The complete deobjectification of this would mean that 'I am not formed by God out of any material foreign to Him, so that my refusal of Him may not be traced back to that source', an interpretation which does, indeed, bring out the significance of the doctrine for my life. But Henderson enquires if that is all there is to it, and enquires if it says nothing about the material world? The latter is a reality and so is God – there must be some relation between the two. Henderson's judgement is that if demythologizing were pushed to its farthermost limit the result would be that Christianity would have absolutely nothing to say about this relation – which includes, it must not be forgotten, God's relation to man in so far as the latter, having a body, is himself in some sense part of the material world. If this were carried out, the result, in Henderson's judgement, would be that there would no longer be any conflict between science and religion, for religion would cease to make statements about the material world and this field would be left entirely to science. (It is pertinent to recall what was said earlier in this chapter of one of Ritschl's main motives for formulating his value-judgement theory – anxiety to prevent a science-religion conflict.) But he is doubtful that Christianity can make any such withdrawal from the material world and at the same time remain Christianity, for what it believes about creation, providence, prayer and miracle imply that for it God is Lord not only of the individual life but of the material universe – and a completely or exhaustively demythologized Bible would give no basis for such an implication.[119] Now it is true that Ritschl nowhere says, any more than does Bultmann, that the world of nature is downright profane or godless, or that salvation means being saved *out of* or *from* the world, or anything of the kind. On the other hand, it is hard to read what he has to say on the matter without feeling that in some sense or other he leaves us with a certain *dualism* between, on the one hand, the supramundane Kingdom constituted entirely by moral agents, and, on the other, the world of nature and of natural society entirely comprehensible on their own terms, about which he has not much more to say than that they are a means to God's and man's final end. It may be so, as Garvie insisted, that he did not intend any dualism of this sort; nevertheless, he conceded that at points Ritschl's theology does *seem* to withdraw religion into a restricted area of its own, and abandon to 'irreligious' (i.e. profane) science or philosophy the wider realm of 'human knowledge'. And if we turn to a modern theologian who has been notable for the sympathy he has extended to the nineteenth-century German tradition, Paul Tillich, we find Garvie's reluctant judgement corroborated.[120] Tillich has described Ritschlianism as 'a withdrawal from the ontological to the moral'; it was 'a theology of retreat'; it implied a 'negation of ontology'; it was motivated by 'anti-ontological feeling'; it completely denied 'the element of power in God'. In the twentieth-century process of secularization, we have observed some of the consequences when religion hands over the intellectual reins completely to the natural and human sciences!

NOTES TO CHAPTER III

1 *J. & R.* III, p. 193.
2 ibid., p. 194.
3 ibid., p. 195.
4 ibid.
5 ibid., p. 196.
6 ibid., p. 197.
7 ET by Olive Wyon, *The Mediator*, London 1934.
8 See pp. 56 f.
9 For the reasons, see Tillich, *Systematic Theology* I, London 1953, pp. 47 f.
10 *J. & R.* III, p. 199.
11 ibid., p. 200.
12 *Instruction*, para. 23.
13 *The Mediator*, p. 136, cf. pp. 138–9.
14 See below, pp. 251 f.
15 *J. & R.* III, p. 11.
16 See *Types of Modern Theology*, pp. 150 f.
17 *Our Knowledge of God*, London 1939, pp. 17 f.
18 *Systematic Theology* I, pp. 67–70.
19 *J. & R.* III, p. 226, n. 1.
20 See *Our Knowledge of God*, pp. 166–7; cf. St Thomas, *Summa Contra Gentiles*, i, 11.
21 *Systematic Theology* I, p. 68.
22 *Essays: Philosophical and Theological*, London 1955, p. 86.

23 ibid., pp. 112, 150, 154, 181, 228.
24 R. Bultmann, *Faith and Understanding*, London 1969, p. 74.
25 See ibid., pp. 160 f.
26 We are reminded once more of Barth's scathing reference in *Kerygma and Myth* II to 'Ritschl, dry-as-dust'.
27 *Types*, p. 151.
28 *The Ritschlian Theology*, pp. 9–13, 25, 95–7.
29 ibid., p. 25.
30 *The Ritschlian Theology and the Evangelical Faith*, pp. 6–7.
31 Introduction to *Three Essays*, pp. 6 and 34.
32 James Richmond, *Faith and Philosophy*, London 1966, p. 80; for the cultural background to Ritschl's theology, see pp. 76–81.
33 The *Relevance of Science*, Gifford Lectures 1959–60, London 1964, pp. 21 f.
34 *J. & R.* III, pp. 209–10.
35 *Philosophy of Religion*, Englewood Cliffs, NJ 1963, p. 37.
36 *Theology and Metaphysics*, p. 156, italics mine.
37 *Instruction*, para. 8.
38 The Moffat New Testament Commentary, London 1928.
39 ibid., pp. 12 f.
40 p. 199.
41 p. 215.
42 p. 291.
43 p. 317.
44 *Letters and Papers From Prison*, Collins Fontana Edition, London 1959, p. 164.
45 J. Macquarrie, *An Existentialist Theology*, London 1955, pp. 50 f. and 69 f.
46 Sören Kierkegaard, *The Sickness Unto Death*, translated by Walter Lowrie, Princeton 1951, pp. 49 f.
47 See pp. 83–4 *supra*.
48 *Types*, p. 154.
49 A. Ritschl, *A Critical History of the Christian Doctrine of Justification and Reconciliation*, pp. 401 f.
50 *Speeches*, pp. 31–6.
51 *J. & R.* I, pp. 203 f.
52 *Essays: Philosophical and Theological*, p. 8; for Bultmann's views on this see his entire paper, 'The Crisis in Belief', pp. 1–21, especially pp. 6–10.
53 *J. & R.* III, pp. 203–4.
54 See *supra*, p. 30.
55 *Some Aspects of Christian Belief*, pp. 140–1, italics mine.
56 ibid., p. 143, italics mine.
57 ibid., p. 144.
58 *J. & R.* III, p. 205, italics mine.
59 See Tillich, *Systematic Theology* I, pp. 47 f.; Martin Redeker, *Schleiermacher: Life and Thought*, ET by J. Wallhauser, Philadelphia 1973, pp. 113 f.; R. R. Niebuhr, *Schleiermacher on Christ and Religion*, pp. 116 f.; J. Macquarrie, *Studies in Christian Existentialism*, London 1966, ch. 3, 'Feeling and Understanding', pp. 31–42.
60 Macquarrie, op. cit., p. 32.

61 Introduction to *Three Essays*, p. 41, italics mine.
62 *J. & R.* III, p. 7.
63 ibid., p. 8.
64 ibid., p. 204.
65 ibid., p. 205.
66 ibid., p. 206.
67 See *supra*, pp. 84–5.
68 *J. & R.* III, p. 194; the Kantian term 'to postulate God' would not be inappropriate here.
69 ibid., p. 199.
70 ibid., p. 226.
71 *Types*, p. 154.
72 *The Ritschlian Theology*, pp. 188–91.
73 See the discussion, ibid., pp. 191–3.
74 *Die philosophischen Wurzeln der Theologie Albrecht Ritschls*, pp. 248 f.
75 *Faith and Philosophy*, pp. 169 and 171.
76 *Church Dogmatics* I: 2, para. 17, pp. 280–361.
77 *The Mediator*, p. 59.
78 *An Introduction to the Theology of Albrecht Ritschl*, p. 167.
79 ibid., p. 168.
80 ibid., p. 169.
81 See, for example, L. Malevez, SJ, *The Christian Message and Myth*, London 1958, pp. 157 f.; for the entire discussion as this has affected Bultmann, see Macquarrie, *The Scope of Demythologizing*, London 1960, IV, 'Demythologizing and Dogma', pp. 102–53; for references to Ritschl in the discussion, see pp. 117 and 123.
82 *J. & R.* III, p. 228.
83 ibid., p. 232.
84 vol. i, p. 504.
85 *J. & R.* III, p. 233.
86 ibid., p. 234.
87 ibid., p. 235.
88 ibid., p. 236.
89 ibid., p. 470.
90 ibid., p. 236.
91 ibid., p. 237.
92 ibid., p. 271.
93 ibid., p. 273.
94 *The Ritschlian Theology and the Evangelical Faith*, p. 115.
95 *The Ritschlian Theology*, p. 256.
96 ibid., p. 259.
97 ibid., p. 257.
98 *J. & R.* III, p. 276.
99 ibid., p. 279.
100 *Ritschlianism*, p. 168.
101 *The Ritschlian Theology and the Evangelical Faith*, p. 255.
102 op. cit., p. 256.
103 *The Ritschlian Theology*, p. 259.
104 *J. & R.* III, p. 277.
105 Orr, op. cit., p. 255 n.
106 Mueller, op. cit., p. 56; cf. *J. & R.* III, p. 306.

107 Garvie, op. cit., p. 262.
108 See *The Mediator*, pp. 56–63.
109 *Twentieth-Century Religious Thought*, London 1963, pp. 92–3.
110 See *supra*, pp. 107 f.
111 For a discussion, see my *Theology and Metaphysics*, VI.42 and VI.43.
112 *J. & R*. III, p. 298.
113 *Instruction*, para 14.
114 *J. & R*. III, p. 299.
115 *Instruction*, para. 15, italics mine.
116 op. cit., para. 16.
117 Orr, op. cit., p. 256.
118 *Kerygma u. Mythos* I, Hamburg 1951, p. 183.
119 Ian Henderson, *Myth in the New Testament*, London 1952, pp. 31–3.
120 *Perspectives on Nineteenth and Twentieth Century Protestant Theology*,
    pp. 217 f.

CHAPTER IV

Man and Justification

Our concern in this chapter is with Ritschl's view of man as sinner and of his salvation by God. The stereotype of Ritschl's doctrine of sin, through which his teaching has been transmitted to modernity, runs along these lines: Ritschl was essentially a Pelagian, who admitted the possibility of human sinlessness; he rejected the traditional doctrine of original sin, erased from his theology the notion of God's wrath (except as a distant eschatological possibility for the finally unrepentant), and denied that human sufferings have any penal or retributive aspect. He came within a hairsbreadth of reducing guilt *coram deo* to awareness of guilt (guilty feelings), and except for the sin of finally and defiantly rejecting the divine purpose, affirmed that the origin of sin is ignorance, which allowed him to hold that sin is 'pardonable'. He was interested only in *sins*, but not in 'organic' *sinfulness*. The result of such a diluted and superficial doctrine of sin was that it required the upheaval of the post-1919 theological revolution to reinstate the orthodox doctrine of sin which spoke in transcendental tones to twentieth-century man. But why, precisely, is this a 'stereotype' or a 'caricature'? It is not that it is factually inaccurate, insupportable by isolated statements to be located in his texts. It is that it is *frightfully ahistorical*, constructed only by wrenching Ritschl from his historical *milieu*, by ignoring the *Zeitgeist* which was the matrix of his thinking, by overlooking his apologetic intentions, all of which could be described as the abandonment of historical scholarship and understanding. The truth of the matter is that theologians of Ritschl's generation were 'fighting with their backs to the wall', in order to make an intelligible case for the sinfulness of human nature in a world of hostile opinions and theories, anything but mutually compatible among themselves. To a brief exploration of that world we must now turn. First of all, notice must be paid to the application of the notion of evolution to human cultural and moral development, leading to a group of theories generically describable as *evolutionary ethics.*[1] The common core of such theories was the regarding of what centuries and millenia had referred to as 'evil', as somehow *illusory*. If 'evil' could now be regarded as an evolutionary residue from more primitive, less civilized stages in the human process, it could be abandoned as a definitive predicate of human nature. While such views have long since been abandoned as erroneously superficial, in Ritschl's day they were regarded as exciting and interesting hypotheses which produced widespread scepticism towards much traditional theological and ethical teaching, which involved theologians in making out a case for human sinfulness from sound experiential, rational and social materials. While such evolutionary theories were optimistic in tone, others, deriving from contemporary materialistic and naturalistic metaphysics, tended towards forms of ethical pessimism. For if human beings and processes were exhaustively explicable in material terms, this was incompatible with much traditional theological talk of the freedom of the will. In practical terms, this involved hard-pressed theologians in defending human freedom and the moral striving and responsibility based on it. Again, it would be unjust to overlook the operation within Ritschl's *milieu* in the 1860s and 1870s of *ethical rationalism*. There were produced countless hostile works (of which the most significant in these islands was W. E. H. Lecky's *History of the Rise and Influence of Rationalism in Europe*),[2] deploring the Churches' attempts to block the progress of the natural sciences since the Renaissance, and the offence given to the developing ethical sensitivity of Europeans by the personal and social implications of doctrines like original sin, the penal character of suffering and death, the consignment of the unbaptized to Limbo, the unpredictable capriciousness of 'religious' phenomena, the priority claimed by theology over ethics, the fate of the heathen, and the rest. In Germany as in England, a doctrine like original sin (considered by European intelligentsia to have been derived from a discredited piece of 'history' like the Genesis Creation Narrative), was regarded as an irrational notion cutting at the root of moral freedom, responsibility and effort. Theologians of Ritschl's generation felt strongly obliged therefore to reinterpret the doctrine so that it would make sense in the context of contemporary psychological and sociological analysis. Mention has already been made of contemporary *anti-Protestant* agitation, with its charge that the doctrine of justification by faith promoted moral inaction and libertinism, and that it compared unfavourably with medieval Catholic ascetic spirituality directed towards good works. Hence Ritschl's heavy underscoring of the view that justification by God is but the threshold of a life of moral responsibility and striving. To fill this latter point out, Ritschl felt obliged to respond to the general accusation by historians of culture and ideas that Protestantism from its inception had been a negative and anti-social movement, destroying not only an ancient, rich and universal Catholic culture, but also German and European unity, by affirming that the aim of protestantism is a spiritually and morally renewed person, liberated and energized by God towards a new life, working out his faith by prayer, humility and patience, in that vocation in which he had been placed by providence, working towards God's and man's final end of that supramundane commonwealth in which all men will finally be united with God, bound together by the bonds of mutual care and loving service. This then is a brief description of Ritschl's *Zeitgeist*, to which, according to Barth and his followers, he and his followers 'capitulated'. For, according to Barth, nineteenth-century German theology had as its *decisive* and *primary* concern 'confrontation with the contemporary age', leading to reductions and over-simplifications which threatened and undermined theology and Church with impoverishment and triviality. This was because such theology ascribed 'normative character to the ideas of its environment'.[3] But this is not the judgement of an objective and unbiased historian, but of a hostile theological opponent. The present generation, disillusioned by Barth's own solution to the Church and culture problem (the abrupt separation of the former from the latter, the only positive 'contact' between the two being the proclamation of the former to the latter), and appalled by galloping secularization, recognizes that the problem of the relation of the *Zeitgeist* to the Gospel is back with us again in urgent form, so that we could do much worse than return enquiringly to those theologians of the nineteenth-century tradition who, in Barth's words, 'wrestled with the challenging issues of their times'.[4] Doubtless, at points, Ritschl's concessions to modernity may have been over-generous;

but this does not mean that in various ways his reinterpretations have not been corroborated by recent research and are irrelevant for contemporary and future theological work.

To return to the stereotype, the first item in it is Ritschl's alleged 'Pelagianism'. Brunner used to refer to him as 'a complete Pelagian' and 'a full-blown Pelagian'.[5] The accusation is possible only by ignoring evidence which points in the opposite direction. There is his view, for example, that from the point of view of Christianity 'it must be presupposed that *all men* are sinners', and that 'even those who enjoy reconciliation must acknowledge that they are sinners who never cease to need it'.[6] It is true that he is hostile to the Augustinian version of original sin and to any doctrine that makes God (the universal author of goodness) the author of sin. He turns, therefore, predictably, to *experience*, which teaches us that 'the fact of universal sin on the part of man . . . is established by the impulse to the unrestrained exercise of freedom, *with which everyone comes into the world*, and meets the manifold attractions to self-seeking which arise out of the sin of society'. 'Therefore,' he continues, 'it happens that some degree of self-seeking takes form *in every person*, even before a clear comprehension of the state of society's self-consciousness is awakened in him.'[7] Pelagius is judged unsound, as he recognizes exclusively the individual will as the form of sin, and the attention he gives to the transmission of sin through example and imitation is inadequate, for 'example operates only when one *receives* and *welcomes* it from another, and thus by the path described the dissemination of sin does not transcend the limits of the individual will'.[8] Pelagius is blind to the communal aspect of sin, an insight preserved only inadequately by Augustine's teaching. 'Pelagianism' has been suggested by Ritschl's celebrated (or notorious) statement: 'Neither *a priori* nor yet in accordance with the conditions of experience, is it to be denied that there may be a sinless development of life.'[9] While this statement tends towards ethical optimism rather than pessimism, this does not mean that he was a 'Pelagian'. For the statement is philosophically significant. In an intensely empiricistic age, he could not possibly defend the statement 'all men are sinners' as both *a priori* and (as we should say nowadays) *synthetic*. He was also most anxious not to fall into the error of teaching that sin was somehow on a par with

God – sin is an aberration, not a necessary, constitutive attribute of the human. Sin is, so to speak, *dysteleological*: 'Sin has no real end, either for the individual life or for the advancement of the whole.' The way to proceed is *a posteriori*, experientially or existentially; 'it is only by reckoning up the sum total of experiences that we arrive at our conviction of *the universal prevalence of sin*'. The hypothesis of an 'innate propensity to sin', like Zwingli's, 'would have to be established by means of observation'. If it were so corroborated 'nothing more would be reached thereby than what ordinary experience ascertains, even without such means of interpretation', (i.e., without beginning from the hypothesis). Ritschl demands of his opponents an intelligible account of the business: 'how ignorance (i.e., in infants) can be a sinful propensity, prior to all activity of the individual will, is unintelligible.'[10] (It is ironical to notice that Brunner, in defending 'orthodox' views of sin against Ritschl in *Dogmatics II*, is at point after point obliged to do so *a posteriori*, notably by citing C. G. Jung's researches into collective psychology.[11])

We turn now to Ritschl's alleged rejection of the doctrine of original sin. Taking his stand on a form of theological empiricism, he declares that as Christians 'we have not to believe in sin in general, or in a general conception of sin as would fall *outside of experience*', and that 'if original sin is an article of doctrine which we believe, then this belief, *if it cannot be tested by experience*, is a mere opinion'.[12] He was in fact defending an *existential* rather than an *ontological* approach to sin. Like modern theological existentialists, he contrasts an existential awareness of sin, evoked by preaching, and an objective or ontological analysis of sin: 'Before we attain to faith in Christ, it is perhaps possible to acquire from the law a theoretical knowledge of the characteristics of sin, but not that estimate of it which should express itself in the decisive estrangement of the will from it.'[13] He anticipates much twentieth-century theology by insisting that knowledge of sin comes from Christianity, with its stress on God's and man's highest good, the Kingdom of God. Indeed, the Christian notion of sin is derived, not from the Genesis Creation Narrative, but from the Person of Christ; 'in Dogmatics Christ's

Person must be regarded as the ground of knowledge to be used in the definition of every doctrine'.[14] Christology is therefore central for Ritschl's anthropology; if Christ is the normative source of Christian doctrine, 'the common destiny of man, through which they attain their distinction from nature and their lordship over the world, was first realized in its full compass in the self-consciousness of Christ, and through Him made manifest and effective'.[15] If, therefore, 'the kind providence of God and man's trust in it' is the *basal form of religion*, then its opposite, sin, essentially 'a defect in reverence in and trust in God, or indifference and mistrust of Him', is the 'basal form of the sin of our first parents'.[16] It is this, the 'basal form of original sin', which has been *transmitted to all men*, and as *sin* (rather than mere social wrongdoing or crime) must be regarded as deriving from indifference towards or mistrust of God. Ritschl did not, therefore, 'reject' the notion of original sin, although he did, to be sure, *reinterpret* it, by replacing the Augustinian-metaphysical notion by his own social doctrine of the 'Kingdom of Sin'. This latter doctrine may be expressed thus: the kingdom of sin is humanity as the sum of all individuals; the wrongdoing of each interacts with and reinforces that of others; it corrupts customs, principles and institutions; this is an essentially cumulative process which progressively undermines each succeeding generation, especially those with 'as yet undeveloped characters'.[17] Ritschl's Johannine inspiration comes out here in a reference to some New Testament passages which refer to the world as being subject to the evil one – e.g., 1 John 5: 18, 19; John 12: 31; 16:11. He affirms strongly that this doctrine is vastly superior to those of Pelagius and Augustine, on the grounds that neither underscores the *horizontal* spread of sin, indicated by his own term, 'thorough-going reciprocation'. More particularly, the Augustinian doctrine is not existential-dynamic: it omits reference to the actual corruption of the will and the quite empirical development of evil habits and inclinations. Hence Augustine's doctrine is to be judged 'intellectually unproductive': it is not sociological enough, analysing the 'illimitable interaction of sin in society'; it ignores that there are 'distinct degrees of evil in individuals', and so fails to express 'the highest sense of sin'. His analysis enables him to illumine and extend a central concept of his system described in the previous chapter, 'the world'.[18] His important identification of 'world' and 'kingdom of sin' is expressed thus:

> This whole web of sinful action and reaction, which presupposes and yet again increases the selfish bias in every man, is entitled 'the world', which in this aspect of it is not of God, but opposed to Him.[19]

Ritschl has little difficulty in showing that the classical biblical passages favoured by St Augustine simply will not bear the weight which the latter wished to place on them. Of the obscure and isolated fifth verse of Psalm 51 ('Behold, I was brought forth in iniquity, and in sin did my mother conceive me'), he remarks with justice that it cannot 'form the basis of any universal doctrinal truth'.[20] The phrase 'children of wrath' of Ephesians 2: 3 is disposed of sensibly by remarking that, to use a modern term, it is a *heilsgeschichtliche* metaphor: Christians, once living in a history of wrath, now live in a history of grace. Of Paul's statement in Romans 5: 12 (and its parallel in v. 19) he says that exegetes are still divided about its meaning, which leads him to say, not unreasonably, that 'dogmas can be based only on clear statements of Scripture'.[21] Of Augustine's authoritatively normative exegesis of these verses Ritschl makes two incontrovertible statements: first, Paul does not say, as alleged by Augustine, 'that all have sinned in the person of Adam'; second, what lies beyond all doubt 'in Paul's presentation of the subject is . . . the fact that he says not a word about the transmission of sin and the inheritance of bias by natural generation'.

What then is our estimate of this second item in the stereotype? Quite clearly, Ritschl did not 'reject' the notion of original sin. On the contrary, his reinterpretation of it may be defended as superior to the older version on various grounds. First, over against the harsh criticism of ethical rationalism, his empirical, psychological and sociological theory does not undercut moral freedom and responsibility. Second, in an empiricistic age, his theory did not depend on any metaphysical dualism as applied to the self – he explicitly rejects the view that human persons consist fundamentally of a hidden, imperceptible, intangible *substantia materialis*, contrasted with the 'mere' observable, historical, spatio-temporal *accidens* conceived of as existing somehow in a plane 'in front of' the substantial dimension, which lies somehow 'behind' or 'beyond' the plane of historico-temporal reality. Doctrinally, for such a viewpoint humanity was sometimes viewed as essentially this substantial substratum in which 'accidents' like reason and will 'co-inhere', and which itself is the bearer of *original* sin, while *actual* sin, affecting merely the will, is regarded as something accidental to man's essential being! Ritschl attempts to cut himself out of this tangle by positing man's essential being as volition and feeling issuing in concrete historical intentions, by committing himself to 'the rule for knowledge that a thing is known through effects which manifest themselves and that, therefore, a spiritual person exists in his volition as it is visible and present to us'.[22] Such a standpoint possesses a high claim to intelligibility in a culture like ours, deeply affected by logical empiricism, insisting that talk of the self must begin with discourse referring to observations, perceptions, behavioural descriptions and the like.[23] And it possesses a higher measure of relevance in a theological *milieu* more or less affected by philosophical existentialism, with its stress, not vastly different from Ritschl's, on the self as a historical, temporal, intentional, volitional, transitional being or principle.[24] Third, it is worth recalling that Ritschl's contemporaries, like Garvie, generally recognized his contribution to social ethics.[25] David Mueller has recently done the same: he links the doctrine of the kingdom of sin with the turn-of-the-century Christian Socialist movement of Ragaz and Kutter, which for a time heavily influenced not only the young Tillich but the young Barth; forty years after Ritschl's day, Walther Rauschenbusch and Reinhold Niebuhr wrote of 'the corporate kingdom of evil which corrupts men and institutions'. Mueller adds: 'But all of them surely learned much from Ritschl, who spoke with prophetic power at this point.'[26] In speaking as he did, Ritschl was answering contemporary critics who alleged that protestantism was essentially a negative, destructive and antisocial movement. Fourth, the theory of Ritschl does not at all depend on the historical literalness of the Genesis Narrative, whose Adam and Eve tale is now widely regarded as *mythical*. (It is significant that one of the two exegetical pioneers who first applied the category of 'myth' to the Genesis Creation

Narrative was one of Ritschl's Göttingen predecessors, Johann Gottfried Eichhorn (1752–1827), Professor of Oriental Languages and Biblical-Exegetical Science from 1788 until 1827.)[27] In modern theology, it is widely accepted that in the Fall narrative of Genesis the term 'Adam' refers to human being or mankind collectively (rather than a first man), and that while man may inherit the nature and/or the situation in which sin is inevitable, he does not become guilty until he acts so as to alienate himself from God.[28] The situation is not dissimilar in modern Catholic theology. Hence, Karl Rahner and Herbert Vorgrimler, in expounding the ancient doctrine in its traditional form, nevertheless stress Adam's *representative* function, and that Adam's sinful disposition 'is ratified in fact by every individual man through his personal sin (see Romans 5: 12)'.[29] In view of the contemporary powerful inclination to defend the significance of the ancient doctrine by some *a posteriori* demonstration of *wilful sinfulness*, it is hard not to judge that Ritschl was an unappreciated pioneer in this matter. Finally, there is the question of his long-term influence, in this context, on modern theology. Without a doubt, this comes out most obviously in Bultmann's wrestling with the problem of Romans 5: 13 f., that of differentiating between that sin for which man is responsible and that for which he is not. There is therefore an uncanny echoing of Ritschl's teaching in Bultmann's treatment of the 'universality of sin':

> At the base of the idea of inherited sin lies the experience that every man is born into a humanity that is and always has been guided by a false striving. The so-derived understanding of existence applies *as a matter of course to every man*; and every man brings himself under it by his concrete 'transgression', thereby becoming jointly responsible for it. Since human life is a life with others, mutual trust is destroyed by a *single* lie, and mistrust – and thereby sin – is established; by a *single* deed of violence defensive violence is called forth and law as organized violence is made to serve the interests of individuals, etc. – ideas at least hinted at by 1 Corinthians 5: 6: 'do you not know that a little leaven ferments the whole lump of dough?' So everyone exists in a world in which each looks out

for himself, each insists upon his rights, each fights for his existence, and life becomes a struggle of all against all even when the battle is involuntarily fought.[30]

Apart from the trifling matter of style, there is no reason why these words could not have been composed by Ritschl in his attempt, a century ago, to reinterpret the notion of original sin.

The third item in the hostile stereotype of Ritschl requiring treatment is his alleged *rejection of the penal or retributive character of human suffering*. The judgements of Orr are that 'Ritschl rejects absolutely the punitive aspect of the divine character' and that in his works 'the doctrine of a government of the world by reward and punishment is explicitly rejected'.[31] Garvie, surprisingly, is equally hostile; 'a feature of Ritschl's doctrine of sin which is opposed to the general teaching of the Christian Church is his refusal to connect the wrath of God at present with sin, and so to regard the evils of life as penalties'.[32] 'Ritschl,' writes J. K. Mozley, 'rejects the idea of any present punishment of sin by God, especially in the way of material evils.'[33] And David Mueller, very much more recently, writes descriptively rather than critically: 'Ritschl dissociates himself from a major segment of Christian tradition, which views evil as the punishment for sin'.[34] In Ritschl's thought, writes H. R. Mackintosh, 'there is no idea of divine punishment, of a divine righteousness manifested in punishment, of a divine wrath'.[35] Now while it would be hard to maintain that Ritschl's position here is entirely satisfactory or acceptable, it is not difficult to demonstrate that statements such as 'Ritschl *absolutely rejected* the penal aspect of sufferings' are untrue and therefore un-scholarly. For Ritschl made no such rejection: what he did was to replace a traditional *objective-ontological-metaphysical* theory (of the relation of suffering to sin) with a *subjective-existential* one. Here, as at other points, the key to Ritschl's thinking is the Wrzecionko thesis that Ritschl, disillusioned with metaphysics as the science which supplies theology with its orientation, turned to human self-consciousness as the area in which historical theology finds its contemporary anchorage, a decision which has had unpredictable consequences for twentieth-century theologies

of human existence. We deal first with his treatment of the former
of these theories. The terms 'objective', 'ontological' and 'metaphysical' are descriptive of a process wherein the theologian,
adopting the stance of an observer or spectator of historical
processes, correlates instances of suffering with antecedent items
of sinful behaviour. Ritschl has little difficulty in discrediting
the theory. For example, he tells us, it fails to distinguish ethically-
merited from ethically-unmerited evils. 'A man should be practised,' is his advice, 'in forming moral judgements on any given
case.'[36] He is clearly appalled, as were the ethical rationalists of
his day, by the judgement that between suffering and sinfulness
there is probably a direct, observable and quantitative relation.
Hence we are bound to reject 'the old doctrine that *all* evil is the
penalty of sin, in the sense that by God's dispensation it is bound
up with wickedness in the general order of things'.[37] Jesus
rejected, he reminds us, as a Jewish and pagan error, 'that the
amount of evil corresponds in the case of every individual, to that
of sin'. Indeed, the theory, in practice, undermines Christian
charity; so he writes in the *Unterricht*: 'The Christian view of the
world differs therefore from the heathen and Jewish views in that
tenderness of feeling which prevents us from reckoning a man's
personal sufferings as divine punishments.'[38] Even if primitive,
ancient religions connected tragedies such as natural events (e.g.,
earthquakes), pestilences, deluges and congenital infirmity with
divine penalties for sin, a member of a Christian society 'in consequence of Christ's express declarations (John 9: 13; Luke 13:
1–5) . . . will decline to have evils of that kind set down to him by
others as Divine punishments'.[39] He comes close to agreeing with
the ethical rationalists on the unhappiness perpetrated by
Western religion by inferring from the capricious phenomena of
nature to antecedent sinfulness;[40] a rigid and narrow quantification of sin with suffering 'leads in practice to people's torturing
themselves with the attempt to put a penal construction upon all
evils which befall them'.[41] In like fashion, in the light of the grave
charges brought against Western religion by nineteenth-century
ethical rationalism, he grapples with the affirmation of *the penal
nature of death*. Roughly speaking, his procedure is to draw the
sharpest possible distinction between that view of death pre-

supposed and taught by the Old Testament on the one hand, and, on the other, that which he derives from reconciliation with God through Christ. Hence, the judgement of Christians 'that we must indeed die, but that we die unto the Lord (Romans 14: 8), is entirely unaffected whether we regard that destiny as a dispensation of nature, or as the consequence of Adam's transgression'.[42] In Christianity, death no longer appears 'as the sheer opposite of that purposeful life in which the soul is conscious of its worth'. (No implication is intended here that Ritschl's treatment of death is entirely satisfactory. There is little in his views pointing forward to the treatments of the theme by Reinhold Niebuhr, Emil Brunner, Karl Barth and Karl Rahner. The truth is that Ritschl so concentrates upon death as a *physiological* process – *vis-à-vis* nineteenth-century biology and rationalism – that he loses sight of death as a spiritual phenomenon, of the abiding validity of the Bible's insight that death remains a spiritual enemy even of the Christian, and of the death of Christ as the victory over sin and death. At this point he was doubtless limited by the insights of his own time. Wolfhart Pannenberg points out that the neo-Protestant theologians of the nineteenth century, Ritschl included, 'are no longer concerned with the conquest of death'.[43] But then we have already conceded that Ritschl, like most of his contemporaries, adhered to ethical optimism rather than ethical pessimism.)[44] Second, we deal with the latter of these two theories. The words 'existential' and 'subjective' are used here with the intention of indicating the affinity between Ritschl at this point and the existentialist theologians, particularly Bultmann. In other words, Ritschl attempted to 'existentialize', to 'deobjectify', and so to 'demythologize' the relation of sin to suffering. The precise meaning of these terms is spelled out by Bultmann in the following attempt to define *demythologizing*:

> If the action of God is not to be conceived as a worldly phenomenon capable of being apprehended apart from its existential reference, it can only be spoken of by speaking simultaneously of myself as the person who is existentially concerned. Since human life is lived out in time and space, man's encounter with God can only be a specific event here

and now. This event, our being addressed by God here and now, our being questioned, judged and blessed by him, is what we mean when we speak of an act of God.[45]

In Ritschl's terms, he wished the proposition 'God punishes sin' to be interpreted, not as an objective truth about the external world, but as an *existential* confession; the proposition is not a *theoretical* but a *value-judgement* which, we recall, is rooted in spirit's subjective awareness of itself over against the natural world. He can express his meaning with admirable terseness:

> Strictly speaking, *only the individual person himself* can determine that the misfortunes which come upon him are divine punishments for sin, when he thus reckons them to himself because of a feeling of guilt.[46]

(He deplores the opposing doctrine, which obtains when a sinner 'regards deserved misfortunes as injustice, or connects no thought of a divine government of the world with his experience'.)[47] He in no way wishes to deny that the world is a moral order, where sin evokes pain as its consequence; he brings this out by insisting that the sinful suffer by reinforcing and extending social evils (the kingdom of sin), partly by helping to produce the aggregate, partly by adopting it. But he does wish to insist strongly and unambiguously on the existential anchorage of it all:

> True, the acceptance of Divine teleology seems to demand that we should ascribe, though not to evil in every case, at least to a signal and conspicuous instance, the significance of a special Divine intention to punish . . . In such cases the Christian view of the world comes out, rather, when we infer from our consciousness of reconciliation that God is educating us in patience and humility and in manifestation of that sympathy which becomes Christians.[48]

Ritschl's theory leads him to place a quite unprecedented emphasis on the *feeling of guilt*. This emphasis is given expression in his affirmation that 'a feeling of unrelieved guilt is the only thing which enables the individual, if he thinks about God at all, to recognize his condition as penal, and set it to his own account'.[49] For him the most frightful consequence of sin is forfeiture of Divine sonship or access to God, but this, he insists, is inconceivable 'unless the forfeiture is consciously recognized as such by the individual affected by it'. The quite exceptional status enjoyed by the guilt-feeling in Christian thought derives from the fact that it is 'not so much one penal state among others, but is itself that of which all external evils are but the concomitant circumstances'. He sharpens his meaning when he writes: 'Divine punishment must be constituted precisely by the consciousness of guilt, as being an index of the forfeiture of access to God.' Such then is Ritschl's so-called subjective–existential theory of the relation between suffering and sin. In judging it, care must be taken to note that the notions which inspire it are in the main derived from his reasoned objections to that extreme and dangerous form of *objectivism* (which, as a distinguished historian, he had identified in the Christian tradition in the West from the sixteenth to the nineteenth centuries),[50] which treats of sin, guilt, justification and reconciliation as though man's spiritual life is essentially transacted within a transcendental dimension above man (so to speak) *which does not significantly impinge upon human consciousness.* It was, as Wrzecionko has so convincingly argued, in trying to overcome this hazardous trend throughout his entire theological programme that he so significantly anticipates modern theologies of human existence. Such perilous *objectivism* has been dubbed by Karl Rahner in our day 'extrinsicism', defined as the view that spiritual realities, although 'real', nevertheless belong to a realm that transcends everyday consciousness. *Extrinsicism*, which in Rahner's view has practically become the average 'textbook' orthodoxy of much post-Tridentine Catholic theology, is defined by him thus: 'The relationship between nature and grace is conceived in such a way that they appear as two layers so carefully placed that they penetrate each other as little as possible.'[51] Rahner spells out the dangers for Christianity implicit within extrinsicist theologies, and links them up with the atrophy of modern man's interest in the spiritual life. If extrinsicism is valid, it is 'not surprising that man should take very little interest in this mysterious superstructure of his being':[52] within the extrinsicist framework, the contact between the two layers is considered to be a 'purely external "decree" commanding the acceptance of the supernatural' which is known 'only through verbal Revelation',[53] interpreted by man as 'merely a disturbance,

which is trying to force something upon him'.[54] It is interesting
that Ritschl, a prodigious researcher in the same post-Reformation period, underlined not dissimilar dangers implicit in much
Lutheran and Reformed orthodoxy, dangers highlighted in the
Kant-Schleiermacher stress on experience. Hence his attempt to
integrate the ingredients of the Christian tradition firmly into
experience and the religious consciousness. Nevertheless, important questions must be put about the acceptability of his
subjective-existential theory. For example, is the believer so confined to the circle of his own subjectivity (in linking his *own*
sufferings with his *own* sinfulness), that he is forbidden to make
any judgements concerning calamities in the 'external' world,
social, political or economic in nature, on a national, international,
or even global scale? Or, is Ritschl's position compatible with the
prophet's judgement of disasters within his own civilization as
rooted in social or economic iniquity, in disobedience to the
divine law? And what of the Christian analysis of World War I
as the inevitable outcome of nineteenth-century greed, cut-throat
competition, imperialistic megalomania, economic injustice and
national pride? Or what of Karl Barth's interpretation of the
Russian Revolution of 1917 as God's chilling 'No!' to that
Western capitalism which brought so much ghastly inhumanity
to millions? Is it compatible with Barth's Exegesis of Romans
1: 28–31 in the *Römerbrief*, that

> the true nature of our unbroken existence is here unrolled
> before us. Our ungodliness and unrighteousness stand under
> the wrath of God. His judgement now becomes judgement and
> nothing more; and we experience the impossibility of men as
> the real and final impossibility of God?[55]

Or what of those contemporary theologians who warn us that
Christianity may stand or fall, as a world religion, in the next
generation dependently upon how it relates itself to the legitimate
moral demands of the socially and economically oppressed?

The comprehensive answer to such questions is that *theoretically* his views are not quite incompatible with such standpoints,
but that *practically*, for very complex reasons, his general standpoint was unsympathetic towards a Christian ethical critique of
social and international disaster. In theory, Ritschl applied no

absolute ban on the Christian attempt to interpret suffering in the external world under a penal, retributive aspect. Despite his anxiety about 'judging others', he nevertheless freely concedes that we may identify outside our own lives 'ethically merited evils', but that we should become 'practised in forming moral judgements on any given case'. He affirms, indeed, that the world is a divinely-appointed teleological moral order where sin brings suffering, although he hastens to plead that our Christian attempt to interpret suffering should confine itself to signal and conspicuous instances (such as, for example, a world war or the Russian Revolution?). Evils, he plainly teaches, may have a punitive as well as an educative function. Nevertheless, *in practice*, it cannot be denied that the entire trend of his theological thinking took a different direction. His highly *individualistic* approach to the question was overwhelmingly strong. His concessions to the opposing line were reluctant and minimal exceptions to a hard general rule. As we shall discover in Chapter VI below, there was in Ritschl, by nature and experience, an exceptionally strong politically and socially *conservative* strain which significantly affected his life's work. But, perhaps most significantly, as noted above, a highly speculative aspect of his doctrine of God (as overwhelmingly, even monistically 'loving purpose') turned out to be, in the last analysis, nearly incompatible with the Pauline-Lutheran stress on 'the Wrath of God displayed from Heaven against sinfulness'. Even the extremely moralistic Herrmann deplored the master's assertion that the Christian's experience of being under Wrath was rooted in a subjective (i.e., *experiential*) misapprehension which is incompatible with God's *actual* attitude to humanity ('loving will'), as the speculative abandonment of the experience not only of the New Testament authors but of Luther and his colleagues.[56] It was Ritschl's kind of teaching here that led to the dialectical theologians' rejection of, in the words of Brunner, his 'rational, one-sided view of the idea of God' in favour of 'the Christian conception, in which the equal stress laid on the holiness, as well as on the love, of God suggests the mystery of the Godhead'.[57] To conclude then, problems there are in plenty in Ritschl's teaching on the connection of suffering and sin; but to say that he 'denied the retributive or penal aspect of suffering' simply will not do.

The next item requiring treatment is Ritschl's alleged *reduction of guilt to a feeling of guilt*. It is here unambiguously clear, as Wrzecionko has shown, that he, over against an 'extrinsicist' understanding of guilt, tried hard to bring guilt within the orbit of the religious consciousness. Quite crucial importance attaches itself to the key terms *reduce* and *reduction* in the stereotyped allegation. Did Ritschl in fact *reduce* guilt *to* guilt-consciousness? This is a notoriously difficult question to answer, requiring meticulous analysis of his terminology. Someone has written,[58] with reference to an experiential approach to the doctrine of God, that to say that God is an ingredient *in* experience is not the same thing as saying that God is *identical with* or that he can *be reduced to* that experience, or that he does not significantly transcend the experience. Analogously, to say that guilt is an ingredient *in* experience (or consciousness) is not to say that guilt is *identical with* or can be *reduced to* that experience or that it does not significantly transcend the experience. Is Ritschl faithful to this insight? This is a hard question to answer, but a defensible answer might be that so far as his *intention* is concerned (as compared with his actual *achievement*), he did, indeed, try to be faithful to it. His opponents may have been misled by his occasionally startling statements, of which the following is a notorious example: 'We have not to believe in sin in general, or in a general conception of sin such as would *fall outside of experience*.'[59] But he at once rushes on to explain that he is referring to a doctrine of original sin *so far removed* from experience that it could not be tested by it, for the belief in original sin 'if it cannot be tested by experience, is a mere opinion'. Elsewhere, his actual terminology clearly reveals his intentions. For example, he is fond of the term *index* for the guilt-consciousness, which is 'an *index* of the forfeiture of access to God or of Divine sonship'.[60] But the term *index* is not necessarily a reductionistic term. Indeed, he is fond of distinguishing between 'guilt' and 'guilt-consciousness' in discussing forgiveness:

> Moral guilt will necessarily come into consideration here *along with* the feeling of guilt, since unless it is distinctly presupposed the forgiveness of guilt cannot be thought as *operating in* the guilty.[61]

Nowhere does the distinction come out so clearly as where he uses the terminology of *marked by* in his formal definition of guilt:

> Guilt, in the moral sense, expresses the disturbance of the proper reciprocal relation between the moral law and freedom, which follows from the law-transgressing abuse of freedom, and as such is *marked by* the accompanying pain of the feeling of guilt.[62]

He uses the analogous terminology of *expressed* in an alternative definition:

> Guilt is thus that permanent contradiction between the objective and the subjective factor of the moral will which is produced by the abuse of freedom in non-fulfilment of the law, and the unworthiness of which is *expressed* for the moral subject in his consciousness of guilt.

Again, he can use the terminology of 'guilt being *recognized as present through* the guilt-consciousness'.[63] In the same place, he refers to the consciousness of guilt *as expressive of* 'that separation of men from God which enters in instead of their proper fellowship'. Against Scotus, he speaks of 'the contradiction of God and our own moral destiny which is *expressed in* the conception of guilt, and is *felt with pain in* the consciousness of guilt, and is marked as a real disturbance of human nature'. The quintessence of his view could not be better expressed than by reproducing his own words:

> The consciousness of guilt *attests* both the lasting validity for the will of the good final end, and also the real injury which freedom has sustained through the production of evil. Thus, in the domain of the will, sin, as the disturbance of the ideal relation of the will to its final end, or to God as representing that end in the world-order, is a real contradiction.[64]

So far then as Ritschl's *intention* is concerned, so good. He took great pains to maintain a sharp distinction between actual, objective guilt and its impingement up (or intrusion into) the religious consciousness. He intended, that is, not unsuccessfully, to stress that objective guilt transcended the feeling of guilt. To what elements, then, is the question, is the feeling of guilt a reliable index? First, it indicates a real, rather than fictional or imaginary, disturbance of human nature, rooted in injury to the freedom of the will, an objective debility which has infected the will. Second, it bears witness to separation from God, forfeiture of access to God (or divine sonship), rooted in a real, objective contradiction between the human creature and God. Third, it expresses a fracture or dislocation of the intended reciprocal relation between freedom and the law, rooted in non-fulfilment of the law. And fourth, it testifies to a dislocation, real and objective, between the striving self and that self's highest end or good. Why then has Ritschl, in his actual *achievement* (as compared with his intention) been so widely accused of *reducing* guilt to the feeling of guilt? The accusation is rooted in the conviction, articulated by twentieth-century neo-orthodox opponents, that Ritschl was a direct child of the German *Aufklärung* and that (despite his misleading biblico-credal terminology) his thought did not significantly advance upon Enlightenment and Rationalistic attempts to come to grips with Christianity.[65] Hence it might plausibly be argued that three, if not all, of these four elements might as conveniently be derived from the moral theology of Kant as from the Christian tradition rooted in the New Testament. Of course, this would not necessarily condemn Ritschl, since that would be to assume that Kant did not possess a unique insight into Christianity as an ethical religion. Nevertheless, scepticism, ancient and modern, remains about Ritschl's claim simply to be expounding the New Testament's doctrine of sin in the light of Luther's Reformation. But against what has it been directed? Not, certainly, to the formal accuracy of his teaching, so far as it goes; there are genuine elements in the Christian doctrine of guilt which Ritschl has justly stressed. It is directed rather to Ritschl's failure to do anything like justice to certain depths and dimensions in the biblical teaching on sin. Before the turn of the century Dr Orr had complained that in Ritschl's teaching sin loses the *catastrophic* character attributed to it by the Bible, as a natural and unavoidable development which is rooted in ignorance and therefore readily pardonable; the feelings and fears which it engenders are easily dispelled by a just view of the character of God, which lies, as we shall see in the following chapter, at the heart of Ritschl's view of the Atonement. But to evangelical Christianity, sin and guilt are 'terrible' realities which evoke God's judgement against them; the truth of the matter, biblically considered, is that the so-called 'guilt-consciousness' but *inadequately* mirrors an objective divine condemnation even more awful in its nature and consequences than the sinner's *imperfect* guilt-feelings permit him to grasp![66] That is, the empirical guilt-consciousness is a poor index of that awfulness of sin which is *disclosed in the biblical revelation as a whole*. It is important to observe here a distinct move away from the *subjective-existential* estimate of sin rooted in a value-judgement of man towards an objective declaration of the hideous, even cosmically hideous, character of sin derived from divine revelation set forth in scripture and reflected in the history of the Christian tradition as a whole. This move reached its farthest extent in Karl Barth's adamant rejection of Ritschl's position in his *Kirchliche Dogmatik* IV: 1, where Barth affirms Ritschl's inability to perceive that 'the actuality of sin is a truth of faith, and that we have a knowledge of it *not so much as we compare ourselves with Christ but as He Himself compares us with Himself before His judgement-throne*'.[67] Despite the unacceptable extremity of Barth's viewpoint here – unacceptable because of the way in which he almost eliminates the experiential pole from the divine-human relation – he has nevertheless put his finger on something important; namely, that Ritschl's heavy stress on man's subjective self-estimate as sinful caused him to overlook certain objective characteristics in the biblical account of sin and guilt which rendered his view defective. If we turn to a contemporary, by no means overtly hostile or unsympathetic interpreter of Ritschl's position, David Mueller, we find him judging that Ritschl's excessively 'psychological' description of sin leads to the excision of those New Testament portrayals of sin as something transcending man and even more powerful than man's collective sin found in Ritschl's kingdom of sin. Mueller's final judgement is harsh: in the final analysis, discourse concerning sin is descriptive of man's feelings and do not refer to an actual separation between God and man.[68]

It now becomes clear why Ritschl has been widely and roundly accused of having *reduced* guilt to guilt-feelings. The point of any caricature is that it does contain a significant element of truth, and this is evident in the case under discussion. The reasons for Ritschl's theological procedure are many, but there can be little doubt that most of them derive from his excessive loyalty to his nineteenth-century *Zeitgeist*: his keen wish to show that Christian teaching on sin was not morally ennervating nor counter-productive; his epistemological agnosticism which inhibited him from probing the 'ontological bases' of experienced spiritual realities; his reluctance, which he shared with Schleiermacher, to admit into his monistic Christianity anything which smacked of dualism as incompatible with *Aufklärung* rationalism and ethical optimism.[69] But the final reason is the weightiest. If Wrzecionko is right, the key to much of Ritschl's thought is his hermeneutical stance. In the context of the doctrine of sin, this means that he brings to the biblical texts a set of presuppositions so heavily influenced by the post-*Aufklärung* nineteenth-century *Zeitgeist* that he fails to do justice to the breadth and depths of the texts themselves. This hermeneutical theory is neither quite new nor original, for it was anticipated germinally by the incisive Orr in his acute account of Ritschl's value-judgement theory.[70] Now the term 'sin' is for Ritschl a 'value-expression'; we could describe statements referring to sin as 'judgements of disvalue'. Orr identifies an important ambiguity in Ritschl's use of the term 'value' (*Werth*), which is a source of confusion in his work. He fails to perceive the difference between *intrinsic* and *imputed* values. In the case of the first, we *recognize* merely what is there, and intrinsic value may belong to a work of art, or a holy character, irrespective of whether it is recognized or not. On the other hand, there are values *imputed by us*, which may be fictitious, artificial, conventional or the result of association. Exactly – the classic criticism of Ritschl has been that, in the doctrine of sin as in other doctrines, he so stressed *imputed* values (cherished by convention or association in his historical *milieu*) that he sat too lightly to *intrinsic* (abiding, perennially valid, eternal) ones. To spell this out in historical terms, the allegation is widely made that Ritschl's loyalty to his *Zeitgeist* is so great as to be incom-patible with the intentions and content of Scripture, an allegation to which we shall return at later points. That he *reduced* guilt to the guilt-feeling simply will not do – there is more to his teaching than that, but whether this 'more' is satisfactory or not is a question which invites a sceptical answer.

The next item requiring treatment is Ritschl's classification of the great bulk of sin as *ignorance*. The main question here is whether, by fastening on 'ignorance' as a key term, he was guilty thereby of a linguistic infelicity, or unwittingly 'let the cat out of the bag', and allowed us to glimpse his fundamentally optimistic view of sin? Once more, his *intentions* turn out to be far superior to his *achievement*, in that he did not try to treat sin superficially. He divided sin into two categories: first, those sins, classified as *ignorance*, which have not yet rendered the sinner finally, firmly and incorrigibly opposed to God's known will and purpose. These sins are pardonable. Second, there are those sins which are the product of a volitional disposition which is finally, fixedly, deliberately and therefore irredeemably settled upon opposition to the divine loving purpose. This is unpardonable and for it is reserved the divine wrath. 'It is,' he insists, 'just this negative relation that is expressed by the predication of ignorance – and nothing more.'[71] In all fairness to him, he makes it clear that for him sin does not originate merely in ignorance – as noted above, it involves disobedience, atrophy of the will, alienation from God and from one's destiny. What were Ritschl's motives for producing this classification? Two of these are patently obvious. First, in response to the charge of contemporary ethical rationalists that Christian doctrines were morally ennervating, he was obliged to reject any suggestion of the omnipotence of sin.[72] Second, as noted above, he repeatedly rebuked his Christian contemporaries for 'judging others'. Hence, he affirms that the assumption of sin as ignorance 'has the significance *only of a standard for God* – a standard, therefore, which is conceived only negatively, *because its specific application does not belong to us*'. So, speaking of the irredeemably hardened, he affirms: 'Whether there are such men, and who they are, are questions that lie beyond our practical judgement and our theoretical knowledge.' Such statements, and his extremely unfortunate use of the key term 'ignorance', have attracted to his teaching the severest of criticisms from his sympathetic interpreters, both ancient and modern. Garvie,[73] Mozley[74] and Mackintosh[75] all judge that there is here clear evidence that Ritschl took an optimistic view of sin, failed to perceive the significance of Scripture on abounding sin and superabounding grace, and consequently undermined the absolute necessity for an act of sheer saving grace on God's part and the utter necessity of the indwelling Holy Spirit. A contemporary sympathetic commentator, Mueller, concurs,[76] but takes the criticism a stage further. While Ritschl holds, as Mueller observes, that the twofold distinction between types of sin holds good in the first place as a standard for God's judgement *alone*, he goes on to affirm that since men are so much in the dark about God's judgement of individuals, 'we ought to be satisfied with comprehending *all these instances of sin* under the negative category of sin as ignorance'.[77] In other words, for all practical and theoretical purposes, 'all sin is ignorance'! So that his choice of the word 'ignorance' was not just linguistically infelicitous, but doctrinally revealing. The word *Unwissenheit* points to his optimistic estimate of sin. While the statement 'sin is ignorance' possesses interpretative power, Ritschl was beyond question blind to the extent to which sinfulness is rooted in clear-sighted adoption of ends which we know, in our heart of hearts, are abominable in the sight of God. When he pleads for utter agnosticism about the existence and identity of the irredeemably hardened, it is hard not to sense that he is throwing the possibility out of court as so fantastically improbable as not to warrant serious consideration in a theological system. A further consideration clinches the matter: the optimism of Ritschl's doctrine of sin is clearly reflected in his teaching on justification and the atonement, both of which will be examined in the following pages. In defending the proposition that sin is ignorance, he certainly did not *try* to belittle the gravity of the former, but in his *achievement* he was unable to conceal that he was an ethical optimist rather than a pessimist.

The final item in the stereotype of Ritschl requiring treatment is the allegation that he was exclusively interested in concrete sins, not sinfulness. Hence Karl Barth:

> (For Ritschl) sin is deed and only deed. It is man's deed, performed in opposition to the action taking place in the Kingdom of God.[78]

Elsewhere, Barth writes:

According to Ritschl there are only active or concrete sins. There is no being of man in sin, in enmity against God.[79]

Now, as a descriptive summary, this simply will not do. To be fair to Barth, in *Church Dogmatics* IV: 1 he so heavily qualifies these bald, stark descriptions that one wonders if he has not abandoned the stereotype. He mentions all too briefly the reciprocity involved in Ritschl's 'kingdom of sin', but complains that this is not so much an interpretation of original sin as something that crowds it out and replaces it. The complaint is hard to understand; after all, Ritschl explicitly intended the kingdom of sin concept as a reinterpretation of and substitute for the older, in his view, discredited and embarrassing doctrine of hereditary sin and guilt. Barth qualifies his bald statement that 'there is no being of man in sin' by conceding that Ritschl 'can speak of the development of an evil character in man'. But his fundamental objection really reveals that he wishes to hark back to the older doctrine of original sin, which he describes as the notion of 'an evil inclination which preceded the evil act', and the doctrine of 'innate' sin. Thereafter, Barth's sketch of Ritschl on sin is designed to show that the latter is overwhelmingly indebted in this matter to the rational theology of the *Aufklärung* rather than to the New Testament or the Reformers, a demonstration to which we return at later points. For the present, we conclude that Barth's charge that Ritschl has no doctrine of general sinfulness cannot be substantiated. This brings us to the conclusion of our sketch of the stereotype of Ritschl's doctrine of man as sinner. We conclude that there is much in it that is thoughtful, permanently valuable, and perennially interesting in his work. The force behind the classical criticisms of his work in this area derives from the indubitable fact that he positions himself firmly on the side of Christian optimism rather than Christian pessimism. Why this is so is a matter which we must take up in later sections of this work.

We proceed now to an account of Ritschl's teaching on justification, which must be somewhat tentative, since we shall see the implications of justification unfolding in our treatments of soteriology and the Christian's lifestyle. The first thing we have to grasp is that for him justification is to be interpreted *teleologic-*

ally; it is to be seen as a means to an end lying beyond itself; it is to be seen in close connection with its fruits in the moving, changing, ongoing flux of human life. We begin by noting that here, as elsewhere in his system, his method is thoroughly *empirical* and *phenomenological*. A systematic theology like his, he claims, must involve the following methodology:

> We must exhibit the operations of God – justification, regeneration, the communication of the Holy Spirit, the bestowal of blessedness in the *summum bonum* – in such a way as shall involve an analysis of the corresponding voluntary activities in which man appropriates the operations of God.[80]

That is, he intends to integrate justification firmly into human existence. His empirical orientation comes out clearly in another way when he writes: 'Three points are necessary to determine the circle by which a religion is completely represented – God, man and the world.'[81] As we shall perceive at point after point, Ritschl is insisting that justification necessarily implies a change in attitude not only to God but also to the world. In tackling justification, the Lutheran Ritschl was obliged naturally to write every sentence of his system with one eye fixed upon the Reformers' insistence upon the *Sola Fide*. Even a hint that salvation might minimally depend upon moral achievement had to be assiduously avoided. Hence his strenuous insistence upon the continuing significant theological breach between the Protestant churches and Rome. Despite the strongly ethical tone of his entire system, he most sharply distinguished his teaching from any form of legalism which implies that God's promise is in any way contingent upon man's moral activity. Hence, the Reformers' account of justification diverges from the Roman one 'which professes to state the causes and means through which a sinner becomes actively righteous' or which tries 'to explain the moral activity of the Christian life'. Such a doctrine, in his view, is not sufficiently *religious*. So that for him, there is a real, not an apparent, difference between the Evangelical *Rechtfertigung* and the Catholic *Gerechtmachung*. Protestant doctrine tries to explore the *religious* character of the Christian's life as *radically* independent of moral activity, and that character 'includes the certainty of eternal life; and instead of dependence on the world through sin (the

Christian) has obtained freedom over the world and trust in God's providence, and therefore forms the precondition of the discharge of moral tasks'. Justification is then the *conditio sine qua non* of moral activity. His insistence upon this is worthy of brief comment, in the light of the reiterated accusation that he was a Kantian or neo-Kantian moralist, or that he had 'moralized' Christianity. David Lotz has argued convincingly that behind Ritschl on justification and moral activity Luther stands firmly.[82] And David Mueller has protested most vigorously at this point against the 'disguised Kantian moralizer' accusation; he points to Ritschl's admirable clarity on the faith-ethics correlation, on the insistence that although they must be held together, they must not be confused, interchanged or commingled one with the other.[83] One can best be convinced of Ritschl's unambiguous clarity on the matter by considering his own words from the *Unterricht*:

> The freedom and independence of this divine judgement consist in this, that on man's part, situated as he is, no moral work (merit) is conceivable which might call for this positive judgement of God or actually establish it. Rather, this judgement needs only religious faith or confidence in the free grace or righteousness of God in order to become actual and effective.[84]

The fact that later in his system (Chapter VI below) he does try to bring ethical action into an intimate relation with faith ought not to blind us to the fact that fundamentally he has distinguished between the two and has affirmed, in vigorous Lutheran tones, the priority and superiority of the latter over the former.

Before drawing to a conclusion Ritschl's rather complex and diffuse teaching on justification, it might be helpful if we offered some kind of scheme which, hopefully, would introduce a certain order into his somewhat lengthy and formidable discussions. There are, it is suggested, *five* themes running through his work worthy of careful attention. First, it is illuminating to observe the way in which his thought moves rhythmically between the subjective and the objective, a surprising fact for those who have uncritically accepted the stereotype of him as *the* subjectivist *par excellence*. No doubt he sat rather too lightly to those elements in Christianity not readily amenable to being existentialized, and no doubt at points his aversion to *extrinsicism* is somewhat excessive. But he is no subjectivist, unaware of the current sharp criticism of Schleiermacher and Feuerbach, insensitively unaware of the objective anchorage of Christianity. A recent commentator has perceptively described this objective-subjective rhythm in his doctrine of justification and reconciliation:

> For Ritschl every moment in the circumference of Christian existence is a function both of the graceful indicative and of the moral imperative. Christ restores sinners to fellowship with God, but he also enlists their discipleship for the Kingdom. The imperative defines the sin which alienates us as well as the goal which engages our no longer alienated freedom. The indicative overcomes our alienation and bestows upon us the power freely to embrace the imperative as our own.[85]

Second, in view of the bitterly hostile complaint that he had *moralized* Christianity (which caused him endless irritation),[86] it is astounding to observe how he staunchly refused to identify religion with ethics, and utterly subordinated the latter to the former. Third, in view of the charge of *subjectivism*, it is astonishing to observe how, in rejecting the individualism both of monk and quietistic sectarian, he affirmed the priority of the Church over the individual and his experience, evoking the unwarranted accusation that he had forsaken the Reformation standpoint for an almost Romanist ecclesiology. Fourth, worthy of notice is his significant teaching that the Christian life is a gradual development, education or training from life's beginning to its end. Fifth, there is his fundamental teaching that justification, to be worthy of the name, must issue in a new and decisive relationship to the world. Hopefully, this five-point scheme will enable us to render Ritschl's somewhat discursive explorations into the ramifications of justification more intelligible than many of his readers have experienced them to be.

First, there is the matter of the rhythmic movement between the objective and the subjective discernable in Ritschl's discussions of justification. It comes out strongly in his identification of justification with the forgiveness of sins. He speaks of the *objective* side of justification like any traditional Lutheran. He can speak of the penalties of sin as the separation of sinners from

God, the ultimate withdrawal of God's presence from the sinner, and so on.[87] Conversely, forgiveness is God's operation restoring separated sinners to his presence and proper fellowship. But he immediately swings over to speak of the *subjective* side of things: he deals with the *correlation* of the objective with the subjective in the religious consciousness, with special reference to his key area, the feeling of guilt. Forgiveness therefore removes or abolishes the guilt-consciousness; indeed, for him, it would be inconceivable in the absence of a guilt-feeling in which the un-redeemed recognize evils as penal, and recognize them rightly so. This is quite different from the case of civil judges who are ordinarily indifferent as to whether the convicted acknowledge their sentences to be just or not, although he makes the point that it is dangerous for civil society when no one regards civil punishments as just deserts, but as arbitrary and violent acts of revenge. He has no desire to deny the universality of sin and the need for redemption, but to affirm that these notions 'can only be proved from a lively feeling of guilt'. He labours hard to give the guilt-feeling an objective referent, by affirming that it is an *expression* of 'the separation of sinners from God which is counter to their ideal destiny'. True, some of his swings towards the subjective are disconcerting; there is, for example, his notoriously misleading statement that 'we ought therefore to transpose "the removal of the separation of sinners for God" into "the removal of the consciousness of guilt" '! It is not fair to read into this the idea that he is pleading for the *reduction* of guilt to the feeling of guilt. Such statements of his are (admittedly) over-reactions from one-sidedly *extrinsicist* redemption theories in which guilt and its abolition are pictured as occupying a dimension detached from the everyday consciousness of man (Karl Rahner). He is in fact pleading with objectivists for a meaningful place for the guilt-feeling in systematic theology. It is impossible, he tells them, 'to form a complete, universal, and practically applicable conception of moral guilt without the element of the feeling of guilt'. His point is that we must never overlook that point within existence where real, objective guilt *intrudes into* or *impinges upon* self-consciousness. If it is over-looked, we are left either with theological extrinsicism (which is a contributory factor to secularization), or a secularized self-consciousness which progressively finds all talk of 'being guilty' meaningless or irrelevant. Although he does try to 'existentialize' or 'deobjectify' guilt, he takes great pains to avoid implying that he has subjectivized it into a mere psychological state of affairs. To the contrary, the guilt-feeling is *cognitive*; through it the sinner is made aware of a real, objective, dislocation of his will and God's. The sinner actually *feels* 'the logical contradiction of the will to God, which is contained in guilt, as a real contradiction, and as a real defect of will'. We could hardly do better than set down Ritschl's own summary of the matter:

> Thus in the domain of the will, sin, as the disturbance of the ideal relation of the will to its final end, or to God as representing that end in the world-order, is a real contradiction.

The same movement is discernible in his rebuttal of the charge (made by certain nineteenth-century ethical rationalists) that justification by faith involves a *fiction* – namely, the declaring righteous of those who are in fact nothing of the kind. In Ritschl's own words, 'the removal of guilt and the consciousness of guilt would be in contradiction with the validity of the law of truth for God and for the sinner's conscience'.[88] On the *objective* side, first of all, he points to the Old Testament metaphors (God 'covering', 'veiling', and 'blotting out' sin) as expressing the fact that God 'renders it inoperative in relation to Himself'. He at once swings to the *subjective* correlate by affirming that 'the *memory* of that contradiction of sin to God which is expressed in the consciousness of sin continues to operate'. Hence, forgiveness is not to be construed as 'the eradication of the feeling of guilt altogether, but as its removal in a certain aspect'. (That is, justification is neither insincere nor productive of ethical insensitivity.) What aspect of sin is eliminated by God's forgiveness? The answer can only be derived from the process of giving and receiving pardon in interpersonal relations:

> Pardon is an act of will by which there is cancelled that aspect of an injury received which interrupts intercourse between the injured person and the offender on condition that the offender must have perceived and confessed his wrong and thus besought pardon.

That is, God's pardon does not allow the objective contradiction between sinners and himself 'to hinder that fellowship of men with Him which He intends on higher ground', and although it does not totally eradicate the guilt-consciousness, it eliminates that mistrust which spoils man's fellowship with God. We can discern both the objective-subjective movement and his sensitivity to ethical rationalism operating in his treatment of the positive side of pardon, in the notion of the imputation to sinners of the righteousness of Christ.[89] He unambiguously rejects the traditional *ethical* interpretation of this as the annulment of the 'basal presupposition of Christianity':

> This idea is altogether false, because it treats the personal moral lifework of a person as a thing which has no essential connection with its author, and may change its owner without having its essence or value altered.

He was also here, he believed, following in his master Luther's footsteps in denying that 'God enters into no real fellowship in religion save with morally perfect men'. The crucial point made by the imputation doctrine is that the position enjoyed by Christ relative to God – as existing in the love of God as Lord over the world – is shared in by his disciples:

> The point at issue is the imputation of the position relative to God which Christ likewise occupied through His practice of righteousness, to those who as His disciples belong to Him through faith, in order that they may be taken up effectively into the love of God.

Christ, as we shall see in our next christological chapter, achieves this position relative to God through perfect obedience to God in the fulfilment of his *vocation*. We shall have to wait until our penultimate chapter to observe the *subjective* correlate of this in the Christian's concrete response to God's gift, expressed in his worldly vocation or calling.

The same movement is apparent also in Ritschl's remarks on *reconciliation* and on *faith*. In treating reconciliation, he deplores the excessive *objectivism* of the older Lutheran theologians, whose 'thought of justification comes to be isolated from all practical relations . . . and condemned to barrenness'.[90] Their fundamental error was their failure to understand justification *teleologically*; they did not perceive that justification was a means to an end, God's and man's. In other words, they overlooked that 'the conception of reconciliation has a wider range and greater definiteness than that of justification', because, on the *subjective* side, it must issue in a concrete, historical *lifestyle*. Hence, for Ritschl, reconciliation 'expresses as an actual result the effect *aimed at* in justification or pardon, namely, that the person who is pardoned actually *enters upon* the relationship which is to be established'. There is to be no escaping, on the subjective side, the definite result of justification in action in the business of daily living; as Ritschl puts it:

> We may count on it that the justification which is successfully dispensed by God finds its manifestation and response in *definite functions of the persons reconciled.*

He can summarize this in technical theological language; the antithesis of justification is guilt (expressed in the guilt-consciousness); but the antithesis of reconciliation is actual, *active* contradiction to God *in the conduct of life*. He is here being no 'Kantian moralizer'; justification is aimed primarily at the elimination of that mistrust of God which issues in active and willing disobedience to God, and at the production of a new confidence in him and a new obedience towards him. This is what is involved in 'reconciliation with God', which eventually gives rise to functions of a more specifically moral stamp. That is, he is aiming at an account of justification and reconciliation under their *religious* aspect, and takes pains to make it plain that their *moral* implications are secondary to and derivative from the fresh relationship with God aimed at in justification. Indeed, he tries explicitly to avoid what he calls the 'moralism' of Roman Catholicism and Socinianism, in insisting on the Reformation doctrine that justification is, in form, a *synthetic* judgement; it is a creative act or resolve of the divine will which, when it declares a sinner 'righteous', gives to him a predicate not already included in the subject 'sinner'.[91] This synthetic judgement is directed, not in the first instance towards moral transformation, but towards a radical transformation in the sinner's relationship to God. Hence his insistence that Protestantism aims primarily at exhibiting

Christianity not as *the* supreme ethical system available to men, but as 'the perfect spiritual and moral religion', as 'the true religion'. It is therefore theologically illegitimate to compare religions (or different manifestations of the same religion) under the aspect of *Gerechtmachung* (making-righteous), in order to judge which is ethically the more potent or fruitful, for this would be to concede the superiority of ethics to religion. But, in order to ward off the misinterpretation that he was trying to divorce religion from ethics, he adds that justification 'is not to be looked for apart from the moral obedience of faith'. It is important to notice here that his teaching is extremely hard to reconcile with Brunner's charge, already noted – that underlying Ritschl's systematization of Christianity there is an 'ethical metaphysic' of which Christianity is the most perfect instantiation,[92] or Weiss's charge that he was a 'Kantian moralizer' of Christianity! No, Christianity is rendered *the* uniquely perfect spiritual and ethical (in that order) religion by the doctrine of justification, which is all-pervasively determinative. Indeed, the Christian's very conception of God is determined by the process of justification; the leading concept for God is *Father*, and the primary model for understanding God's relationship to his people is the *family*. This goes far to explain the strong anti-juridical strain which runs through his system as a whole:

> The title of Judge as applied to God has therefore for Christians no real place alongside of, or over, the relation in which he stands to them as Father.[93]

And since 'the real analogy for the Kingdom of God should be sought, not in the national State, but in the family', it follows that *justification must be considered equivalent to adoption*:

> The adoption of the believing signifies their reception into that peculiar fellowship with God which is represented under the analogy of the family.

The same objective-subjective movement is discernible in his treatment of *faith*, the human condition of justification.[94] Ritschl concurs with those *objective* statements made by the Christian tradition: God himself is the author and creator of faith; he restores the sinner to fellowship with himself, abolishing the consciousness of guilt and its concomitant mistrust. But, on the *subjective* side, such divine operations would be meaningless unless, in his own words, they were accompanied by 'a consenting movement of the will towards God', a movement identified in the Reformation view with faith. Hence we have a formal definition of faith:

> Faith is emotional conviction of the harmony between the Divine purposes and the most intimate interests of man.

Or, to put this in sixteenth-century terms, in justification God is revealed *pro me* or *pro nobis*. The term 'emotional' is used, predictably, in order to distinguish religious faith from the disinterested, unemotional knowledge of the world involved in 'theoretical judgements'. Or, faith is 'emotional' because it involves a 'feeling of moral pleasure' at the satisfaction bestowed on spirit by the redemptive process. Subjectively, faith implies *trust*, for faith is directed to 'the saving will of God, bound up with the characteristic mark of a clear purpose'. Ritschl agrees with the Catholic formula *fides caritate formata*, for 'faith, regarded as trust, is no other than the direction of the will towards God as the highest end and the highest good'. But the alleged 'Kantian moralizer' of Christianity significantly breaks with the Catholic tradition in its Thomist form at an interesting point: he concurs with St Thomas that acts of love extended to men are simultaneously extended to God, but disagrees that charitable acts directed to God are at the same time directed to one's fellows:

> Love to God is not in itself bound up with love to one's fellow men; but the latter is a special resolution of the will, quite distinct from love to God.

We must be careful not to misinterpret him here, as he was misinterpreted by Orr,[95] who complained, unjustifiably, that in Ritschl's view religion has one origin and morality another and independent one; since the two lie apart in their root, they can only afterwards be mechanically combined. For Ritschl makes the ground of the separation unambiguously clear, 'that the characteristic marks which distinguish Christianity *as a religion*, and those which denote *its ethical purpose*, are therein confused with one another', leading to distortion and falsification. As noted already, he guards against the 'moralizing' accusation by insisting sharply that Christianity's uniqueness resides in the new *religious* relationship to God brought about by justification and not in its alleged ethical superiority to competing ethico-religious systems. True, when he speaks thus, he always covers himself against the kind of misinterpretation popularized by Orr. For example, he insists that in Reformation theology it is maintained 'that the impulse to love one's fellow-man . . . is essentially bound up with the very idea of justification', and that 'wherever entrance into the specifically Christian status before God is realized, Christianity brings into exercise also the corresponding moral impulse'. But this is not at all to say that active love to men might be regarded as the *condition* for the religious relation to God implied in justification. It really is time that modern interpreters of Ritschl heeded the plea of David Lotz that it is more fruitful to consider him essentially as a follower of Luther than as a slavish disciple of Kant.

Our third theme concerns the attempt of Ritschl to overcome the subjective individualism characteristic of the eighteenth-century *Aufklärung*, already initiated in the nineteenth century by Schleiermacher, in his characteristic doctrine that the datum of theological work is supplied in the religious consciousness of the actually existing Christian community. In Ritschl's case, hostility to the *Aufklärung*'s individualistic stress is blended with another motive, derived from his life-long researches on pietistic individualism, published in his *Geschichte des Pietismus*. The core of his disapproval of mystical pietism is expressed in the following statement:

> Wherever men give way to mystical states or aspirations, they imagine that the sphere of the preached Word and the promises of grace, therefore the necessary subordination to the public Revelation in the Church, is transcended and may be forgotten.[96]

He appeals, predictably, to statements of Luther, who had experienced fanatical and mystical sects as a thorn in the side, and 'accordingly represented the justification of the individual as conditioned by the existence of the community', and had therefore described the Church as 'a mother, who bears and nurtures every individual through the Word'. From this he formulates the principle, 'that one cannot arrive at and maintain individual conviction of faith in isolation from the already existing community of faith, and that the community is coextensive with the spread of the Gospel, that is, the public preaching of the forgiveness of sins'. The following terse statement is an admirable summary of his final opinion of the matter:

> The individual can therefore appropriate the forgiveness of sins by faith only when he unites in his faith at once trust in God and Christ and the intention *to connect himself with the community of believers*.

But, and here we encounter a grave difficulty, he goes very much further than these generally mild statements, and affirms plainly that the *object* of justification is the community itself:

> Justification, or reconciliation . . . is related in the first instance to the whole of the religious community founded by Christ, which maintains the Gospel of God's grace in Christ as the direct means of its existence, and to individuals only as they attach themselves by faith in the Gospel, to this community.[97]

Not that his interpreters have quarrelled with the obvious truth contained in his general view of the priority of the Church. Nor can we extend much sympathy to Ritschl's contemporary opponents who urged that he had reverted to a later medieval doctrine of the priority of the Church – for nowhere does he identify 'the community' with a juridically constituted hierarchical order or caste. The difficulty is that his views allow him to do much less than justice to the historical phenomenon of *individual Christianity* as a valid religious phenomenon *over against the Church*, or within but *against the prevailing teaching in* the Church. His monolithically ecclesiastical Christianity would hardly have room for a Wesley, a Kierkegaard, or, ironically, a Luther, and is therefore hardly sympathetic towards a radical interpretation of the Reformation principle, *ecclesia semper reformanda*. Moreover, his implacable hostility to pietism made him insensitive towards the significance and worth of a sudden, sharp, decisive, and historic Christian 'conversion' in the life of the individual, an experience central to understanding Paul, Luther, Wesley and Kierkegaard. This point serves as an introduction to our exposition of the fourth theme in his doctrine of justification. It is impossible to defend him against the charge that he grotesquely over-emphasized the Christian life as a gradual, slow, developing, evolving, progressive education or training, whose firm and indispensable context is home, Church, school and organized society.[98] Critics, arguing that his exclusively *social* conception of Christianity was almost grotesque, have pointed to his startling teaching that when theology speaks of 'humanity' it must do so under the categories of 'races and nations, of grades and species within the genus'.[99] He argues that 'Christianity must win over the nations as a whole'; but this is a difficult business in the light of 'the ascertained facts of ethnology'. In order to become a universal world-religion, Christianity would have to 'bring under its influence all the social conditions under which the spiritual life of individuals exists'. For the present, therefore, it is hard not to identify the domain of Christianity with those Western nations which together comprise 'Christendom' and to concede that Hindus, Buddhists and Muslims 'lack the disposition towards Christianity'. It is difficult to deny that this is a fantastically narrow conception of Christianity, and that Ritschl could not imagine its occurrence apart from the ethos, educational systems and social institutions of Europe, that the spread of Christianity was contingent upon the nineteenth-century Westernization of the non-Western nations, and that his theological views were coloured by the prevailing and unchallenged nineteenth-century assumptions of cultural, ethical, linguistic and religious superiority of the European West to non-European cultures. Even Dr Garvie rebuked him sharply, and complained of a view which dismissed the greater part of the human race as incapable of appropriating Christian salvation, and which pictured God as so involved in care for the *community* as to disregard, apparently, each individual member of the human race![100] The incisive Dr Orr is even more critical, accusing Ritschl of philosophical inconsistency, embracing here a *realism* rather than his usual *nominalism*, leading him to posit the community as an entity by itself on which, as a collective unit, justification is confirmed, so that the individual partakes of this saving benefit, not individually nor immediately, *but only as a member of the body*.[101] This leads Ritschl, in Orr's view, into grave theological error: he stresses God's will and deed grotesquely as *static*, eternal and unchanging, at the expense of specificity; there can be no specific, concrete, individual, interpersonal saving encounter between the believer and Christ.[102] In the light of much recent theology, it is hard to acquit Ritschl of insensitivity to the significance of intra- and extra-ecclesiastical experiential and mystical movements, which oppose the tendency of the Churches to identify current, finite, and historically conditioned modes of thought and life with absolute and final revelation, and which have contributed a certain creative dynamism to the history of Christianity. He was oblivious of what Tillich has called 'the impact of the anti-demonic fight of mysticism', in which it is 'the permanent function of mysticism . . . to reject the demonic identification of anything finite with that which transcends everything finite'. Tillich observes significantly:

> It is unfortunate that those in the Kant-Ritschl and those in the neo-orthodox schools in theology have pointed only to the possible and actual abuses of the mystical approach without acknowledging its world-historical function of transcending the concrete mediums of revelation towards the mystery which is mediated by them.[103]

Our conclusion on this then is as follows: in the last chapter we observed a tendency to identify God with the impetus towards the Kingdom of God immanent in humanity; not dissimilarly, we observe here an almost exclusive identification of the activity or work of God with the functions of the Christian community. Here is one point at any rate where there is a gulf between his thinking and one aspect of that Christian existentialism rooted in Kierkegaard – the notable stress placed on the existing and heroic individual over against all communities, not excluding the organized Church. At the same time, we must not overlook that his theology represented a positive thrust towards those twentieth-century German systems which insist on the Church as the necessary locus of redemption and revelation, and that revelation determined by God's Word proclaimed in and by and for the

Church claims absolute, even exclusive precedence over any and every claim to the knowledge of God.

We deal finally with the fifth theme which Ritschl, as a *Lutheran* theologian, simply could not avoid in his treatment of the subjective side of justification, namely, *the assurance of salvation.* He dealt with it thoroughly for, broadly, two reasons. First, it dominated Lutheran theological debate in the seventeenth and eighteenth centuries. Second, in so far as he was methodologically an *anti-extrinsicist,* he could hardly overlook the issue. Basic to his discussion is the admission that assurance cannot derive from experienced *freedom from sin* in members of the community. The Christian Church 'makes daily prayer for forgiveness of sin a fitting thing'.[104] Indeed, his entire system affirms that 'the forgiveness of sins is the necessary basis of the Christian religion, both as a whole and in detail'. Predictably, he displays hostility towards pietism, to which he attributes unseemly introspection, leading to a morbid state of disgust at one's own sinfulness, which makes all assurance impossible. Remarkably, in one sense, he is an anti-subjectivist, for he affirms that 'the subjective *certainty of justification* springs only from a vision of the object of faith', which is the promise of God. Emotive subjectivism will not do; he agrees with Melancthon that assurance may vary in intensity and quantity, but dismisses the notion that it can thereby *objectively* invalidate justification grounded only in God. His *objectivism* comes out strongly when he writes bluntly, 'Justification is held to be valid even when the subjective certainty of it varies.' He confesses that his own view of the matter approximates to that expressed in the joint Lutheran-Roman Catholic declaration of the Colloquium of Regensburg (1541), to the effect that the assurance of faith depends upon 'the evidence of divine grace furnished, not merely by the sacraments, but *by the good works we do*'. He concurs also with Calvin, who was strongly objectivist in insisting that justification is grounded on the vision of the justifying God, but nevertheless conceded that subjectively faith is incipient, developing, relatively imperfect, within which the *visio dei* becomes only progressively clearer and sharper. But for Calvin as for Melancthon, 'the consciousness of good works done by the believer serves to support and to confirm faith, because in these fruits of our calling appear evidence of Divine favour'. (It is interesting to compare Ritschl's consideration of the place of good works in the Christian life, derived *directly* from Melancthon and Calvin, with the charge that he was a 'Kantian moralizer' of Christianity.) But why, it must be asked, have there been such fierce disputes over the assurance of salvation? Salvation flows from the preaching of the Word 'which is the *general* promise of grace'. The problem is that 'the *general* truth of the forgiveness of sins leaves its actual compass undetermined'. Hence disputes (especially in the post-Reformation period) about the actual, definite, concrete application of justification *to individuals* have inevitably occurred. In sketching such disputes he is once more predictably hard on the solutions to the problem advocated by pietism – he will not have, for instance, an acute individual conversion experience as proof of justification, since this would be to sit lightly to the Christian community as the locus of justification. He deplores pointing to outstanding conversion experiences as proof of salvation, since these are rare exceptions to the general rule, just as sporadic religious revivals, highly valued by pietists, are also quite exceptional.[105] Likewise, he is convinced that introspective meditation leading to inactive morbidity is a denial of the Reformation, which discovered that 'justification in actual fact becomes a matter of experience through the discharge of moral tasks, while *these are to be discharged in the labours of one's vocation*'. He rejects the category of 'good works' as inadequate to the task of conveying the full message of the Reformation, and substitutes for it one of his own key categories, that of *Lebensführung* (lifestyle). 'The real question,' he writes, 'is whether our life-work (*Lebenswerk*) is manifested in the individual visible actions which we have before us.'[106] As we shall discover in Chapter VI below, the justified Christian life worthy of the name always issues – not merely in particular, discrete, disparate ethical actions or works – but in a concrete, well-rounded, coherent, worldly role or vocation, in which the justified individual is aware of a new relationship both to God and *to the world*.

This last phrase brings us close to the heart of his teaching on this matter: *Christianity, in common with all religion, must be defined in terms of a twofold relation, to God and the world*. Ritschl himself puts the matter unambiguously:

It is impossible that justification by faith can express the relation of men to God and Christ without at the same time including a peculiar attitude of the believer to the world.[107]

He appeals to St Paul in Romans 5: 1–5 and 8: 32–9 in support of the view that justified Christians are, through God's power, enabled to triumph over all *worldly* sufferings, forces and dispensations. This must be understood always in *an active*, never in a *passive* way. It follows:

Faith verifies the forgiveness of God experimentally when it *reaches out to grasp* God's care and providence over the whole of life, and relies thereon even under those sufferings involved in the believer's situation in the world.

The transition from 'inauthentic' to 'authentic' existence (if we may so describe it), or from mistrust of God (which leads to dependence on the world) to trust in God, can be demonstrated or proved 'only if with that trust there is combined *a new lordship over the world* due to confidence in God's all-embracing care'. His heavy stress on the *active functioning* of the Christian comes out in this statement:

The real change in the sinner is proved by the fact that he is impelled, by the forgiveness of his sins, by the Divine decision that for Christ's sake he is *deo acceptus*, to *exercise* that reverent trust in God which is the characteristic activity of the new life.

He is insisting that the most notable characteristic of Reformation Christianity (as found in the early works of Luther and Melancthon) was just this practical emphasis, this insistence that genuinely Christian existence *must* find expression in a new, concrete, historico-temporal lifestyle (*Lebensführung*), in which faith in God is exhibited by a new, triumphant and transcendent attitude to the world, its temptations, trials, tribulations and hardships. His answer to the question of assurance of salvation consists of his teaching that *one indispensable index* of our closeness to and communion with the justifying God is the measure of our *independence from the world*, understood as the source of impediments and obstacles.

Not that he has not been much misinterpreted on this matter.

It is astounding that the perceptive Dr Garvie should have been critical of him at this point, rebuking him for failing to notice that for the Christian his relation to God is what most concerns him, *and his relation to the world matters very little!*[108] It is to J. K. Mozley's credit that he saw exactly what was at issue here.[109] Ritschl, he points out, would have agreed with Garvie that, in the Pauline sense, the Christian's relation to the world matters very little – for 'lordship over the world' means complete security of faith, complete victory over any conceivable event or circumstance in the world which might challenge Christian confidence in God.

NOTES TO CHAPTER IV

1 For what follows, I am indebted to Ian G. Barbour, *Issues in Science and Religion*, London 1966, ch. 4, 'Biology and Theology in the Nineteenth Century', pp. 80 f.; and in John Dillenberger, *Protestant Thought and Natural Science*, London 1961, ch. VIII, 'The Darwinian Aspect', pp. 219 f.

2 London 1865; second revised edition, 1869, and reprinted fifteen times until 1910.

3 See K. Barth, 'Evangelical Theology in the Nineteenth Century', in *The Humanity of God*, London 1961, p. 19.

4 op. cit., p. 18.

5 *Dogmatics* II, 'The Christian Doctrine of Creation and Redemption', London 1952, pp. 96 and 117.

6 *J. & R.* III, p. 327.

7 *Instruction*, para. 28.

8 *J. & R.* III, p. 335.

9 ibid., p. 378.

10 ibid.

11 Brunner, op. cit., pp. 119 and 138.

12 *J. & R.* III, p. 328.

13 ibid., p. 329.

14 ibid., p. 331.

15 ibid., p. 332.

16 ibid., p. 334.

17 ibid., p. 335; *Instruction*, para. 30.

18 See *supra*, pp. 90 f.

19 *J. & R.* III, p. 350.

20 ibid., p. 344.

21 ibid., p. 345; for the obscurity of these verses and the difficulty of getting consistency out of Paul's statements, see R. Bultmann, *Theology of the New Testament* I, London 1952, pp. 250 f.

22 *Three Essays*, pp. 203–4.

23 Gilbert Ryle, *The Concept of Mind*, London 1949.
24 For links between empiricist and existentialist views of the self, see John Macquarrie's paper 'Selfhood and Temporality', *Studies in Christian Existentialism*, pp. 59–76.
25 Garvie, op. cit., pp. 19 and 20.
26 Mueller, op. cit., p. 73.
27 Wilhelm Ebel, op. cit., p. 105; the other pioneer was Johann Philipp Gabler (1753–1826), *Privatdozent* in Theology at Göttingen from 1781 until 1783, before his translation to Altdorf. For a brief historical discussion of the application of 'myth' to biblical exegesis, see Ian Henderson, *Rudolf Bultmann*, London 1965, pp. 6–11.
28 See articles 'Doctrine of Man' and 'Guilt' in *A Dictionary of Christian Theology*, London 1969, pp. 204 and 150.
29 *Concise Theological Dictionary*, Freiburg 1965, p. 330.
30 *Theology of the New Testament* I, p. 253.
31 *The Ritschlian Theology and the Evangelical Faith*, pp. 138–9.
32 *The Ritschlian Theology*, pp. 307 f.
33 *Ritschlianism*, p. 206.
34 *An Introduction to the Theology of Albrecht Ritschl*, p. 74.
35 *Types*, p. 159.
36 *J. & R.* III, p. 353.
37 ibid., p. 355.
38 *Instruction*, para. 32.
39 *J. & R.* III, p. 356.
40 For a brief treatment of this charge in English-speaking circles, see Lecky, op. cit., p. 279.
41 *J. & R.* III, p. 357.
42 ibid., p. 360.
43 *Jesus – God and Man*, p. 45; the reason, Pannenberg rightly comments, is that, as we shall see in Chapter VI, theologians of Ritschl's generation concentrated on the expression of Christianity in a concrete, distinctive 'Ideal of Life' (*Lebensideal*).
44 For twentieth-century views, see William Hordern, article 'Death' in *A Dictionary of Christian Theology*; Karl Rahner, SJ, *On the Theology of Death*, Freiburg 1961, ch. II; Martin Heidegger, *Being and Time*, London 1962, pp. 279–311.
45 *Kerygma and Myth* I, London 1953, p. 196.
46 *Instruction*, para. 33.
47 ibid.
48 *J. & R.* III, pp. 356–7.
49 ibid., p. 364.
50 It is one of the great merits of Philip Hefner's *Faith and the Vitalities of History* that it has shown conclusively that Ritschl understood himself as a theologian of the Christian tradition *in its entirety*. See also his Introduction to *Three Essays*, pp. 18–19.
51 'Nature and Grace' in *Theological Investigations* IV, London 1966, pp. 165–88; also 'Concerning the Relationship between Nature and Grace', *Theological Investigations* I, pp. 299–317.
52 op. cit., IV, p. 168.
53 vol. i, p. 299.
54 ibid., p. 300.

55 *The Epistle to the Romans*, London 1933, pp. 53–4.
56 David Lotz, *Ritschl and Luther*, p. 185, n. 6, although appreciative of Ritschl's contribution to the understanding of Luther, nevertheless deplores the fact that he 'failed to grasp Luther's profound doctrine of God in which the divine love and wrath were held together in dialectical tension'. Lotz asks, significantly, if this 'does not mark Ritschl's own reversion to theological speculation?'
57 *The Mediator*, p. 58.
58 John E. Smith, *Religion and Empiricism*, Milwaukee 1967, pp. 52 f.
59 *J. & R.* III, p. 328.
60 ibid., p. 365.
61 ibid., p. 57.
62 ibid.
63 ibid., p. 58.
64 ibid.
65 We are reminded again of Brunner's aphorism that 'the Ritschlian Theology is a Rationalistic system clad in scriptural garments'.
66 Orr, op. cit., pp. 266–7.
67 *Church Dogmatics* IV: 1, Edinburgh 1956, p. 382, italics mine; this volume contains an informative, if hostile, account of the views on sin entertained by nineteenth-century Protestant theologians, pp. 374–87.
68 Mueller, op. cit., p. 172.
69 *J. & R.* III, pp. 367 f.; cf. Schleiermacher, *The Christian Faith*, pp. 161–70.
70 See Orr, op. cit., p. 244, n. 3.
71 *J. & R.* III, p. 383.
72 ibid., p. 380.
73 Garvie, op. cit., p. 315.
74 Mozley, op. cit., p. 221.
75 *Types*, p. 176.
76 Mueller, op. cit., p. 172.
77 *J. & R.* III, p. 379.
78 *Protestant Theology in the Nineteenth Century*, p. 659.
79 *Church Dogmatics* IV: 1, p. 382; for the discussion that follows, see pp. 382–3.
80 *J. & R.* III, p. 34.
81 ibid., p. 29.
82 *Ritschl and Luther*, p. 33.
83 Mueller, op. cit., pp. 80–1.
84 *Instruction*, para. 36.
85 A. Durwood Foster, *A Handbook of Christian Theologians*, ed. by Dean G. Peerman and Martin E. Marty, Cleveland 1965, p. 64; quoted by James C. Livingston, *Modern Christian Thought*, New York 1971, p. 255.
86 See his argument against Weiss of Tübingen in *Theology and Metaphysics, Three Essays*, p. 198.
87 See *J. & R.* III, pp. 42 f.
88 For what follows, see ibid., pp. 60 f.
89 ibid., pp. 69 f.
90 ibid., pp. 74 f.
91 ibid., pp. 80 f.

92 *The Mediator*, p. 59.
93 *J. & R.* III, pp. 94 f.
94 ibid., pp. 100 f.
95 op. cit., p. 159.
96 *J. & R.* III, p. 113.
97 ibid., p. 139.
98 ibid., pp. 145–6.
99 ibid., pp. 133 f.
100 Garvie, op. cit., p. 330.
101 Orr, op. cit., pp. 169–70.
102 op. cit., p. 172.
103 *Systematic Theology* I, p. 156.
104 For what follows, see *J. & R.* III, pp. 140 f.
105 ibid., p. 157.
106 ibid., p. 164.
107 ibid., p. 168; for the discussion that follows, see pp. 168 f.
108 Garvie, op. cit., p. 332.
109 Mozley, op. cit., p. 229.

CHAPTER V

The Work and Person of Christ

Ritschl would have approved of the word-order of this title, rather than the traditional 'The Person and Work of Christ', and would have claimed that it expressed the view of Luther and Melancthon that in christology we must *begin from below and move upwards*. Or, in modern terminology, 'there can be no christology prior to soteriology'. Right at the outset, it is worth noting that his christological method has received much corroboration in the history of recent christological research. Recently, Wolfhart Pannenberg has sketched the development of christologies that begin 'from below'; in the nineteenth century, he remarks, Ritschl was the first to build his christology on the question about the divinity of the historical man Jesus; his example has been followed not only by the Ritschlians down to Herrmann but by Walter Elert, Paul Althaus, Emil Brunner, Carl Heinz Ratschow, Friedrich Gogarten, Gerhard Ebeling, Rudolf Bultmann, and Pannenberg himself.[1] And David Mueller has remarked that Ritschl's thesis that the deity of Jesus is to be understood in the light of his saving work has been widely accepted.[2] Before exploring his christological doctrine proper, four comments might appropriately be made. First, we note carefully Pannenberg's statement that Ritschl really and truly tried *to build a christology*. (Pannenberg's entering into serious critical dialogue with the writings of Ritschl has been an important factor within the Ritschl Renaissance in Germany.) This means that those who have been taught to regard him as a 'typical' nineteenth-century 'liberal Protestant' who tried to locate Jesus' unique significance in his sublime, timeless, religious and ethical teaching, or in his example as a pattern for moral imitation, would be severely shocked if they open-mindedly examined his christological texts.[3] Second, there are significant *negative* implications, it need hardly be said, of his 'from below upwards' methodology. The principal one is his repudiation of the Chalcedonian christology of the two natures in one person, as a classic piece of disinterested, scientific, metaphysical (i.e. *non-religious*, in his sense) speculation, which can only obscure the *religious-valuational* quest for the divinity of Christ manifest in his concrete, public, historical existence witnessed to in the New Testament. While this is historically important for the implementation of the dehellenization programme by members of his school, it is greatly significant for the case of Ritschl himself. It is impossible to examine his christological work without feeling that his unreasonable fear of the intrusion of the 'metaphysical' into theology was a damagingly restrictive influence upon his system, and that it obscured from him the importance, even the indispensability, of the ontological for theology. How this fear operated we shall see at several precise points below. Third, worth noticing at the outset is the Denney-Garvie controversy of the 1890s, sparked off by Dr Denney's allegation that Ritschl intended to deprive the doctrine of Christ's divinity of all objective characteristics.[4] There are four items in the allegation – that he either denies or sits dangerously lightly to the Virgin Birth, the Pauline statements on Christ's pre-existence, the Johannine doctrine of the Incarnation of the Logos, and the notion of Christ's heavenly exaltation. In response, Garvie attacked Denney's sense of 'objectivity': if these elements establish 'objectivity', there is a serious lack of objective attestation in Scripture to the Virgin Birth, a doctrine which, together with the Pauline pre-existence doctrine and the Johannine Logos doctrine, did not form part of the most primitive versions of the apostolic faith. Correctly, he insisted that these four themes were, from the point of view of nineteenth-century apologetics, those which were stressed the least as evidences for Christ's divinity, a fact which led him to place a high value upon Ritschl's christological contribution. Further, he showed that as a matter of fact Ritschl did *not* explicitly deny the Virgin Birth doctrine (nor the notion of Christ's sinlessness supposedly implied by it), that he did try to come to grips with the pre-existence passages in Paul, that he dealt seriously if critically with the Johannine Logos christology within the context of the history of dogma, and that Denney simply ignores the effort expended by Ritschl to make sense of the doctrine of Christ's exaltation and contemporary activity. The controversy is important for two reasons. The first is that the sweeping allegations made by Denney (in lectures delivered in Chicago only five years after Ritschl's death) are a classic example of the early hasty misinterpretations of his work, which contributed to the detriment of his name and the reputation of his christology. The second concerns an important element of truth in Denney's charges. Despite his overt hostility to Ritschl, he puts his finger firmly on two elements of extraordinary difficulty and controversy in his christological construction – the themes of the pre-existence and the exaltation of Christ, themes which must be examined in depth below. Fourth, and finally, it is worth noting that Pannenberg links up Ritschl's fundamental christological approach with that of more recent *existentialist* theologians, notably Friedrich Gogarten and Rudolf Bultmann. Indeed, it is hard to read Bultmann on christology without acknowledging the extent to which Ritschl fruitfully anticipated significant twentieth-century approaches to christological problems.[5]

Even those with only a passing acquaintance with Ritschl's christology know that one of his key terms is the word *Beruf*, translated usually as *vocation* and sometimes as *calling*. Precise analysis of the term will be undertaken in the next chapter, but a brief word must be said about it here. He deals with the humanity of Christ almost exclusively in terms of Jesus' acceptance and fulfilment of his divine *vocation*, and has evoked considerable criticism for so doing. Even Wolfhart Pannenberg, by no means an *a priori* hostile critic of his, having described Ritschl's emphasis on Jesus' perfect adherence to his divinely-given vocation to found the Kingdom of God, remarks: 'one perceives in the background of these ideas the impressive ideal of life (*Lebensideal*) of the bourgeoisie of the late nineteenth century.'[6] Elsewhere, although Pannenberg concedes that his own christological term 'Jesus' office' is 'closely related to Ritschl's concept of the "ethical vocation" of Jesus', he insists that 'we still prefer to speak of "office" rather than "vocation"'.[7] Several comments on this seem apt. First, as argued in the next chapter, it has not been proved by modern scholarship that Ritschl's attachment to the term 'vocational obedience' was *exclusively* determined by his uncritical acceptance of the social ideals of the late nineteenth-century Prussian bourgeoisie.[8] The influence of such ideals cannot be ruled out of court, but it does not tell the full story. It is one of the merits of the Ritschl Renaissance to have attempted a recovery of his original intention and meaning over against the damning interpretation of the Barthian school. Second, as just indicated, the Barthian historians have never doubted that Ritschl's concern with vocation and *Lebensideal* stemmed exclusively from his preoccupation with nineteenth-century German anthropocentrism which stemmed from the affirmation of the *human* by Kant.[9] This affirmation will be examined and rejected in the next chapter, but a word might appropriately be said here about the much-maligned effect of the *Aufklärung* upon Ritschl, with special reference to one concept of crucial christological importance – that of *substance*. The development of a highly sophisticated empiricism during the *Aufklärung* produced not merely many philosophical casualties but also fatalities. Well known to philosophical theologians are casualties like *causality* and the philosophical concept of *God*. Less well known and pondered is the conceptual casualty of *substance* or *substantial nature*. This was rendered a casualty by the development of modern British empiricism from Locke to Hume, a development communicated to Kant by his reading of Hume in translation. It is hard, and hazardous, to summarize in a word the *Aufklärung*'s conclusions on the epistemological status of substance, but perhaps its verdict may be expressed by 'unknowable', whether we prefer the definition of Locke as 'something . . . we know not what, which underlies the accidents or properties of things', or some other formula.[10] Thereafter, in the case of substance as of other themes, in post-Enlightenment German theology the attempt is made to take seriously and come to grips with the tough-minded philosophical demands of the Enlightenment.[11] It is impossible to read Ritschl's christological texts and his *Theologie u. Metaphysik* without perceiving that he saw the implications of all this with crystal clarity. He opposes, for example, that Christian metaphysical tradition 'in which everything is deduced from above by means of general concepts', and within which 'knowledge of Christ is subordinated to a general concept of his pre-existent divinity . . . and then the futile attempt is made to authenticate the divinity of Christ in his historical existence'.[12] For him, there is 'behind' or 'underneath' reality no generally nor publicly knowable substratum identifiable as divine as distinct from human) *substance*, manifest in the historical Jesus, knowable *prior to or independently of* such a historical manifestation, and he would have claimed for his position support not merely from Enlightenment epistemology but also from the christological teachings of Luther and Melancthon. Hence, he rejects the suggestion 'that the reality of the human spirit is not to be grasped in its volition which, naturally, includes knowing and the dominant feeling of self-consciousness but, rather, that one must conceive of man's real and authentic being "behind", "under" or "over" these functions in an objective form that is also proper to nature'.[13] In other words, genuine cognition of human being is not dependent upon *independent* and *prior* knowledge of a general, human, substantial substratum which is subsequently manifested in concrete and particular human existents. Our cognition of other persons is dependent upon our experience of the following (the terms have been abstracted from the text of *Theologie u. Metaphysik*) – of disposition (in which purposes and designs are formed and which calls forth and directs activity), of will, of individuality, of calling, of activity of work, of relationships, of states of self-consciousness, 'of a, broad perspective that emerges from the observation of the individual and the particular',[14] of function, of feeling, of appearances, of motivation, and the like. That is, for Ritschl the distinctively *human* is volitional, intentional, active, dynamic, relational, individual, purposive and self-conscious throughout. Now if knowledge of Christ is really and truly to proceed *from below upwards*, this epistemological scheme must apply not only to discrete human existents but also *to the humanity of the man Jesus*. The term which he selected to describe the distinctive being of the human is *vocational*, indicating a concrete, decided, specific, directed, purposive, individual existence to which one is *called*, and in which one selects and attains one's life's end. Ritschl and his nineteenth-century contemporaries did not understand Christ's deity in terms of *substance*, nor of *consubstantiality* with God, simply because such terms had become in post-Enlightenment Germany unintelligible, not to say meaningless. No one knew better than Ritschl that the Chalcedonian definition of Christ's divinity, far from expressing in a positive, kerygmatic or persuasive way the fullness of what was involved in the Incarnation, was a negative, theoretical prohibition of approaches which from the outset could only do less than justice to the being of God in Christ. His own attempt to understand Christ's person in the light of his vocational work was intended to be a *positive-kerygmatic* exposition of the core of biblical Christianity for his contemporaries. That Christ's life was a rounded and completed whole is brought out by Ritschl when he writes:

> In so far as Christ, by His duly ordered speech and conduct realises His personal self-end, it follows from the special content of the latter that in this form He also realised the end of others, i.e. has ministered to the salvation of mankind as a whole.[15]

Jesus' full humanity is affirmed, not by urging that there was in him a fully human *nature* (coexisting with a divine *nature*), but by teaching that he is man as man ought to be, as he would be were it not for the presence and activity of sin. His humanity is *archetypal* rather than *substantial*. Man's attainment of eternal life, through the personal self-end of vocation and lordship in the Kingdom of God, has all been *prefigured* in the work and person of Christ. There is here expressed again the closest possible connection of the objective with the subjective, the objectively given with subjective appropriation, the gift with the task, the christological with the existential.

One problem which the Lutheran Ritschl could not avoid was the allegedly honourable place given by Luther to the doctrine of the two natures, criticized by Ritschl as a disinterested and objective 'scientific' theory of Christ's person.[16] His solution is to point out that Luther's approach is very different from the Catholic one, in that he attaches to every apparently objective statement about Christ the *pro me* formula. Luther's objective-subjective approach is summarized in the *Shorter Catechism* in the following sentence:

> I believe that Jesus Christ, very God, eternally begotten of the Father, also very man born of the Virgin Mary, is *my* Lord, by whom *I*, a lost and condemned man, have been redeemed, gotten and won.[17]

For Luther as for himself, he insists, God's redemptive activity only becomes apparent through the activities of the man Jesus. The congruence of Luther's christological position with his own can therefore be summarized:

> It really is in Christ's human achievement that His Godhead becomes for His people manifest, conspicuous, intelligible, winning our faith, not in the form of assent to an unintelligible dogma, but of personal trust for our salvation.[18]

Accordingly, he, like other nineteenth-century German Lutheran theologians, is anxious to dispose of one ancient but fallacious *either/or*: *either* Christ is a union of two natures (Chalcedon) *or* he is a mere man (christological heresy).[19] Rightly or wrongly he, followed by members of his school, drew the sharpest possible distinction between what they described as scientific, disinterested, speculative and objective christological approaches and their own, focused on trust in Christ, on the *beneficia Christi*, on Christ's value for salvation, on his historical, ethical life's work. In Ritschl's own celebrated summary:

> We must *first* be able to prove the Godhead that is revealed *before* we take account of the Godhead that is eternal.[20]

He *intended* then, in *beginning from below*, to produce a modern, kerygmatic and apologetic affirmation of the divinity of Christ. In our examination of his christology, this must be maintained, even in face of the not unreasonable challenge, which will be assessed sympathetically below, that he, in his *achievement*, because of a stubborn and insensitive aversion to anything smacking of the metaphysical in christology, failed to perceive that the Chalcedonian definition of Christ's person, far from being 'disinterested' or 'speculative' in character, may have been an experientially-based defensive formula intended to exclude from the Church the notion that redemption can be wrought by *anyone less than God*.

His basic christological affirmation is that the contemplation in depth of the historical Jesus reveals the divine ground of Jesus' being:

> That Christ overcomes his fate, reveals to us in Him the Creator of the world; that he endures indignities which He has

not deserved, of course for the good of men, reveals in Him the Creator, the wise Ruler, the gracious Protector of the world; finally, that He does not withhold his benefits from the unthankful and unbelieving, that He prays for those who crucify Him, proves His connection with the perfect God, who bestows His favours both on the evil and the good. The God-man has all the Divine attributes.[21]

In treating the *Munus Triplex* doctrine, it is well known that he followed Luther, Melancthon and Calvin in exalting the office of King over those of Priest and Prophet, and of giving the former two much greater dogmatic significance than the latter, and that almost entirely because of his overall *interpretation of Christianity as a world-conquering phenomenon*. But the objective statement that 'Christ is King' must have its subjective correlate in our lives:

> What Christ is *for* us, must verify itself in the transferring of His worth *to* us. The recognition of Jesus as the Christ has *for us* no meaning unless through Him we know ourselves raised to kingship or dominion over the world, and to priesthood or undisturbed communion with God.[22]

If Jesus is, as maintained by the Church, truly human, his humanity, his ethical freedom and subjectivity, must be safe-guarded. And while Jesus, as prophet, was indeed similar to the Old Testament prophets in giving his free assent to God's will and purpose in fulfilling the role of God's instrument of self-revelation, it must be made clear that he exercised a closeness of will to God's never possessed by any mere prophet of old.[23] But so close does he conform his will to that of the Father without displaying contradiction or strain, that we cannot rest content with the view that 'Christ was an *instrument* of Divine revelation'. The fourth evangelist, in expressing for the Church the impression on him of Christ's life as a whole, affirms the judgement 'that the Divine revelation is a human person'. The Johannine prologue bids us recognize in Jesus' personality as form the substance of grace and truth, the distinctive marks of Godhead.[24] But Christ must not be seen as some automaton viewed, as it were, from the divine standpoint. While judging that the characteristic activities of Jesus are the activities of God, we must qualify this by insisting upon his ethical independence under the category of human freedom.[25] For how otherwise could we follow the procedure of Luther ('from below upwards'), which is to adopt a truly *historical* starting-point which presupposes that a human ego can only be grasped in the light of its inherent unity as judged by ethical laws? His standpoint, he insists, is identical with that of Reformed theology, which holds 'that Christ rendered obedience to the law, in the place of the elect, as Head of the Church'.[26] In common with his post-*Aufklärung* contemporaries, he regards an authentic human life as essentially a *teleological* one; in it a personal self-end (*Selbstzweck*) is pursued and attained. Christ's personal self-end is his obedience to the divine vocation, understood as all of his 'doings and sufferings', it being understood that his sufferings, having been accepted freely and vocationally, constitute a kind of doing.[27]

We perceive another swing from the objective to the subjective in Ritschl's attempt to bring the *Beruf* of Christ and that of Christians into the closest possible correlation.[28] The concept of 'vocation' may be defined thus:

> Inasmuch as each man's vocation forms for him the special sphere within which he regularly fulfils the universal moral law, it follows that each man, in the ethical exercise of his own vocation, at once attains his own ethical self-end and renders his rightful contribution to the ethical end of society as a whole.[29]

As we shall see in Chapter VI, there can for Ritschl be no fulfilment of the universal except through the particular and the concrete. Ordinary mortals may practise several vocations simultaneously, but not Christ: 'Christ combined no other vocation with that to which He was conscious of being called.'[30] While our ordinary civil and private vocations may fulfil this or that aspect of the final good, the vocation of Christ is directed to 'the ethical as a whole', to God's and man's final good, the Kingdom of God. This brings us close to the heart of his teaching on the work of Christ. Jesus' *vocation to found the Kingdom of God* is for Ritschl *the* key to every phase and detail of his life and ministry – the abandonment of fixed dwelling and family, his neutral attitude to most secular interests, his comparative indifference to the *minutiae* of the Pharisaic law, the temptations – every incident must be interpreted in the light of his unshakable resolve to fulfil his *Beruf*, including his sufferings, particularly those he brought upon himself by appearing in Jerusalem. Although we cannot think that this did not involve a continual conflict between vocation and self-preservation, 'He steadfastly endured, without once proving untrue to his vocation, or failing to assert it'.[31] The material content of the *vocatio Christi*, then, 'was the establishment of the universal ethical fellowship of mankind, as that aim in the world which rises above all conditions included in the notion of the world'.[32] And in support of the notion of a complete identity of will, purpose and function between Christ and God, recognized and confessed by Christ himself, he quotes the Johannine saying of Christ (4: 34), 'My meat is to do the will of Him that sent Me, and to finish His work'. This leads to the following christological pattern: we begin by contemplating the life-work of Christ empirically, historically and ethically; in so doing, we encounter Christ's judgement of his own life-course, to the effect that his personal self-end coincides exactly with God's, in whose knowledge and love he has existed 'from the beginning'; this content is the foundation of the Kingdom of God, the area of spiritual lordship over the world. This leads to the following extremely important christological statement:

> Since, as the Founder of the Kingdom of God in the world, in other words, as the Bearer of God's ethical lordship over men, He occupies a unique position towards all who have received a like aim from Him, therefore He is that Being in the world in whose self-end God makes effective and manifest after an original manner His own eternal self-end, whose whole activity, therefore, in discharge of His vocation, forms the material of that complete revelation of God which is present in Him, in Whom, in short, the Word of God is a human person.[33]

In conclusion, the ethical contemplation and estimate of Christ 'run out into a religious judgement', or, as Ritschl expresses it, 'the former finds its necessary complement in the latter'.

Even though it is hard to withhold admiration for the systematic, tightly argued way in which Ritschl tried to move from the historical to the religious, one cannot help, even at this early stage, sensing gaps in his account. How is it, we want to ask, that Jesus possessed and enjoyed this transcendentally privileged knowledge of God, and unique experience of God's all-encompassing love and support? Can we rest content with a flatly empirical and historical account of the origin of Jesus? Does not christological reflection impel us towards the use of a quite different language which indicates, however unsatisfactorily, that purely human, social, natural and historical categories are inadequate for answering christological questions? To such matters we shall return below in our critical assessment of his christology. But here it is worth noting that he was vividly aware of the existence and significance of such questions and that, far from allowing even tentative answers to them, he firmly refused to recognize the religious or theological validity and viability of the questions themselves. In this connection, there are two classic statements from him:

> The origin of the Person of Christ – how His Person attained the form in which it presents itself to our ethical and religious apprehension – is not a subject for theological enquiry, *because the problem transcends all enquiry.*

> The correlation of Christ with God His Father is not a scientific explanation. And as a theologian one ought to know *that the fruitless clutching after such explanations* only serves to obscure the recognition of Christ as the perfect revelation of God.[34]

This can be nothing other than an expression of ontological scepticism and agnosticism. That philosophical agnosticism is operative christologically can be easily proved from a cursory examination of the christological discussions in the *Theologie u. Metaphysik*, where, for example, he affirms that the christological datum must be confined to Christ's historical *Lebenswerk*. He remarks:

> One must avoid all attempts to *go behind this datum*, that is, to determine in detail how it has come into being and empirically how it has come to be what it is. These attempts are superfluous because they are ineffectual; and it is dangerous to give oneself to these attempts since they are superfluous.[35]

Analysis of his ontological scepticism in the christological context will be undertaken below. For the present, it is not unimportant to note that along the scale 'from below upwards' Ritschl rather abruptly imposes an upper epistemological limit beyond which he forbids others or himself to travel.

What are the characteristics of Christ's deity, manifested in his historical existence, which prove Ritschl's christological results? As the expression of the love of God, Christ is the bearer of that 'grace and truth' spoken of by John in connection with the divine Word. Since the love of Christ is unshaken by all worldly influences and hindrances, 'it follows that the "grace and truth" in Christ's whole activity is the specific and complete revelation of God'.[36] If the divine Word has appeared in a human life, there must be an *analogical similarity* between God and man, located in certain common attributes. These, he insists, are concepts like spirit, will and love:

> Since the being of God is spirit, will and above all love, it can therefore become effective in a human life, for human nature as such is laid on the lines of spirit, will and love.[37]

The *spiritual* unity between Jesus and God enables him to make an important point about the nature of the Kingdom. This spiritual unity enabled Jesus to go beyond the limited messianic expectations of the Old Testament, the Jewish expectations of a messianic Kingdom guaranteeing to the Jews political and material superiority, in other words, a merely mundane order. Jesus' spiritual unity with God enabled him, in his life and vocation, *to transcend the merely mundane*:

> Jesus rose above this standpoint, and introduced a new religion, by setting free the lordship of the supramundane God from national and political limitations, as well as from the expectation of material well-being, and by advancing its significance for mankind to a spiritual and ethical union, which at once corresponds to the spirituality of God, and denotes the supramundane end of spiritual creatures.[38]

This affirmation has social and even political implications. Christ did not exercise a material or natural lordship, through his miraculous powers, in dramatic interference with or alteration of the natural system of the world. His lordship is spiritual in nature, and to explain it Ritschl turns to its *subjective correlate* in the triumphant claim of Paul in Romans 8: 38, 39; 'I am persuaded, that neither death, nor life, nor angels, nor principalities, nor powers, nor things present, nor things to come, nor height, nor depth, nor any other creature, shall be able to separate us from the love of God, which is in Christ Jesus our Lord.' His comment on this is:

> The independence of the religious consciousness over against the world, and the supremacy over the world which is to be realized within the sphere of this religion, are identical.[39]

Christ's lordship, that is, consists essentially of a victory over all worldly impediments (natural or social in origin) to the attainment of man's supranatural end. It is interesting that Ritschl, in locating the worldly sources of such impediments, should single out for special attention the *family* and the *natural state*. In his ministry Jesus raised himself above, transcended, these, and attained to radical inward freedom from them, in order to achieve that universal human nature required by his vocation. And this teaching, that Christ and Christianity essentially transcend national differences and boundaries, is *typical of Ritschl's works in their entirety*. This is a matter of singular importance for our assessment of the history of Ritschl interpretation, with special reference to the *demise* of 'Ritschlianism' in the years after 1919. For we have to reckon here with the widely-accepted image of a group of German 'Ritschlian' academics, with strongly nationalistic leanings, devoted not only to the articulation of a distinctively Germanic Christianity, but also to active support for Wilhelm II's imperialistic efforts towards a *Mitteleuropa*, Germanic in language, culture and religion. Among the twelve theologians of the 93 German academics who signed the manifesto of 4 October 1914[40] in support of the Kaiser's war aims do we not find the names of three 'Ritschlian' signatories: A. v. Harnack, W. Herrmann and R. Seeberg? Is there not therefore some connection between 'Ritschlianism' in religion and early twentieth-century German nationalism, a connection not unconnected with the *demise* which overtook discredited Ritschlianism in the decade or so after World War I? In answer to these questions, it is advanced here that to suggest such a connection is *almost to indulge in a defamatory libel against Ritschl.* On the one side it is true that there *are* elements in his thought capable of a certain circuitous, long-term, nationalistic interpretation – for example, his undoubted stress on the continuity between human moral values and God; there is also his emphasis, to be examined in depth in the next chapter, on the Christian's obedience to civil law as the outcome of his vocation. But there are sound grounds for drawing the sharpest possible distinction between the impossibly vague term 'Ritschlianism' and *the teachings of Ritschl himself,* in order to rescue his name from undeserved calumny! For an unbiased examination of his writings convinces us that his central standpoint was that of a *Kantian international universalism* which was, in point of fact, anathema to his excessively nationalistic Göttingen colleague, Paul de Lagarde.[41] Robert Lougee, in his study of Lagarde, places us in his debt by plotting the relationships between that pan-Germanic nationalism which Lagarde symbolized and certain members of 'Ritschl's school'. Ritschl, as noted already, Lagarde could not abide; neither could he Kant, whom he peremptorily dismissed as 'lacking in substance'.[42] His main convert from Ritschl's school was in fact Adolf von Harnack, who, in the year after Ritschl's death, wrote to Lagarde commiserating with him on his long struggle with Ritschl, which had ended only with the latter's death in 1889.[43] Thereafter, the main converts to Lagarde's specific brand of Germanic Christianity within systematic theology were Ernst Troeltsch[44] and Friedrich Gogarten.[45] But the commitment of all three to ethnic Christianity was in spite, not because, of their links with Ritschl's systematic theology.

Even a cursory look at Ritschl's texts shows this to be so. He rejects the State as a model for comprehending the Kingdom of God; the duty of universal love to man transcends the limits of nationality and that natural hereditary friendliness which men direct to their compatriots.[46] Indeed, Christ's teaching on the Kingdom means that 'He transcends the view of the national State, and *takes up an attitude essentially opposed to it*'. Civil and moral law are quite distinct; there are actions pleasing to civil law which are contrary to moral law, and vice versa.[47] Within the

Kingdom, social action prompted by Christian love 'is no longer limited by considerations of family, class or *nationality*'.[48] And when the Christian selects and pursues moral ends, 'self-determination exclusively by regard for family feeling, the interest of a class, or *patriotism, may be bad* if it sets itself in opposition to common ends, that are higher still'.[49] He makes his meaning lucidly clear when, in the *Unterricht*, he gives a formal definition of the Kingdom:

> The Kingdom of God which thus presents the spiritual and ethical task of mankind as it is gathered in the Christian community is *supernatural*, insofar as in it the ethical forms of society are surpassed (such as marriage, family, vocation, private and public justice, or *the state*), which are conditioned by the natural endowment of man (differences in sex, birth, class, *nationality*) and also offer occasions for self-seeking.[50]

Indeed, Christ's supremacy over the world implies his supremacy over the nations;[51] moreover, 'the Christian religion is *not* a national religion', for its God is a 'supramundane spiritual God, free and independent with regard to the world'.[52] It is no wonder that these teachings, published as early as 1874, and expressing a *Christian-Kantian ethical universalism*, horrified Lagarde and his pan-Germanic Christian sympathizers. And they would have been regarded as sedition by many 'German Christians' during the period of the Third Reich. But for the modern interpreter of Ritschl the theologian their significance is this: they bring unavoidably to his attention yet another distorting stereotype, the adjective *Ritschlian*, whose use in this instance perpetrates a slander. No wonder that his inter-war sympathizers spoke of the *vilification* of his name.

We return to his christological interpretation of Jesus' earthly career and ministry. Ritschl places unprecedented stress on Christ's *patience under affliction* as proof that *he has overcome the world*. The *Victoria Christi* has little to do with the exercise of political and legal influence by the *ecclesia militans* in the secular order. Indeed, despite the emphasis on the community within the justification process, he has a singularly low estimate of the working of the ecclesiastical establishment as revealed by Church history, for, in his view, the methods it employs 'come under strong suspicion of falsifying the intention of Christ'.[53] The Kingdom must be distinguished from the empirical Church; it is 'only a really strong faith in the invisible that, amid the miry abominations and miserable trivialities of Church history, can trace the advancing power of Christ over this world at all'. Rather, Christ's and the Christian's supremacy over the world are *spiritual* and 'cannot become palpable or evident in any corresponding degree'. He was fond of quoting John 16: 13 – 'I have said this to you, that in me you may have peace. In the world you have tribulation; but be of good cheer, I have overcome the world' (RSV).[54] Christ's encounter with worldly affliction *symbolizes* all human existence. Christ never allows it to divert him from fulfilling his vocation, but accepts it as the dispensation of God. He accepts all such with *long-suffering patience*, reveals thereby that the world has no power over him, and so *overcomes the world*. In this encounter, Christ's immediate opponents represent the entire world of men in so far as it is in revolt against God. There is an immediate, and predictable, swing towards the *subjective*, for he proceeds to *existentialize* the victory of Christ. Any individual suffering of ours has existential Christian significance for us 'only in so far as it represents at the same time the opposition of the system of nature as a whole'. When we are struck or slandered, 'the whole mechanical and organic connection of the individual with the world is involved'. In such a situation, Christ's call to us is to *share in his patience* so that we may lift ourselves above our misfortunes and the world which administers them. Therefore, the defining characteristic of the deity of Christ may be expressed thus:

> According to the hints given in the New Testament, the grace and truth (faithfulness) manifested in the discharge of His vocation, and the loftiness of His self-determination as compared with the particular and natural impulses which spring from the world, are the features in the earthly life of Christ which are summed up in the attribute of His Godhead.[55]

Needless to say, he takes a strongly *teleological* view of the work of Christ, which is aimed at producing the Kingdom of those who share in Christ's lordship, conduct themselves according to universal brotherly love, and in their *Lebensführung* exhibit their dependence on Christ through their independence from and lordship over the world. The attribute of Christ's divinity is one that was first applied by, and can only be comprehended by, members of this community.[56] But the work of Christ is intended to produce very much wider consequences – in the religious effects of the divine community on the world, the effect of Christian love on the public conscience, the penetration of public institutions by this, the emancipation of men from captivity to nature, and the progressive utilization of nature for human ends.[57]

It is widely known that, in his treatment of the *priestly* office of Christ, Ritschl would have nothing to do with the notion that Christ *propitiated* or *satisfied* the righteous wrath of God. While it is tempting and easy to ascribe this merely to 'Enlightenment rationalism', other motives at work ought not to be overlooked. For example, in *Justification and Reconciliation* I he analysed in depth an atonement-theory such as Abelard's, and, through a point-by-point comparison, judged it in most ways religiously superior and intellectually more cogent than a satisfaction-theory such as Anselm's.[58] Then again, there is his axiom that what Christ does for others he must first have achieved for himself.[59] Also, as a systematic theologian, he had to interpret Christ's priestly office in accordance with his over-all system. The dominating idea here is his notion of God's righteousness, which, as already noted, is strongly anti-juridical:

> God's righteousness is His self-consistent and undeviating action on behalf of the salvation of the members of His community; in essence it is identical with His grace.[60]

His anti-extrinsicism operates strongly in his criticism of older, objective theories of atonement – they set forth a transaction which necessarily fails to 'effect for any man that personal attitude to God which pervades the consciousness of Jesus', or, in other words, lack the necessary subjective correlate in believers' lives. The positive meaning of the death of Christ is that it is the glorious outcome of his life-long dedication to his vocation – he willingly accepts as the dispensation of God his death at the hands of violent adversaries 'as the highest proof of faithfulness to his vocation'.[61] In denying the penal nature of the sufferings and death of Christ he observes 'that for the believer all evils are disciplinary in character, and serve to purify and try the soul'.[62] Moreover, the wooden notion of purely retributive punishment may obscure for the believer certain vital religious truths; for example, the notion of the 'inward crucifixion' of believers in which the old man, through painful self-denial and the attainment of virtue, is transformed into the new, when 'dying to the flesh is recompensed by living to the spirit'. (The similarity here to the teaching of Bultmann is so obvious as not to require comment.) And occasionally, because, we may guess, of his sensitivity to the criticism of ethical rationalists, he tries hard to preserve the integrity of *personal responsibility* (which, he observes, 'we must regard as one of the strongest motives of the Christian religion'):[63]

> Just as the assumed conception of original sin obscures the particular guilt of individual men, so the penal satisfaction offered by Christ is made the equivalent of the eternal damnation due to all mankind, and is by no means fitted to counteract the sense of guilt of each separate individual.

Here we perceive clearly again the swing from the objective to the subjective, the attempt to find the subjective correlate of the death of Christ in the life not only of the community but also of the individual believer. In treating the relationship of forgiveness to the death of Christ, while conceding to Socinians that there appear to be cases in the New Testament where Christ's spoken word alone conveys divine forgiveness, independently of and prior to his death, he nevertheless insists that there is no such thing as a valid 'natural religion', rooted in the superficial assumption that God is a mild, indulgent will naturally inclined to forgive as a matter of course.[64] Such is not the product of positive Christianity, but of the *Aufklärung*'s 'philosophical naturalism and moral individualism'. The Christian community attaches the general validity of forgiveness to Christ's death, as suggested to it by Christ's eucharistic discourse. But his death and life hang together, all of a price, so that his death is the fulfilment of his vocation – his perfect willingness to die for his vocation supplies the only sense in which his death is to be regarded as a 'sacrifice'.[65]

In his treatment of the application of the work of Christ, his sensitivity to nineteenth-century ethical criticisms of Christianity is strongly operative. In facing the problem of the continuation of sin in the Christian community, he concedes that evidently the work of Christ does not alter sinfulness in believers in anything like the same way or to the same extent that it does man's relation to God as regards the status of sin.[66] But, he adds hastily, removal of guilt implies subjectively a redirection of the will to God, so that forgiveness 'becomes the basis of the *positive possibility* of a life no longer sinful as a whole'. He therefore introduces the distinction between *general* and *special*: a *general* inclination of the will towards God is inadequate, if there is a lack of *special* moral decisions which are not the *automatic* outcome of faith in *general*. *General* conversion does not necessarily come to grips with *special* vices – each individual must grapple with each of these concretely in the *willed* formation of the appropriate opposite resolutions.[67] No violence is done to the term in describing Ritschl's approach as *quasi-existentialist*: in character formation, ethical universals are inadequate, for there is not simply a *common* but a *special* depravity in each man. The *genus* of evil does not disclose what is involved in the *species* of evil without empirical considerations. His overall conclusion is that special, concrete, unique, individually personal manifestations of evil are by no means *at the outset* immediately, automatically or actually eliminated by the universal or general atonement, wrought by the life-work and death of Christ. As an empirical historian, he feels himself unable to dissent much from those nineteenth-century ethical rationalists who pointed at the *gap*, in the history of Christianity, between high ethical demands and claims on the one hand and, on the other, actual ethical achievements. If, he concedes, the theological notion of 'the communication of the sinless perfection of Christ' were to be understood as the imparting of 'active moral righteousness', then, 'it would have to be objected that such communication was *altogether contrary to experience*, and inconsistent with the necessary condition of moral righteousness'.[68] However much, he warns the Church, is attributed to the divine initiative in the salvific process, 'we still experience the formation of our moral character, and the separation of it from the impulses of sin which are peculiar to us, *as an act of our own will*'. With Schleiermacher before him (who lived much closer, admittedly, to the very source of that fierce blast of ethical criticism of religion so characteristic of the Enlightenment),[69] he expresses doubt as to the fitness of the Christian community for discharging its divine commission. Ritschl's problem is that he has given such a high place to the community in his entire system that he must now reconcile this with widespread nineteenth-century scepticism and cynicism about the actual ethical fruits of organized Christianity:

> The Christian community, however, in the course of its history, has carried with it so much actual sin, that the question must be raised *whether it has not altogether forfeited* the relation of Divine sonship bestowed upon it through Christ's work of reconciliation, and accordingly become unfit in any sense to mediate for the individual the religious benefits which proceeded from Christ.[70]

These words might have been lifted straight from the pages of Schleiermacher's *Glaubenslehre*, as might his twofold solution to the problem. First, he pleads with believers to penetrate through the conventional activities of the Church (proclamation, teaching, etc.), to make contact with the living figure of Christ, available in many kinds of moral and aesthetic forms. Second, with Schleiermacher, he expresses the charitable hope that there is in every believer an inclination towards the final end of Christianity, one which we see erupting from time to time in various *reformations* of Christianity aiming at the establishment of Christian humility and moral purity.[71] His sensitivity to the contemporary ethical dismissal of Christianity has an important bearing on his treatment of technical atonement theories. He criticizes, for instance, the so-called patristic theory of the atonement[72] – that in his life, death and resurrection, Christ once-for-all (*EPHAPAX*) broke the power of and triumphed over the Devil.[73] So afraid is he of the interpretation that Christ's work eliminated once-for-all sin in the Christian community that he writes:

> How . . . can it be asserted in the face of Church history that Christ by His victory over the devil altogether withdrew His believing followers from the latter's power?[74]

The patristic account must therefore be *demythologized* or *existentialized*: it points to 'a spiritual conflict with the untruthfulness and wickedness of others', and its language symbolizes 'the loathsome calumny which constitutes the most characteristic mark of Satan in the adversaries of Christ'.[75] All talk of the conflict of Christ with Satan must be transposed into *existential* discourse referring in the first instance to Christ's vocational fidelity, long-suffering patience and the like, in the face of 'demoniacal' or 'satanic' impediments and sufferings, accepted by Jesus as occasioned by divine dispensation.[76] But, we remind ourselves, such fidelity and patience *must* find their subjective correlates in the lives of Christians. It must be conceded that probably the most used phrase to describe Ritschl's interpretation of the work of Christ is 'Moral Influence'. There are important senses in which this is true, for he stood self-consciously in the tradition of Abelard. But if the phrase is taken in the sense of an *Imitatio Christi* then it must be heavily qualified. The classic medieval *imitatio* practised by St Francis was possible only at the cost of distortion, for Francis 'laid hold upon the outwardly perceptible circumstances of Christ's life of poverty, and exaggerated them'.[77] Nevertheless, Francis was right to the extent that he saw clearly that Christ's work involved a twofold relation, to God and to the world, expressed in Franciscan world-renunciation. In 'modern' theology, Schleiermacher's 'feeling of absolute dependence' implied a relation of neutrality towards the world, which in his excessively psychological disciples has been interpreted as teaching that man's relation to God can dispense with any reference to the world whatever. Our *Imitatio Christi*, if it be attempted, must fulfil the condition that we cannot, like Jesus, 'be religiously dependent upon the supramundane God without at the same time experiencing our religious freedom relatively to the world', or, conversely, 'spiritual dominion over our situation in the world is the obverse side of our Divine sonship'.[78] His overall conclusion is that in seeking for our *subjective correlate* of Christ's work and person, the *Imitatio Christi* concept is severely limited, and that mainly for three reasons. First, the utter *uniqueness* of Christ's vocation to found the Kingdom of God is strictly speaking *inimitable*, yielding 'nothing but fidelity in the moral vocations which is assigned to *everyone* as *the special field of his contribution to the Kingdom of God*'.[79] To use modern but not wildly anachronistic terminology, Ritschl, like modern existentialists, held that each human existent is historically unique, and that his

Lebenswerk is providentially allotted to him in his place and situation, and that a slavish *Imitatio Christi* might obscure this fundamental truth. As we shall see in the next chapter, the culturally-conditioned overtones ascribed critically to his term *Beruf* ought not to conceal this from us. Second, it ought not to be overlooked that as mere humans we are involved in the sin of society, a sin which we are obliged to overcome in ourselves, but one in which Christ never participated. Third, and finally, excessive stress on the *imitatio* might obscure the fact that the starting-point and central doctrine of Christianity is justification by faith:

> We are justified in the assurance of Divine sonship, in spite of our sense of guilt, because we belong to the community which is founded by Christ as the community of reconciliation with God.[80]

We are now perhaps in a position to attempt a critical estimate of Ritschl's christological work. Now it is a plain fact that most criticisms of this, ancient and modern, cluster around one critical affirmation: that in the last analysis, *Ritschl's christological reconstruction is determined overwhelmingly by the philosophical interests of the Enlightenment, rather than by the mainstreams of Christian tradition, an affirmation conclusively demonstrable by what he says of the pre-existence and exalted status of Christ.* To put this more simply, Ritschl's picture of Christ is that of a most unusual man, an unsurpassable and archetypally significant one indeed, but, at the end of the day, *no more than a man* who did not significantly transcend those spatio-temporal limitations that belong to human existence as such. This criticism of his christology is inestimably important and demands careful consideration. In so far as twentieth-century neo-orthodoxy has been overwhelmingly christocentric and incarnational, it is no surprise to find that this criticism was the principal one which its adherents directed against Ritschl from the beginning of the inter-war period onwards. It is illuminating to glance at three versions of this criticism as formulated by Brunner, the 'early' Bultmann, and by Barth. A famous, and influential, version of it is to be found in Brunner's 1927 text, *Der Mittler* (ET 1934), which, as its title implies, is principally a plea for Christianity understood as an incarnational-mediatorial phenomenon, determined in root and branch by the work and person of Christ. Judged by this criterion, Brunner found the mainstream nineteenth-century German christological workers painfully defective. We have already noted Brunner's point that Ritschl, despite his severe criticism of Schleiermacher's fundamental conception of *Religion, failed to perceive* that his own work also presupposed a general conception of religion of which Christianity was the highest manifestation.[81] Therefore, his Christianity does not really 'contain any reference to an unique historical event', and is, as noted earlier, but 'a Rationalistic system clad in scriptural garments'.[82] His rationalism is most evident in Ritschl's stress on the concept *Idea* – the 'idea' of God as love, or the 'idea' of the Kingdom of God. All such 'ideas' are eternal, existing eternally in the mind of God, but introduced into history in a definite historical event, in the life of Jesus. Brunner seizes upon Ritschl's statement 'that historically this Idea first received shape and form through Christ'.[83] Brunner argues for the relativism implied in Ritschl's view by insisting that although every rational idea, at some time or another, is expressed for the first time in history, it is by no means certain that Jesus was the first to express the 'Christian Idea' in history, and that he did in fact express it is dependent on the results of (sceptical) historical research. In the Jesus of history, in Ritschl's view, we have the effective representation of the Idea in history for the first time, which generated a great historical movement – Schleiermacher's 'collective life', the 'Kingdom of God', the 'great historical phenomenon' of the Christian community. Ritschl shrank from predicating divinity of the community; but Brunner points out that his colleague and disciple Hermann Schultz had no such compunction: 'The Deity of Christ appears throughout only in connection with the deity of His community. It does not apply to Him as an isolated personality, but as the starting-point of the new humanity.'[84] Schultz's interpretation was possible, Brunner insists, only because of the master's clear teaching that the community is the sole depository of Jesus' redeeming activity, and that the Christian can only receive forgiveness within it. In Brunner's submission, the content of Ritschl's 'historical element' is 'nothing more than the rational and ethical idea of purpose, only here it is clothed in definite historical garb'.[85] Its garb (historical and personal forms) ought not to conceal from us that it is the bare, rational, ethical idea essentially unconnected with history; it is 'only effective in connection with history', in the senses that history is always the source of ideas for the individual, and that the idea becomes 'effective' only in the life of the experiencing individual. Ritschl's view is that historically 'this idea first received shape through Christ'.[86] Brunner severely criticizes the adequacy of this christological statement. First, it is dubious historically and fails to do justice to the *uniqueness* of Christ. Second, in discussing Christ's alleged 'uniqueness', Ritschl reduces this to Christ's alleged *temporal priority* over others in generating a historical movement of momentous consequence:

> For if a *second* could be produced who, really, was on a level with Christ in grace and truth . . . etc., he would yet stand in historical dependence upon Christ and therefore, logically, would be *subordinate* to Him.[87]

A later 'Christ', even though equal in religious and ethical value to Jesus of Nazareth, would be 'subordinate' to him only in virtue of his *later* historical appearance. Brunner therefore characterized Ritschl's view as involving something 'gradual' or 'quantitative', and argues that Ritschl's 'unique revelation' in Christianity is analogous to 'the historical dependence of every mathematician of the present day upon Euclid',[88] a christological viewpoint incompatible with classical Christianity. The historical result of Ritschl's christological reconstruction was this:

> That the historical Person of Jesus, from the point of view of ethical and religious humanity, is to a certain extent regarded as the foundation and the centre of the religious life (faith we cannot call it); inevitably this procedure provoked opposition both from the idealist and mystical side and from the Christian side.[89]

This explains why he chose, from all of the titles available in christological tradition, the title of 'royal Prophet' rather than, say, 'priestly Mediator'; on the grounds of his christological presuppositions there was just no room for 'talk of Atonement through a Mediator'. Brunner therefore concludes that in Ritschl's system Christ's relation to the Christian religion is 'causal and factual' rather than 'positive and necessary'.[90] This is a powerful and disconcerting critique, which is reinforced by the two that follow.

The critique of the 'early' Bultmann is contained in his important 1924 paper, 'Liberal Theology and the Latest Theological Movement'.[91] This demands the most careful interpretation, because even though it was composed only several years after Barth's revolt, it must be read in the light of the subsequent disillusionment of Bultmann with the direction that later dialectical theology was to take. Even in 1924 Bultmann was careful to observe (as the editor of the English version underlines) that 'the attack against the so-called liberal theology is not to be understood as a repudiation of its own past, but as a discussion with that past'.[92] Moreover, we must observe that in the skilful hands of Bultmann the term 'liberal theology' is not a pejorative stereotype, which it was later to become in neo-orthodox circles. Bultmann begins with the charge against 'liberal theology' that it failed to perceive that the subject of theology is *God*, and that 'it has dealt not with God but with man'.[93] The word of that God dealt with by theology is the word of the Cross, which, according to the New Testament, is a 'scandal' or 'stumbling-block' to men, and the charge against liberal theology is 'that it has sought to remove this stumbling-block or to minimise it'. Having paid generous tribute to liberal theology's contribution to free historical enquiry, Bultmann is sharply critical of the confidence it placed in the *religious value* of historical research:

> Historical research can never lead to any result which could serve as a basis for faith, for all its results have only relative validity.

> How uncertain is all knowledge of 'the historical Jesus'![94]

It is impossible not to read this as an indictment of Ritschl's rather naïve supposition that a sound religious contemplation of the historical Jesus leads us to see his deity *configured in* his actions and words! Rather, such research should bring us to the realization that the world grasped after by faith is *absolutely unattainable* by means of scientific research.[95] So-called liberal theology failed lamentably to grasp that all historical phenomena are but relative entities which exist only within an immense inter-related complex, which means that the historical Jesus is a phenomenon among other phenomena, not an 'absolute entity'. In its discourse about Jesus, liberal theology speaks of him in terms 'which do not ascribe an absolute value to him'. Bultmann quotes the view of Ernst Troeltsch (from his *Die Bedeutung der Geschichtlichkeit Jesu für den Glauben*, 1911), that while faith in God (in the liberal sense) *leads to* the acknowledgement of Jesus, there cannot be a *necessary binding* of the Christian faith *to* the person of Jesus. Bultmann points out that nineteenth-century liberal theologians were in fact motivated by a certain philosophy of history to which he applies three adjectives – 'vague', 'idealistic' and 'psychological'.[96] Certain spiritual powers or 'forces' (like truth, goodness and beauty) are conceived as immanent in history, and operate thus:

> Through the action of such forces, it appears, mankind develops from a state of nature to civilization and culture. History is a struggle in which the powers of the true, the good and the beautiful are victorious, and it is a struggle in which man participates, in that he is supported by these powers and thus emerges from his bondage to nature to become a free personality with all its riches.

(It is impossible here to believe that Bultmann does not have Ritschl's 'general conception' of religion in mind.) Within this framework God's 'revelation' takes place through those individuals who are 'bearers' of these powers. (We are reminded at this point of Schleiermacher's 'Religious Heroes'.) Such a conceptual framework, described by Bultmann as a 'pantheism of history', is applied to Christianity:

> At the very least, the liberal view of history is assumed to serve Christian faith by demonstrating that such powers as are manifested in Christianity, the powers of love, of self-sacrifice and the like, are the forces actually operative in history.

Only within this conceptual framework may Jesus be said to be the 'bearer' of God's revelation. If so, in what resides the *uniqueness* of Jesus? Bultmann's answer coincides with that to be given by Brunner three years later: the attempt was made by the liberals to prove that *some ideas or impulses entered history for the first time in Christianity*.[97] Of this proof Bultmann remarks:

> Apart from the doubtful nature of the proof in specific instances, *newness* is not a category which is determinative for the divine. That category is eternity. Newness can be claimed equally for this or that imbecility. Newness is never a guarantee of the *value* of what claims to be new.

Hence, liberal theology became trapped in its own conception of history; no matter how it tried, it could not find a way out of that *unending inter-relatedness* in which no single epoch nor single person can claim *absolute* significance. But worse, in Bultmann's judgement, was involved: for such a conception of history, rooted in the 'enrichment' of the human, leads to obsession with and, indeed, *deification* of men, evoking the polemic of Barth and Gogarten aimed directly at this attempt to deify man, in which direct knowledge of God is claimed as an actuality. To particularize, Bultmann selects the Ritschlian christological programme.[98] There, the ability is claimed to prove that history as known through scientific research has a positive value for faith. Bultmann comes within a hairsbreadth of saying that the Ritschlian christological value-judgement theory *fashions the historical Christ in the image of value-seeking man*, so that faith *originates* in man's sense of value:

> Man has not only a yearning for God; he has also a vision of God as the supreme power and the moral will.

But the unfulfilled *a priori* sense of value is of itself frustratingly useless; it requires an external object, a 'bearer' of this value correlating with the innate sense of value – out of this process there develops inevitably the conviction of the existence of an external reality corresponding exactly to that value.[99] It is against this background that the religious individual (in the 'liberal' sense) 'encounters Jesus'; he becomes aware of the reality and meaning of the powers working within himself because he sees them effective in history, in historical personalities. Bultmann analyses a passage from a paper by the Göttingen Ritschlian theologian, Max Reischle,[100] 'Do we Know the Depths of

God?',[101] which demonstrates that in this 'encounter' between believer and the historical Jesus (in which the believer's incompletion, inward division, double-mindedness, vaccilation, sensuality, and predisposition towards secondary motivations are overcome) the final *criterion of validity* is man's own moral consciousness.[102] Since there is no certainty that such personality-enrichment could not result from 'encounter' with other historical personalities of outstanding spiritual or ethical stature, the uniqueness of Jesus is abandoned. 'The contemplation of the historical' is of strictly limited theological value; in the historical the believer contemplates only a *belief* in forgiveness, *acts* of love and forgiveness, *consciousness* of love and forgiveness; but in such contemplation he can know directly neither God's love nor forgiveness. In his sin he stands directly *coram deo*; he can be forgiven only by God's Word directed *towards him*. Liberal theology forgot about an encounter between man and God in which man is miraculously and simultaneously judged and reconstituted by God's Word.[103] To be contrasted with this is Ritschl's grotesque stress on the necessarily smooth *gradualness* of Christian experience, the power of the divine being conceived as immanent within the idealistic influences operative within Christian home, Church and school:

> Out of the practice of humility and trust in parents and teachers the right sense of guilt in relation to Christ and trust in Him *will arise in the maturer period of life*. Accordingly, that which proves itself the comprehensive motive of the Christian life in the later period can neither be directly understood nor experienced in childhood . . . *Faith in Christ can be expected only in maturer life*.[104]

Bultmann considers that liberal-idealistic christological thinking models itself upon Greek idealism. Anyone acquainted with Epictetus, for example, cannot help noticing that this evaluation of Jesus accords with this view of the world and man, for he is accepted as the human *prototype* or *pattern*, like Heracles or Diogenes among the Cynics and Stoics, as one who bore the burden of his labours and 'made something' out of his life.[105] (It is worth recalling here a comment of Pannenberg on the christologies of Schleiermacher and Ritschl: 'The neo-Protestant

theologians are concerned only with making possible the human-
ness of life on earth.')[106] It is as protests against such views that
we must interpret not only the Barth-Gogarten attack, but also
a work like Otto's *Das Heilige*, whose stress on the 'Wholly
Other' God and on 'creature-feeling' is an anti-liberal protest. In
Bultmann's judgement, there are parallels between Otto's *tre-
mendum* and dialectical theology's *judgement*, as between Otto's
fascinans and the latter's *grace*. And it is only against such a
background of ideas that we can understand certain fierce thrusts
within Barth's early polemical theology. For instance, there is his
insistence that *faith is not a state of consciousness*. (Bultmann
hastens to add that 'no doubt, along with faith there is also a
state of consciousness – at least there can be'.[107] Is this a pre-
monition of things to come in the 'later' Bultmann?) As anti-
liberal protest also we must understand Barth's polemic against
all 'religion of experience', piety, sense of sin, and inspiration.

We turn finally to the extremely harsh critique of Karl Barth,
who, we hardly need reminding, interpreted Ritschl's thought as
almost entirely determined by 'the theoretical and practical
philosophy of the Enlightenment in its perfected form',[108] a
judgement heavily criticized by recent writers on Ritschl. Barth
tries to discredit Ritschl's system by comparing it with that of a
typical, if feeble, post-*Aufklärung* systematic theologian, Julius
A. L. Wegscheider (1771–1849), Professor in Halle from 1810
until his death.[109] Wegscheider was *the* nineteenth-century theological rationalist *par excellence*, whose basic relief was in the
lex aeterna planted originally by God in the human heart. For
him, therefore, theology has no hope of making credible to the
homo cultior of the present any doctrine that contradicts the
pronouncements of the *sana ratio*; genuine religion knows only
of one revelation, that which is given to reason. Christ is one of
the 'founders of religion' (we are reminded of Schleiermacher's
'Religious Heroes' and Bultmann's phrase 'pantheism of history'),
all of whom are worthy of reverence and commitment only in so
far as they proclaim pure and unalterable faith in reason loftily
and impressively. The dogmatic value of the Bible depends on the
degree to which it corresponds to reason. The content of Weg-

scheider's doctrine of sin is as follows:[110] Man can *raise himself* to that dignity and divine likeness for which he is destined only with great *effort* and continual application. Despite his knowledge of what is right and his inclination towards the divine likeness, he unfortunately possesses a tragic inclination to listen more to the demands of the senses (Kant's propensity to evil), than to the voice of reason and the known standards of good, a defect traceable to defects in education and culture, social environment, and the like. But we must not, dare not, speak of any 'incapacity of man for the good'! Man *can* and must fight to overcome his *informitas quaedam moralis* and rise *gradually* to true virtue. Within the salvific process man should be informed (not of his sinfulness!) but of his *moral capacity* and be entreated to use it. Of all the wise men who by God's providence have won fame as teachers and lawgivers, Christ merits the highest reverence, because he was a man of the highest religious gifts, who taught and exemplified a purified Mosaic religion.[111] Confronted with Christ, we have to acknowledge as divine the principle at work in his life, and the guidance we perceive that he was given, and to reverence and imitate him as *prototype* of the man filled with genuine religion and true virtue.

For the rationalistic Wegscheider, there is an exact and strict proportion between virtue and divine reward, vice and divine punishment, a proportion that must not be abrogated in talk of *divine forgiveness*! While the sinner may be 'forgiven' previous sins, such 'forgiveness' cannot in this world and in the world to come abolish a certain *quantification* of blessedness proportionate to achieved moral worth. There must be no talk of a 'vicarious satisfaction' wrought by Christ, for his death, apart from its function as a symbol of the inauguration of the new religion, has a strongly moral relevance. In the eucharist, Christ obliges his followers to follow his example in all that is true and noble, *even unto death*.[112] Hence his death is to be preached as a summons to rapid moral improvement. *Grace* derives its meaning from the fact that God is the sole author of the Christian religion with its salvific effects, so that it can be reduced to a general concept of a particular providence or a particular divine concursus. *Justification* indicates that man is pleasing to God and worthy of blessedness, which is the ground of his seriously turning himself to God, not simply through individual meritorious works, but *sola fide*. Now the whole point of Wegscheider for Barth is this: he was no less, in Barth's words, than 'a theological Philistine'; and in Ritschl, who followed closely in Wegscheider's footsteps, we have a *lowering* of the pathetic theological level we find in the latter; Ritschl is worse, theologically speaking, or more banal, than Wegscheider; what he was mistakenly pleased to call 'the Gospel of the forgiveness of sins' was only a disguised form of Wegscheider's natural *lex aeterna*, allegedly inscribed on human hearts; Ritschl, no less, if not more than Wegscheider, was a child of the eighteenth-century Enlightenment.[113] It is hard to believe that any modern, careful student of Ritschl's texts could fail to be astounded by Barth's allegation that there is no more in them than is to be found in the lamentable Wegscheider, or to reach the conclusion that Barth's judgement on the matter is not to be rejected out of hand. Nevertheless, this neo-orthodox critique of Ritschl's christology – by Brunner, Bultmann and by Barth – is exceedingly important, and must be carefully evaluated. But before doing so at the end of this chapter, some attention must be paid to two crucial aspects of Ritschl's christological reflections – the notions of Christ's pre-existence and contemporary activity.

To turn first to the issue of pre-existence, it must be conceded right away that there are philosophical influences at work. We have already noted Ritschl's insistence that the datum of christology is Christ's historical *Lebenswerk* and that the theologian is forbidden to penetrate *behind* or *beyond* it. Accordingly, he is forced into the position of accusing St Paul of expounding *non-religious* knowledge. When Paul, in 1 Corinthians 8: 6, refers to the *Lord* Jesus Christ as him through which all things have been created or come to be, he comes within a hairsbreadth of accusing Paul of expounding theoretic (i.e. metaphysical) knowledge of Christ which 'creates problems rather than solves them'.[114] Christ's 'lordship' refers to Christ's status as the *exalted* (i.e. post-existent) Lord who *has* (in his life's work) achieved *Herrschaft* over the world and is exalted as *Herr* of the Kingdom of God. Ritschl's classic statement on this is:

The thought of Christ's Godhead is *never other* than the expression of that unique acknowledgment and appreciation which the Christian community yields to its Founder.

In other words, it is never more than a communal value-judgement. All theoretic talk of Christ's 'pre-existence' is *GNOSIS*, and invalidates the clear and definite meaning of Christ as *KURIOS*, i.e., as post-existent head of the community. In both exegesis and theology 'the temporal priority of Christ before the world cannot be the thought at issue; that would be a barren thought'.[115] No wonder, then, that most of his interpreters have concluded that there is just no room whatever for a pre-existent Christ in his thought. But this is not quite true, for at one point he did try to give positive significance to the notion:

> The special significance Christ has for us is by no means exhausted in our appreciation of Him as a revelation conditioned by time. On the contrary, it is implied that, as Founder and Lord of the Kingdom of God, Christ is as much the object of God's eternal knowledge and will as is the moral unification of mankind, which is made possible through Him, and whose prototype He is; or rather, that not only in time but in the eternity of the Divine knowledge and will, Christ precedes the community.[116]

Have we here, at last, left mere communal value-judging behind and entered the area of the ontological? On close analysis we find that we have not. Christ (as Lord of the Kingdom, etc.) is *as much* eternally present to God *as* the eventual moral unification of the race! This unification is present to God eternally and Christ also, as *prototype*, but only as that, precedes the historical community. It is impossible to read Ritschl on the subject without concluding that what he intends by talk of pre-existence is something purely *notional, ideational,* or *conceptual*; namely, that Christ exists, *like everything else in history and nature,* from all eternity in the mind of God as an aim, idea, intention, or notion, in close conjunction with, although prior to the correlative concept of the final unification of human creatures in his Kingdom. What appears to be at issue here is the pre-existence in the mind of God of the *Christ-Idea*. (We recall Brunner's complaint that in Ritschl's christology we are moving in the realm of *timeless ideas* – of

'love', or 'purpose', or 'Kingdom of God' – which allegedly
achieved their *first* expression in the person and life of Jesus.)
This is confirmed by our discovery in Ritschl of a singularly
strong tendency to 'de-humanize', 'de-personalize', or 'de-parti-
cularize' Christ. 'Whatever belonged to the natural and generic
limitations of Christ,' he writes, 'cannot be taken as the object of
the eternal will of God.'[117] When we contemplate Christ's vocational life, 'we fail to notice in Him those traces of individual
temperament which are wont to count for something even in the
most perfect of men'. Now in Chapter III we noted the objections
of many to the tendency in Ritschl's thought *to identify God with
his Kingdom*.[118] In similar manner, we here encounter a tendency
to allow Christ, or the Christ-Idea, to *merge into* the Idea of the
Kingdom, the progressive realization of the spiritual destiny of
the race of which he is both Founder and Prototype. It is true
that certain interpreters have protested, and pointed to one
passage at least where he *appears* to go beyond a merely notional
pre-existence:

> The eternal Godhead of the Son . . . is perfectly intelligible only
> as object of the Divine mind and will, that is, *only for God
> Himself*. But if at the same time we discount, *in the case of God*,
> the interval between purpose and accomplishment, then we get
> the formula that Christ exists for God eternally as that which
> He appears to us under the limitations of time. But *only for
> God*, since for us, as pre-existent, Christ is hidden.[119]

J. K. Mozley rejected Dr Garvie's argument that Ritschl is here
reaching out after a *real* rather than a *notional* pre-existence.[120]
Mozley suggested, interestingly, that at this point Ritschl seems
to be reverting to a quasi-Hegelian mode of thought in asserting
that God (for whom there is no distinction between willing and
accomplishing) views everything *sub specie aeternitaris*, so that
the strictly temporal term 'pre-existence' can have no meaning
for God. But Hegelian thought-modes are incompatible with
theological empiricism. Mozley contemplates Ritschl's assertion
that Christ 'pre-exists for God as that which He appears to us
under the limitations of time', and wonders if the statement *does*
transcend any mere assertion that the historic *Lebenswerk Christi*
was the object of God's foreknowledge. It is impossible to suppose

that it does. The *mode* of Christ's pre-existence is not significantly other than the *mode* of the pre-existence of God's *Selbstzweck*, the Kingdom. His statement that Christ's pre-existence is intelligible 'only for God Himself' tells us precisely nothing, theologically speaking, and it is hard to quarrel with those who want to argue that it is only a translation into theological jargon of his epistemological agnosticism with regard to the trans- or superhistorical. While it is true that nowhere does Ritschl explicitly deny a real pre-existence, his failure to say anything positive about it, his near silence on the matter, has, predictably, invited the radical criticism that, for him, in the last analysis, *Christ was a mere man*, the product, like the rest of us, of composite biological, social, and environmental forces, although, undeniably, possessed of unsurpassed and unsurpassable insight into God's mind as willing above all else the unity of men in a 'supramundane' Kingdom inaugurated by himself in his work and words. This was the kind of judgement reached by scholars like Dr Orr while Barth and Brunner were still children.[121] Orr anticipates the criticisms of Brunner thirty years later in arguing that we ought not to be so overawed by 'the exalted language of the Ritschlians about Christ' that we overlook that 'however great the worth of the Revelation of Jesus, it does not imply an origin outside of, or transcending, the inherent laws of the human spirit'.

H. R. Mackintosh offers a telling criticism of Ritschl in insisting that historic Christian talk of Christ's pre-existence, deplored and abandoned by him as 'theoretic' or 'metaphysical', is expressive of an 'ineffable religious fact' or a 'vast evangelical truth', to the effect that in the coming of Christ into human life *God gave us nothing less or lower than himself*; despite the acknowledged shortcomings of human language, credal talk of Christ pre-existing means nothing less than this, and it is theologically insensitive to imagine that the scope and dimensions of the Gospel can remain unaffected when it is omitted.[122] Accordingly, Pannenberg, in a survey of patristic christological theories, points to a reappearance of *patristic adoptionism* since the Enlightenment in Kant, Schleiermacher, Ritschl and Adolf von Harnack.[123] And commenting upon such 'adoptionist' and 'Ebionite' themes, the late Donald M. Baillie makes the point that the reason for the

Church's dissatisfaction with them has been that the formula 'first man, then God' is incompatible with the formula 'first God, then man', which obscures the necessary notion of the *prevenience* of the divine; the theologian has to wrestle with *Incarnation*, not Adoption. It is finally necessary to enquire about the reason for Ritschl's failure in this matter of Christ's pre-existence. In all fairness to him, it is worth remembering that most of his critics (including the unfriendly Brunner) draw a sharp distinction between his admirable *intentions* on the one hand and his rather disappointing *achievements* on the other. It is hard to read his christological efforts and deny that he was trying as hard as his limitations would allow to express the uniqueness and transcendence of Christ for his generation. But in what did these limitations consist? It is beyond question that in this area as in others he was severely inhibited by a crippling dread of the term *metaphysical* which was rooted in a prior failure properly to ponder the meaning of the term. There is no lack of evidence that this dread quite blinded him to the significance for Christianity of the *transcendental* or the *ontological*, and this quite inconsistently. The incisive Dr Orr indicated just how much in fact Ritschl was willing to concede to speculative reason – for example, a transcendent basis for the universe in a living, personal God, or a supramundane Kingdom for the realization of the *Summum Bonum*. If so, why not a little more – a *transcendental* background for the person of Christ, including a pre-temporal as well as a post-temporal state of existence for him? Why should the latter be 'metaphysical' and the former two not?[124] Elsewhere, Orr suggests, with conviction, that Ritschl confuses the 'metaphysical' with the 'transcendental', and fails to recognize that theology simply cannot get on without *transcendental postulates*, of which the most significant is *God* himself; why then forbid us to 'postulate' what may be necessary to explain the person of Christ? If the term 'metaphysical' is thought offensive or misleading, then, Orr suggests, we might name it 'a thought of faith'.[125] The not unsympathetic Garvie argues that certain truths spurned by Ritschl as 'metaphysical' are, strictly speaking, grounded in the 'historical'. He is right in arguing that by force of habit the term 'metaphysical' has come to be used in a loose sense for any notion or idea *not immediately given in ordinary experience*. Strictly from this point of view, the pre-existence and heavenly exaltation of Christ may loosely be called 'metaphysical ideas'. But they are nothing of the kind in the sense of being speculative influences from the data of his life, drawn to 'explain' his personality and influence. For the former may be an *assurance* given by Christ in his own self-testimony, and the latter a *promise* he gave to his disciples for their encouragement; in that case both come within 'historical reality', or may be derived from 'historical contemplation'.[126] This criticism is directed, ironically, against one who claimed above all else that his theology was based squarely upon the bedrock of the *historical* Jesus.

We turn now to glance at Ritschl's treatment of Christ's *exalted status*, and contemporary activity in Church and world. The basic criticism directed against his christology is that for him Christ does not significantly transcend the limits of spatio-temporal existence and is therefore *merely human*. We have just seen that this can scarcely be rebutted on the grounds of significant teaching on pre-existence, so that everything depends, for the defender of Ritschl, on the merit of what he says about Christ's contemporary being and activity. Let us proceed by formulating, in advance, the over-all impression which his writings impart to the impartial reader, which may then be tested by his own words on the subject: this is that, despite rather misleading and ambiguous language, he tends strongly to the view that *Christ's 'contemporary work' is the posthumous prolongation of his life's work in the community founded by him, and that the relation of the contemporary believer to Christ is constituted by memory, nurtured by the 'Christ-image' whose custodian is the Church.* Now so far, once more, as his *intention* is concerned, there can be little question that he sincerely attempted to expound a satisfactory doctrine of *Christus Praesens*; Christian faith 'has its necessary points of attachment always in the present':

> Our faith in Christ is not faith in Him as One Who was, but faith in Him as One Who continues to work, namely under the conditions corresponding to His present mode of existence.[127]

But there can be no question of talk of Christ's contemporary work which *cannot be linked to the historical Jesus*:

This idea of the Godhead of the exalted Christ depends for its convincing power entirely upon whether the marks of this Godhead can be found in His historical existence upon the earth.[128]

When he insists that 'every form of influence exerted by Christ must find its criterion in the historical figure presented by his life', he is right to ensure, as he claims, that Christ's present lordship is not transformed into 'a meaningless formula or the occasion for all kinds of extravagance'.[129] But it soon becomes apparent that this insistence is in reality an inflexibly exclusive *obsession* with his own image of the 'historical' Jesus, which gravely impeded nineteenth-century christological progress. A most disconcerting example is the doctrine of the *cosmic Christ*. He takes issue with Schleiermacher's contemporary Philipp Marheineke for introducing into christological reflection the creative *motif* that Christ represents humanity in that in him is present what is common to man universally.[130] Ritschl concedes that the biblical background of this is the Pauline theme of the First and Second Adam, but insists that it leads towards a *cosmic* or (he adds, tediously) *metaphysical* doctrine of Christ's person. Marheineke argued that Christ is 'the central individual of the human race' and that the point of his appearance is the cosmic point 'which is the centre of receptivity for God', a point where is manifested embryonically world-unity and world-consummation. Marheineke was attempting here a christological interpretation of history, a rudimentary *heilsgeschichtliche* understanding of human history – in the striking words of Lichtenberger, Christ as 'the luminous centre of history'.[131] Despite Ritschl's concession of the Pauline roots of the theory, he tries to demolish it on grounds which should now be tediously familiar. First, in *Rechfertigung u. Versöhnung* I, he opposes the implications of Marheineke's view that 'in Christ the suffering and dying of all may concentrate itself' – a representative theory of the Atonement which he deplored on the grounds of that individualism which is an ingredient of ethical rationalism.[132] Second, he argues, a 'cosmic' Christ makes an end of Jesus' 'human individuality'.[133] Or, to put it critically and conversely, Ritschl's notion of christological 'vocation' (a rounded, intentional life, spatio-temporally limited) makes an end of any understanding of a cosmically significant Christ! Third, his paralysing suspicion of 'metaphysical' theology leads him to attack the theory as 'philosophical' rather than 'religious' – i.e. there is nothing in it of vigorous world-conquering spirit-fulfilment, of the exclusive Lutheran stress on the *beneficia Christi*, and so on. Fourth, if we fix our gaze, he insists, on the 'historical picture' of Christ, on his religious convictions, ethical motives, and visible conduct (those factors which, as he puts it, 'exert an influence upon us'), we do not *perceive* and cannot prove the existence of 'this central individual' in Christ![134] It is difficult at this point totally to withhold sympathy from those of his critics who have denounced his 'historical positivism' as impoverishingly restrictive! From the standpoint of historical theology, his rejection produced disastrous consequences, which have been well brought out and documented by Wolfhart Pannenberg, who writes of Jesus' designation as humanity's 'central individual'.[135] The content of this notion is by no means exhausted by the typically nineteenth-century theory of Christ as human 'prototype' (e.g., as in Ritschl's christology), for it was more important for renewing the biblical idea of the *summation of all things in Christ*. The roots of this idea in the modern period lie in the first half of the nineteenth century, in Hegel,[136] in Marheineke, and in the Hegelian theologian, Karl F. Göschel (1784–1861).[137] The fierce controversy produced by the publication of D. F. Strauss's *Leben Jesu* kept the theory in the forefront of public debate,[138] especially in the writings of Ritschl's predecessor at Göttingen, I. A. Dorner.[139] It also occupied an important place in the thought of Ritschl's Heidelberg teacher, Richard Rothe (1799–1867).[140] But, according to Pannenberg, further development of this christological theory was *abruptly arrested* in the second half of the nineteenth century by that *antispeculative reaction* (which appears today in many respects as intellectual superficiality), typical of and popularized by Ritschl's *Rechtfertigung u. Versöhnung*! If Pannenberg is right, the unfortunate Ritschl was responsible for significantly blocking the progress of modern christological research for several generations, until the publication of works such as Brunner's 1949 *Dogmatik* II,[141] Tillich's *The Interpretation of History*,[142] and Donald Baillie's *God Was in Christ*.[143]

A careful examination of some of Baillie's remarks in this volume usefully clarifies Ritschl's fundamental christological presuppositions, and confirms much of what we have already argued. Baillie insists that christology's concern is with the meaning of history, and that its essential content is Christ as the *centre* or *middle-point* of history, a theme developed variously by thinkers as diverse as Barth, Gogarten, Otto Piper, Hans-Dietrich Wendland, C. H. Dodd, H. G. Wood, and Reinhold Niebuhr, who concur in holding that christology stands for the uniquely and distinctively Christian interpretation of history *as against* *other* interpretations. This interpretation (using a real eschatology, a concrete time scheme) issues in a 'story of salvation' (*Heilsgeschichte*) based upon the conviction that in Jesus Christ, its central character, the divine had actually come right into history. Christian thinkers therefore constructed a *Heilsgeschichte* from Creation, Fall, Promise, Prophecy, the First Advent of Christ in the 'fullness of time', his life, death, resurrection and ascension, the gift of the spirit, the Church and its proclamation, to the Second Advent and the consummation of all things in him. Now this stands, in Baillie's view, in the *sharpest contradiction* to *all other* interpretations, for example, the ancient, classical *cyclical* understanding of history. Baillie argues that in our time such a christological scheme must be defended against *modern* misinterpretations of history, particularly against that view presupposed and expounded by late nineteenth-century, German, 'liberal-Protestant' theology, the view sketched in fact above by the 'early' Bultmann and by Brunner. Such a view is to be characterized as humanistic, evolutionary and *progressive*, and is entertained by those who wish to have 'Christ without christology', a desire bound up with 'a sub-Christian conception of God'. He proceeds to argue that this humanistic-progressive philosophy of history sees Jesus as the religious 'pathfinder', the supreme seeker and discoverer of God, the crown and flower of humanity in its age-long upward struggle. But this view of Jesus, he protests, is not the outcome of meditation on the traditional christological mysteries, but of a purely evolutionist philosophy of progress, of the 'Ascent of Man', culminating in Jesus Christianity speaks of a *Heilsgeschichte* (sacred story) rather than

Fortschritt (progress), a story which refers to divine action 'from Creation to Consummation' rather than 'evolution', which tries to illumine both past and future from the central, determinative point of Jesus of Nazareth. To abandon contemplation of the enigmas and paradoxes of christology is to abandon the Christian view of God and history for that sub-Christian view of 'human seeking and finding, of spiritual progress and discovery, with Jesus as its climax'. Not that this latter view is intrinsically *false*, but *inadequate* to the task of spelling out all that is involved in the doctrine of the Incarnation. This critique is all the more striking, coming as it did from one who was by no means an unsympathetic pupil of Herrmann, and who was never a doctrinaire adherent of the neo-orthodox Barthian school. And it corroborates that understanding of history which, according to Bultmann and Brunner, was the theoretical presupposition of nineteenth-century 'liberal' christologies.

We return to the mainstream of Ritschl's explanation of what is involved in the believer's present relation to Christ *in statu exaltationis*. In admitting this to Christian theology, there are three possibilities. First, we may be *agnostic* about it, and affirm that 'Christ as exalted is beyond our ken'.[144] Second, in affirming it we may be opening the door 'for every form of extravagance', by which he meant naturally (in the light of his voluminous writings on the history of pietism), all those expressions of familiar, intimate, quasi-sexual, emotionally charged relations between the heavenly bridegroom Christ and his earthly bride the Christian community, a 'sickly' form of devotion which he never tired of exposing as based upon the love-play language of the Song of Songs and upon seventeenth-century pietistic literature, rather than the New Testament corpus as interpreted by the confessional documents of the Reformation. This last point is important, for not many of his interpreters, ancient and modern, would deny that his violent over-reaction against *all* such devotional discourse may have reached that point where it paralytically inhibited him from any unambiguous talk whatever about the believer's here-and-now relation with Christ. Third, and this is his only solution to the problem, we may proceed on the following presupposition:

Regard must be had to the fact that between Christ and the community of believers, which He designed by His words, deeds, and patience to establish, there is an abiding relation whereby Christ continues to be the ground of its existence and specific character.

But how do we know when and where Christ is *functioning* in and through the community? This, he insists, 'can only be rightly judged in the light of what is recognized to have been the content of these functions *in his historical life*'. This is highly ambiguous, and for some generations his interpreters have pondered whether he meant 'Christ works in the *hic et nunc*', or that in the community he founded the members share in the world-transcending benefits which derive from communal contemplation of the image of his historical figure. For he comes close to *identifying* the exalted Christ with the subjectively appropriated *beneficia Christi* participated in by believers:

The exalted Christ exercises His Kingship *in the assurance* which believers have of their salvation, in their victory over the enemies thereof, and in their patience under all kinds of evil.

And it is hard to withhold sympathy from those who have complained of a slippery ambiguity in this use of the adjective 'exalted' as applied to Christ. They have pointed to passages in his writings[145] where 'exalted' appears to be interchangeable with 'exercising supremacy' (over the world), 'exercising power' (upon the community and through it upon the world), and 'exercising independence' (of all that is worldly), the validity of which can only be proved 'by some corresponding activity of the earthly Christ' sought in 'the historical portrait of Christ'. Many have pointed to the following classic passage as evidence for his view that Christ's 'contemporary work' is but the *historical prolongation* of his functions within the movement he inaugurated:

For to Him Who wields the lordship of God, or Who, to borrow Luther's phrase, is in virtue of His redeeming work 'My Lord', we must reckon all those to belong who experience this same lordship in themselves; in this connection the community of the Kingdom of God must be regarded as such, in so far as its members, through conduct prompted by universal brotherly love, and through the various possible manifestations of supremacy over the world and independence of the same, display in themselves *the successful issue of Christ's peculiar work.*

And the power for good exercised by Christians in public life and in worldly affairs must be 'ascribed to its *historical* Author'. Jesus is the 'inspiration' of Christians in that he is 'the prototype of that union of the many in the one', that is, the contemporary Kingdom of God. And many have judged that Ritschl has himself eliminated all possible doubt from the matter in the following remarkably frank statement:

> Christ comes to act upon the individual believer on the one hand through the *historical remembrance* of Him which is possible in the Church, on the other hand as the *Permanent Author* of all the influences and impulses which are due to other men, and like in nature to Himself.[146]

Trust in Christ is evoked by 'the tradition *of Christ* propagated in the Church'.[147] That Ritschl's intense personal aversion for emotional devotional discourse is still operative comes out in his complaint that such talk overlooks that 'love very distinctly implies the equality of the person loving with the beloved',[148] which leads to that medieval piety characteristic of St Bernard of Clairvaux 'who expressly states that in intercourse with the Bridegroom awe ceases, majesty is laid aside, and immediate personal intercourse is carried on as between lovers or neighbours', so that we are back once more in the pre-Christian framework of the Song of Songs! Over against this sort of thing, the Reformers affirmed that Christ's Godhead 'is present precisely in the mediatorial achievements of his earthly life'.[149] To be fair to Ritschl, his views on the exalted Christ are by no means exhaustively determined by idiosyncratic personal aversions, for important theological considerations are operative also. For example, his answer to contemporary opponents who argued 'that an immediate personal relation to Christ and to God is the kernel of the Christian life' is theologically significant. He replies that the contemplative relation to Christ they claim 'is possible only because they have been brought up in the Church, have in it become believers, and in it have been furnished with the right knowledge of Christ', and that, in the words of Calvin, 'Christ, even as He is represented in devotion, can be rightly conceived only as invested with His Word'.[150] Our 'love for Christ' is always directed to him *as the bearer of reconciliation and as God's representative*. There should therefore be exercised a control on undisciplined, emotional devotion by the theologian, who 'is obliged to trace back the immediate contemplation of Christ in the exercise of devotion to all the *historical* presuppositions of that act, and to remind his readers of these, in order that devotion may not be taken up with arbitrary distortions of the picture of Christ'. It could be argued that here he was simply and sensibly pleading for historico-theological control over fanciful, ecstatic, arbitrary and purely psychogenic excursions into the Christ-cult. Moreover, his firm insistence that our relation to Christ is always qualified by him as the Word of God was, it can no longer be denied, a significant anticipation of twentieth-century theologies of the Word, and of theological opposition to unbiblical and ahistorical forms of mysticism. Be that as it may, his adversaries and some of his interpreters were painfully chilled by his inflexible prohibition of Christ-devotion *in order to achieve feelings of happiness*, by his insistence that the *end* of reconciliation with God is to achieve a certain attitude to the world, by his unwavering antipathy towards Christian 'conversion' and his austere predilection for systematic education and moral discipline as the normal form of Christian spirituality.[151] In his *Theology and Metaphysics* he affirms that 'the religious evidence of God's presence depends upon a connection of religious community and education with ethical self-formation and self-criticism'.[152] There is perhaps no better, and revealing, definition of the believer's relation to Christ than the following, in his own words:

> Christ consoles me and gives me courage when I sense the work of his example or when I direct myself towards the motives which, since they are focused and made actual for me in his person, make him the originator and perfector of my salvation.[153]

Those who have wished to maintain that the believer's 'relation to Christ' is understood by him to be exhaustively constituted by

memory of the historical Jesus, have pointed conclusively to the
following:

> One person continues to be efficacious in the life of others *and
> is therefore present to them* when they act on the basis of
> education or other stimulation which they have derived from
> him. In the broadest sense, this is the case with the religious
> bond between our lives and God – *mediated through the precise
> recollection of Christ.*

It is in the light of such teachings that we must understand the
bitter accusations hurled against him by adversaries that his
writings on pietism reveal just how little real religion there was
in the man, and that his religious insensitivity was of such an
order that he was simply unable, throughout his life, to see God,
Christ and the Spirit as *ends*, rather than as *means to ends*.

It is not easy to reach a final estimate of Ritschl's teaching on the
exaltation of Christ. Probably the truth of the matter is that, once
again, while he *intended* to give substantial expression to the
doctrine, because of certain fundamental limitations (e.g., over-
reaction to the excesses of mystical pietism, what has been widely
called 'historical positivism', and a basic confusion over the
meaning of the term 'metaphysical'), his actual *achievement* was
disappointingly defective. What lies beyond dispute is that most
of his interpreters, ancient and modern alike, have judged, with
varying degrees of disapproval, that he, so far as his treatment of
Christ's exaltation is concerned, *failed adequately to express that
Christ transcends the spatio-temporal limitations of the human.*
Orr, for instance, while conceding that Ritschl nowhere denied
Christ's contemporary glorified state, judges that he translated it
into terms which equates it with *the posthumous influence of his
historical personality*,[154] and proposed that all talk of Christ *in
statu exaltationis* should be replaced by that of *the perpetration
of Christ's image and influence* in the Scriptures and the Church.[155]
Therefore, the Christian religion has to do *only with Christ's
historical manifestation.*[156] Orr's final estimate is therefore that
Ritschl, by the exaltation doctrine, has failed to establish that
Christ significantly transcends the empirically human. The gener-

ally sympathetic Garvie is embarrassed by Ritschl's performance, and more than once strenuously contradicts that he denied or disbelieved the doctrine – nevertheless, by *over-insistence on the historical media*, he *obscured* the truth of Christ's continued presence and activity.[157] H. R. Mackintosh, predictably, because of Ritschl's 'historical positivism' and his predilection for 'the immanental factors of development', judged that he replaced the *hic et nunc* activity of the exalted Lord with *a merely posthumous influence*,[158] so that what Christ is alleged to be doing now is *the posthumous result of what he did in the first century*.[159] And if we turn finally to a not unsympathetic contemporary interpreter, David Mueller, we find the uncompromising judgement that 'there is no doctrine of the *Christus praesens* in Ritschl'; his alternative was to ask the Church 'to look back to Jesus', the founder of the Church and Kingdom.[160]

Finally, we must attempt, as promised earlier, some kind of evaluation of that 'neo-orthodox' criticism of Ritschl outlined above,[161] from the writings of Brunner, Bultmann, Barth and Baillie, that nineteenth-century 'liberal' theology and christology presupposed a philosophy of history and an anthropology determined by the philosophical needs of the *Aufklärung* much more than by ancient, Christian, biblical and credal tradition. This philosophy of history, whose classic expression was probably contained in Kant's *Religion Within the Limits of Reason Alone*, asserted fundamentally that there exists a general or universal religion of which Christianity is the highest (known) manifestation; closely connected is the conviction that history is a struggle in which man strives to progress from the natural to the ethico-spiritual, a historical scheme to which all religion conforms; within this framework priority is given, not to God or the gods or the divine, but to the overcoming of impediments to the free spiritual development of humanity towards its destiny; but religion, so conceived, would be but an empty abstraction were it not for the appearance of gigantic ethico-spiritual personalities, bearers of inspiration in life and word, renewing and strengthening an eternally covenanted relationship of God to man. Within this framework, Christ is seen as the most significant, even the *transcendentally* significant, of such personalities, the bearer of *Heilsideen* (saving ideas) such as 'love', 'reconciliation' and 'Kingdom of God', whose influence is to be seen, not merely in the teaching of these ideas, but in his life which 'actualizes' them for men. While within this framework it would be hard to say that the person and work of Christ are 'absolute', they are absolutely *unique*, and that for two reasons. First, it is claimed, Christ was the *first* to actualize and impart these ideas with his own incomparable intensity. Second, he inaugurated a *uniquely new* historical movement (Christendom) and 'collective life' (Kingdom of God) destined to serve the deepest of human needs in a 'unique' way. Christology is subordinated to theology, the divine to the human, and history is regarded as a gradual progress from the natural to the ethico-spiritual. The entire viewpoint is strongly marked by optimism and a firm faith in historical progress and innate moral capacity. The scheme has been variously described as 'rationalistic', 'idealistic', 'humanistic', 'evolutionary' and 'progressive'. How then is this criticism of Ritschl to be evaluated? This is an extraordinarily difficult question to answer. A tentative and sketchy reply is all that can be attempted here – for various answers will be suggested in the two chapters that follow. Let it be conceded right away that there are certain lines of connection that can be drawn between this philosophy on the one hand and Ritschl's theology and christology on the other. There are *similarities* between the two. But it is also true that there are *dissimilarities* that ought not to be overlooked. If Ritschl was a child of the Enlightenment, he was by no means a docile and subservient one! For it is going to be argued in Chapter VII[162] that around the turn of the century his theology attracted to itself much disapproval for the extent to which it had criticized and deviated from the philosophy of the Enlightenment – it had become excessively *bibliocentric* and *christocentric*, denying the existence and significance of the *universal* or general religion postulated by the Enlightenment, and Ritschl was condemned for having isolated Christianity and having dealt with it as if there were no other religion in the world. In great measure, the history of nineteenth-century Protestant theology represents a positive, Christian attempt to overcome the rationalistic deism of the Enlightenment by progressively making it more *christocentric* in character. If so, within such a development the christological work of Schleiermacher and of Ritschl would find a significant place. Indeed, there is a judgement in Karl Barth's *Church Dogmatics* which suggests just such a possibility.[163] Speaking of the harm done to Christianity by 'natural theology' (i.e., the natural religion and deism of the eighteenth century), Barth remarks:

> When in due course in the nineteenth century a reaction, sound in itself, arose in the direction of a christocentric theology, first in Schleiermacher and *subsequently and still more outspokenly* in A. Ritschl and his school it was then too late.

Barth is naturally critical of both on the grounds that so much 'natural theology' had already been incorporated into their systems that these must be regarded as gravely defective – in Barth's judgement 'one cannot subsequently speak christologically, if christology has not already been presupposed at the outset, and in its stead other presuppositions have claimed one's attention'. But no matter, Barth is here conceding that in the 'story' of modern christological theology *the contribution of Ritschl must be taken into account*, which is what this chapter has been all about. There is one final point. One christological contribution can only be criticized from the standpoint of another, and each christological construction cannot be understood totally divorced from the *Zeitgeist* in which it is conceived. While it may be true that Ritschl's *Zeitgeist* is no longer ours, it may be equally true that neither is that of Brunner and Barth, of the decades following World War I. Those who are today disposed to deal harshly and dismissively with Ritschl's christological work would do well to remember that it was rejected in a secular era understandably weary of and disillusioned with all talk of 'evolutionary progress', 'ethical idealism' and 'optimistic humanism'. If so, it is possible that the eschatological, *heilsgeschichtliche* christology which replaced it may today in some respects *be just as dated as Ritschl's*. If christology is the heart of Christian theology, what has such theology to say to those who believe in social and economic betterment, who see a connection between Christian faith and social action, who deplore theology's isolation from national and international policy-making and decision taking? In the two chapters which follow, it will be argued that those who today take such issues seriously could do worse than look again at the teaching of liberal theology on the relation between the Kingdom of God and the *worldly activities* of the Church and the believer.[164]

NOTES TO CHAPTER V

1 *Jesus – God and Man*, pp. 36–7.
2 Mueller, op. cit., p. 170.
3 See, e.g., *J. & R.* III, p. 143: 'As a matter of fact, Jesus is not concerned to provide a moral code for the details of life; that is not His business, and any estimate of His person that has this for its starting-point is historically unjust.'
4 See the statements in Denney's *Studies in Theology*, pp. 14, 261–2, and the treatment of them in Garvie, op. cit., pp. 286–95.
5 See, e.g., Bultmann's 'The Christological Confession of the World Council of Churches', pp. 273–90 of *Essays: Philosophical and Theological*, and Rudolf Schnackenburg, 'Christology and Myth', pp. 336–55 of *Kerygma and Myth* II.
6 Pannenberg, op. cit., p. 45.
7 ibid., p. 194.
8 See, e.g., Julien Freund, *The Sociology of Max Weber*, London 1972, especially pp. 200–3, 'Attitudes of different social strata to the religious phenomenon'.
9 Barth, *Protestant Theology*, pp. 655–6.
10 For a useful, if compressed, summary of this development, see the article 'Substance', pp. 209–11 of *A Dictionary of Philosophy*, by A. R. Lacey, London 1976.
11 James Richmond, *Faith and Philosophy*, pp. 46–8.
12 Ritschl, *Theology and Metaphysics*, p. 187.
13 ibid., p. 193.
14 ibid., p. 191.
15 *J. & R.* III, p. 443.
16 See, e.g., Adolf von Harnack, *History of Dogma*, London 1893, p. 558.
17 *J. & R.* III, pp. 392–3.
18 ibid., p. 394.
19 ibid., p. 397.
20 ibid., p. 398, italics mine.
21 ibid., p. 416.
22 ibid., p. 418, italics mine.
23 ibid., pp. 435–6.
24 ibid., p. 438.
25 ibid., p. 439.
26 ibid., p. 441; cf. *J. & R.* I, p. 275 (ET).
27 *J. & R.* III, p. 443.
28 See *supra*, pp. 149–50.

29 ibid., p. 445.
30 ibid., p. 447.
31 ibid., p. 448.
32 ibid., p. 449.
33 ibid., p. 451.
34 ibid., italics mine.
35 Ritschl, *Three Essays*, p. 178, italics mine.
36 *J. & R.* III, p. 453.
37 ibid., p. 454.
38 ibid., p. 455.
39 ibid., p. 457.
40 For the theological effects of the manifesto on Barth, see *Karl Barth*, by Eberhard Busch, London 1976, pp. 81–2, and *Revolutionary Theology in the Making*, pp. 26–7.
41 See *supra*, ch. I, pp. 22–3.
42 Lougee, op. cit., p. 118.
43 op. cit., pp. 223 and 343, n. 8.
44 ibid., pp. 280–3.
45 ibid., pp. 279–80.
46 *J. & R.* III, p. 252.
47 ibid., p. 253.
48 ibid., p. 281, italics mine.
49 ibid., p. 293, italics mine.
50 *Instruction*, para. 8, italics mine.
51 *J. & R.* III, p. 460.
52 ibid., p. 483.
53 ibid., p. 460.
54 ibid., p. 461.
55 ibid., p. 463.
56 ibid., pp. 464–5.
57 ibid., p. 466.
58 *J. & R.* I, pp. 22–41.
59 *J. & R.* III, p. 474.
60 ibid., pp. 473–4.
61 ibid., p. 477.
62 ibid., p. 480.
63 ibid.
64 ibid., pp. 539–40.
65 ibid., p. 547.
66 ibid., p. 556.
67 ibid., p. 557.
68 ibid., p. 559, italics mine.
69 Schleiermacher, *The Christian Faith*, paras. 87, 88; Schleiermacher's actual words are: 'If we regard the Christian mass as a whole, it manifestly shares so largely in the general sinfulness, and this at certain times so saliently and in such specifically heightened measure, that it is doubtful whether there is less of this sinfulness at any one point rather than another, and whether *it might not therefore have been better for the shaping of human affairs if Christianity had not become such a widely spread historical force*', op. cit., p. 364, italics mine.
70 *J. & R.* III, p. 560, italics mine.

71 ibid., p. 564.
72 See, e.g., Gustaf Aulén, *Christus Victor*, London 1953.
73 See the important survey in Ritschl, *J. & R.* I, pp. 10 f.
74 *J. & R.* III, p. 575.
75 ibid., p. 572.
76 ibid., pp. 574–5.
77 ibid., p. 586.
78 ibid., p. 588.
79 ibid., p. 589, italics mine.
80 ibid., p. 590.
81 ET, *The Mediator*, p. 56.
82 ibid., p. 57.
83 ibid., p. 60; see *J. & R.* III, p. 450.
84 *Die Lehre von der Gottheit Christi*, 1881, p. 439, quoted by Brunner,
   pp. 61–2; Schultz (1836–1903), Professor at Göttingen from 1876 until
   1903, was generally regarded as being the most 'extreme' of Ritschl's
   disciples; see Lichtenberger, *History of German Theology in the 19th
   Century*, pp. 586 f.
85 Brunner, op. cit., p. 63.
86 *J. & R.* III, p. 451.
87 ibid., p. 465, italics mine.
88 Brunner, op. cit., p. 64.
89 ibid., pp. 64–5.
90 ibid., p. 97.
91 In *Glauben u. Verstehen* I; ET, *Faith and Understanding*, pp. 28–52.
92 ibid., pp. 28 and 13.
93 ibid., p. 29.
94 ibid., p. 30.
95 ibid., p. 31.
96 ibid., p. 34; cf. the description of the 'liberal' philosophy of history in
   Heinz Zahrnt, *The Question of God*, London 1969, pp. 18–19.
97 *Faith and Understanding*, p. 35.
98 ibid., p. 36.
99 R. Paulus, *Das Christusproblem der Gegenwart*, Tübingen 1922, p. 67,
   quoted by Bultmann, ibid., pp. 37–9.
100 Professor in Göttingen, 1895–7.
101 *Zeitschrift für Theologie u. Kirche*, 1891, pp. 287–366.
102 Bultmann, op. cit., p. 38.
103 op. cit., p. 47.
104 *J. & R.* III, pp. 598–9, italics mine.
105 Bultmann, op. cit., p. 49.
106 *Jesus – God and Man*, p. 45.
107 Bultmann, op. cit., p. 50.
108 *Protestant Theology*, p. 655.
109 op. cit., pp. 476 f.
110 See Barth, *Church Dogmatics* IV: 1, p. 374.
111 *Protestant Theology*, pp. 478 f.
112 Barth bases his interpretation of Wegscheider on the latter's *Institutiones
   Theologiae Christianae Dogmaticae* of 1815; for Brunner's references
   to Wegscheider, see *The Mediator*, pp. 46 f.
113 Barth, op. cit., pp. 476, 480, 655; *Church Dogmatics* IV: 1, pp. 374–5.

114 *J. & R.* III, p. 401.
115 ibid., p. 462.
116 ibid., p. 469.
117 ibid., italics mine.
118 See *supra*, pp. 114f.
119 *J. & R.* III, 9471; for Garvie's defence of Ritschl as teaching a *real* pre-existence, see op. cit., pp. 283 f. and 292–3.
120 Mozley, op. cit., pp. 186 f.
121 Orr, op. cit., pp. 211 f.
122 *Types*, pp. 166–7.
123 *Jesus – God and Man*, p. 121.
124 Orr, op. cit., pp. 196–7; in passing, it ought to be pointed out that the conservative Kaftan – in *The Truth of the Christian Religion* – and the fairly moralistic Herrmann – in *The Communion of the Christian with God* – both part company firmly with Ritschl at this point, and teach unmistakably a personal pre-existence of Christ as a necessary correlate of Christian faith and worship.
125 Orr, op. cit., p. 210.
126 Garvie, op. cit., p. 63.
127 *J. & R.* III, p. 400.
128 ibid., p. 405.
129 ibid., p. 406.
130 See Ritschl's discussion in *J. & R.* III, pp. 411 f.; cf. *J. & R.* I, pp. 600 f. Marheineke's christological views are to be found in his *Die Grundlehren der christlichen Dogmatik als Wissenschaft*, Berlin 1819 and 1827.
131 Lichtenberger, op. cit., pp. 236 f.
132 *J. & R.* I, p. 601.
133 *J. & R.* III, p. 411.
134 ibid., pp. 412–13.
135 *Jesus – God and Man*, p. 388; for the discussion that follows, see Part Three, 10, II, 'The Summation of Humanity in Jesus Christ', pp. 378–90.
136 *Science of Logic* II, pp. 361 f.
137 *Beiträge zur spekulativen Philosophie von Gott, dem Menschen u. dem Gottmenschen*, 1838.
138 See D. F. Strauss, *The Life of Jesus Critically Examined*, London 1973, pp. 777 f.
139 See *A System of Christian Doctrine*, vol. iii, pp. 323 f.
140 *Theologische Ethik*, 5 vols., Wittenberg 1867–70, paras. 555 f.; cf. Lichtenberger, op. cit., pp. 492–526, and Barth, *Protestant Theology*, pp. 597–606.
141 ET by Olive Wyon, *The Christian Doctrine of Creation and Redemption*, London 1952, pp. 196 f.
142 New York 1936, pp. 30 f.
143 See ch. III, section iii, 'Christology and the Meaning of History', pp. 71–9.
144 *J. & R.* III, pp. 431 f.
145 There is a classic one in op. cit., p. 460.
146 op. cit., p. 591, italics mine.
147 op. cit., p. 592.
148 op. cit., p. 594.

149 op. cit., p. 595.
150 op. cit., pp. 596–7.
151 op. cit., pp. 597–8.
152 *T. & M.*, p. 194.
153 ibid., p. 195.
154 Orr, op. cit., p. 133.
155 op. cit., p. 134.
156 op. cit., pp. 134–5.
157 Garvie, op. cit., p. 295.
158 *Types*, p. 158.
159 op. cit., pp. 163–4.
160 Mueller, op. cit., p. 175.
161 See *supra*, pp. 169 f.
162 See *infra*, p. 280 f.
163 *Church Dogmatics* I: 2, p. 123, italics mine.
164 See *infra*, pp. 270–3.

CHAPTER VI

The Lifestyle of the Christian

We have so far had much to say of those 'stereotypes' by means of which Ritschl's theological teaching has been, through several generations, transmitted to modernity. Nowhere is this truer than in the case of his ethical work. Briefly, modernity has inherited the unfavourable judgement that his ethical teaching was, above all, fundamentally and incurably, *bourgeois*: that he unreflectively and coarsely identified Christian existence with our vocational *Lebenswerk* (that is, with our 'job'); that he unimaginatively and dangerously taught that to do our job well is simultaneously and exhaustively to serve God and fulfil our obligations to Christ, a doctrine which confirmed and corroborated the Prussian bourgeois' high conception of service to the State in the nineteenth century. The evidence for such twentieth-century allegations is weighty and impressive, and its classic expression is arguably to be found in Barth's book on nineteenth-century theology.[1] His view, we remind ourselves, was that Ritschl stemmed directly from Kant as an *antimetaphysical moralist*, who motivated Ritschl to understand Christianity as that which preeminently made possible a certain *Lebensideal*; we ought not to be misled by Ritschl's biblico-dogmatic language into believing that this alone was not his *chief concern*; Ritschl took his stand firmly, even immovably, upon that *Lebensideal* which was the epitome of the national-liberal German bourgeois of the age of Bismarck; modern man can strive for God's Kingdom only within those structures that have been naturally determined, particularly within one's *given* 'calling' or 'vocation', and not outside them; it follows that vocational loyalty is the highest, indeed the only, fulfilment of the example of Christ; where such realization (*Behauptung*) or self-realization (*Selbstbehauptung*) as the realization of the *Lebensideal* does not occur, no reconciliation (as God's command) is realized either; and where reconciliation has not been activated, there can be no justification. The much earlier 1927 judgement of Brunner[2] had been briefer: as a

'Kantian', Ritschl had replaced Kant's central conception of 'Law' with the idea of 'the calling', which, despite its similarity to biblical and Reformed notions, is really meant only in the conventional sense of a *daily calling* or *vocation*; God's commandment only demands that the individual shall abide in that place where, by historical processes, he has been situated by God, do his duty, carry out his 'calling' (as a citizen!), at the particular place he finds himself in the historical process; such obedience thus divinely legitimizes the historical stream. Paul Tillich has judged that Ritschl's theology was able to fortify the development of the nineteenth-century bourgeois personality; it undergirded theologically the development of the strong, active, morally-disciplined individual; it had connections with liberal elements in social and political structures, with autonomous thinking in the sciences and with the correlative rejection of authority; it was compatible with the *liberal-personalistic* mood of the time, which did not survive for long into the twentieth century.[3] We have already noted Pannenberg's judgement that perceptible in the background of Ritschl's christological work is the impressive, nineteenth-century bourgeois *Lebensideal*; here, Jesus' suffering is understood as but the highest expression of his vocational faithfulness.[4] It was Max Weber who characterized Ritschl's standpoint (as expressed in his *Geschichte des Pietismus*) as *theological-bourgeois*.[5] Ritschl produced a thoroughly bourgeois account of Christianity by identifying what we should nowadays call Christian existence with 'fidelity to civic vocation', thus effecting what the French call the *embourgeoisement*, and the Germans the *Verbürgerlichung*, of Christianity, so closely connecting God's demand with civic-social activity that he materially assisted in creating a latter-day German *Kulturprotestantismus*, which was eventually charged with aiding and abetting *all* activities of the German State from about 1910 to 1945. Now we have already seen that there is more often than not considerable truth, carefully selected and edited, in all stereotypes. What is dismaying and disconcerting about this stereotype is that it has so violently compressed Ritschl's lengthy and rather involved reflections on ethics, that it is hard not to suspect that it has gravely distorted it. His critics have so concentrated upon his conclusions in the matter, rather unfortunately stated, that they have completely ignored the steps which led him to them. We try now to redress the balance by re-examining what he had to say about such matters in his actual texts.

We have already briefly alluded to Ritschl's central insistence that God's work in Christ does not finish with justification, but goes on to issue in reconciliation understood as a certain 'personal activity' in the world, or a certain distinctive mundane *Lebensführung* (lifestyle). This, as God's work in man in the world, 'is a part of the divine revelation'.[6] Insistence on this, in his view, is what decisively separates mainstream Lutheran-Reformed Protestantism from quietistic pietism and from monastic Catholicism. Before describing the nature of this *Lebensführung*, it is as well to recall clearly that since man stands in an indissoluble double-relation to the world and God, the distinctively Christian *Lebensführung* can only adequately be described and identified as simultaneously *related to these two*. To put this conversely, the opposite of Christian existence is domination by the impersonal natural and social world; Christian existence is *world-transcending communion with God*.[7] In the light of this, his fundamental position on Christian ethics may be usefully summarized: *the authentic Christian proves to himself and others his fellowship with God in Christ through his transcendence over the world, manifested in ethical decision leading to a new lifestyle, constituted by action freed from impersonal worldly restraints and determinations.* In the light of this, we may list the components of the Christian's lifestyle: the achievement of Christian perfection, faith in God's providence, patience, humility and prayer. First, we glance at his treatment of *Christian perfection*. He felt obliged to give considerable attention to this, because two of his theological *bêtes noires*, medieval monastic Catholicism and post-Reformation pietism, had claimed in different ways to have made Christian perfection the ultimate goal of their respective religious systems. It hardly needs saying that Ritschl strenuously opposed these claims.[8] The burden of his case against Catholic monasticism is that for it the achievement of Christian perfection (demanded of us all by the New Testament) involves the abandonment of home, family and civil vocation, and also its teaching that in the non-monastic state the laity are at best capable of an *approximation to* monastic perfection through the imitation of the ascetic practices (derived, in Ritschl's view, from later Hellenism) of the monastery. In contradistinction, he reminds us, the Reformers taught that authentic Christian perfection, achievable in and through worldly existence and activity, is 'an injunction incumbent *on all* Christians'. The principle of the Reformation, he insists firmly, 'is *meant* to exclude every possibility of two kinds of Christianity'. The passionate desire to withdraw from the world is, in his view, based in the last resort upon the medieval *timor filialis*, 'the perpetual terror', as he puts it, 'of disobeying the Divine commandments which confront the soul in all their statutory multiplicity'. Within this ethical framework, worldly relationships are suspect, as dangerous opportunities for transgression, and mundane life is regarded as shot through with nervous terror lest ignorance or temptation should lead to transgression and condemnation. Rejection of such views led him to draw a sharp distinction between *quantitative* and *qualitative* views of Christian perfection. A *quantitative* view regards the ethico-spiritual agent as standing over against the infinite multiplicity of divinely promulgated statutes, commands and prohibitions, *all* of which command infinite and absolute obedience. This, he insists, is false, and has nothing to do with perfection witnessed to by the New Testament and rediscovered by the Reformation. His own *qualitative* view deserves careful documentation and consideration. For one thing, the progressive erosion of the notion through the pietistic infection of Lutheranism goes a long way, in his view, towards explaining the alarming decomposition of the Evangelical Churches during the nineteenth century. The core of the *quantitative* doctrine is that in Christianity each human existent is intended to be *a whole*:

> In Christianity man is destined and is enabled to be *a whole* in his own spiritual order.[9]

> We must uphold man's destiny as one who may attain personal perfection, since this destiny is correlative with the qualitative judgement that the religious-ethical life is a whole in its own right (*ein Ganzes in seiner Art*).[10]

For Ritschl, the life of the individual so considered has a higher worth than 'the whole world':[11]

In (the) coherence of the spiritual life the individual person possesses the significance of *a whole* which exceeds the significance of the entire world which is viewed as the order of a divided and naturally conditioned existence.[12]

What this means in concrete terms is indicated by his statement that the Christian

directs his action towards the end of the Kingdom of God in a particular ethical vocation and authenticates his sonship with God and his dominion over the world *in the particular conditions of life* into which he is placed.[13]

Such an understanding of Christian perfection was, of course, deliberately framed in order to stand in the sharpest conceivable contrast with so-called *dogmatic* perfection (immaculately correct assent to dogmas), or as realizable necessarily *in the cloister*, rather than in those 'conditions of life' into which we are placed *by divine providence*. In sharp contradistinction to such notions, the genuine doctrine of perfection means

that our moral achievement or life-work (*Lebenswerk*) in connection with the Kingdom of God should, however limited in amount, be conceived as possessing the quality of *a whole* in its own order.[14]

The medieval tendency to regard Christ as 'the ideal of self-abnegation' must therefore be rejected in favour of the fundamental truth that

we have to seek in Christ no special moral pattern other than that of *perfect fidelity to our calling*.[15]

At this point it is impossible not to judge that here Ritschl is articulating a view of Christian existence which significantly anticipates accounts of it familiarized in the twentieth century by forms of Christian personalism and existentialism. His teaching that each Christian existent is a qualitative 'whole', transcendent over the merely social and natural orders, shaped and formed in response to the given, particular 'condition of life' into which the individual has been thrust, so that he forges under grace a special, unique, historical, temporal, concrete calling in the world, finds such striking parallels in more recent theology that it is impossible not to regard the former in part at least as the source of the latter. It is one of the merits of Philip Hefner's book based on Ritschl, *Faith and the Vitalities of History*, that it brings this out. His re-reading of Ritschl's texts leads him to regard the term *Lebensführung* as *the* key term for interpreting the latter's view of the historical development of the Christian tradition and community.[16] In describing Ritschl's historical research, Hefner explains his choice of the term *Lebensführung* over the better-known *Lebensideal*: his choice is determined by his rejection of Barth's one-sided emphasis on *Lebensideal* as 'the ideal which man has constructed by his own powers as the goal for his life, towards the realization of which he bends every effort', thus allowing Barth to identify it with 'bourgeois morality' understood in its nineteenth-century sense. Hefner rejects Barth's hostile interpretation because he claims, persuasively, that the root *führen* (to lead, drive, manage, direct, steer, wield) of *Lebensführung* points to Ritschl's *existential concern*, to the fact that for him the Christian faith characteristically deals with the *direction* and *mode* of human existence rather than doctrine or ecclesiastical institution. Of course, Hefner insists, the component *Ideal* of *Lebensideal* does the same, in so far as it refers to the concrete goal that man's *will* sets for his life. (Barth, by ignoring the close connection in Ritschl between *will* – or, as we might nowadays say, *decision* or *resolve* – and a concrete mode of existence, is able to interpret Ritschl pejoratively by saying that man simply accepts his *Lebensideal* from contemporary – Prussian, bourgeois, or whatever – society.) Hefner correctly characterizes Ritschl's historical method as sifting and discriminating between various *types* of Christianity (Catholic, Lutheran, pietistic, and so on) in terms of different 'configurations of existence' (i.e., *Lebensführungen* or *Lebensidealen*) which they call into being. Ritschl had a propensity for personalizing Christianity (what we have described as his *anti-extrinsicist* translation of the objective into the subjective), and this led him to discuss *Lebensführung* in terms which emphasize individual *Beruf*. Barth's misinterpretation derives from his one-sided over-emphasis on the particular forms which vocation takes, and pictures Ritschl as if he were canonizing nineteenth-century *bürgerlich* modes of life. A fairer reading is possible which suggests that Ritschl's all-round use of terms did not intend any glorification of particular forms of life, but meant to stress the significance of Christianity for *the concrete realities of human existence*.[17] Before leaving this discussion of perfection, it is appropriate once more to remark, in the light of his choice of a *qualitative-existential* notion of perfection rather than a *moralistic-quantitative* one, that it is astounding how the terms 'moralizer' and 'moralistic' have been so uncritically and unreflectively attached to him.

We turn next to what Ritschl meant by *faith in the fatherly providence of God*.[18] He at the outset sharply distinguished the Christian's *Herrschaft* over the world from any empirical state of affairs, and his belief in God's providence as an expression of it from any quasi-metaphysical theory derived from detached observation of the world, with a view to identifying the activity of a supreme moral governor of the universe, who publicly recompenses evil with eventual and appropriate punishment, and virtue with eventual and appropriate blessedness, the kind of theory discussed and sought after during the *Aufklärung*. Belief in the Christian's lordship over the world must be formulated in order to prevent it from colliding with the contemporary natural sciences, a collision which he, as noted in Chapter II, was ever most anxious to prevent. Lordship over the world is the intrinsic aim of human spirit as such, and is realizable only through a certain 'supernatural independence of spirit in all its relations to the world of nature and to society'. He gives a classic definition of that lordship exercised by Christians thus:

> Lordship over the world . . . though it is not technical and empirical, but ideal, is not therefore unreal. For the will which exercises religious dominion over the world is the real; and it is at the same time as much ideal as real.[19]

The Christian's interior and unobservable lordship, having to do with a certain exercise of will, issues in faith in providence. He distinguished such faith from mere wishful thinking or whistling in the dark by urging that the rudimentary form of such faith is *cognitive*, that it is an act of *knowledge* because based on a *judgement*. It is so in a twofold sense. First, because such faith is derived from the religious *Weltanschauung* of Christianity, in which the supramundane God is seen as redeeming his children from worldly oppression and limitations, and leading them towards the unity of his Kingdom. It is so, second, because based on the interior, incorrigible experience of the Christian himself, who, believing that everything that happens in the world serves his ultimate good as a child of God, *knows* that a particular oppression or limitation, initially regarded as evil, has in the long run turned out as beneficial within the order of character-formation. The qualification added to this teaching by Ritschl involves us in judging that for him such faith, to use modern terminology, was a thoroughly *existential* attitude. Having urged that the knowledge involved in such faith is uniquely different from every other species of knowledge, he affirms that 'in it we are guided not by observation of the attitude towards the world occupied by others as well as ourselves, *but solely by our own experiences*'.[20] Hence we have his precise definition of the doctrine in the following terms:

> Faith in providence affirms the general truth of the Divine goodness not as a law of phenomena discovered inductively, but as the personal conviction of each individual, drawn from the nexus of the experiences he has made of himself.

We have more than once alluded to Wrzecionko's view of Ritschl as the theologian of the religious *consciousness*; his view is once more confirmed by the way in which Ritschl describes faith in providence as a 'self-feeling' (or 'feeling of self'), or 'tone of feeling', over against the whole world, although care must be taken not to give 'feeling' an emotive content. It hardly needs to be added that his account of faith in providence ought to be read in its *Sitz im Leben*, in the light of that frightful threat posed to nineteenth-century European Christians by various forms of pessimistic materialism and naturalism, which informed them that they had no more control over their lives than inert floating twigs exercised over a swollen torrent. It was to such a generation that Ritschl addressed his final word on faith in providence, which he regarded as a word of comfort in an atheistic world:

> Faith in the fatherly providence of God is the Christian world view in an abbreviated form. In this faith, although we neither know the future nor perfectly comprehend the past, yet we

judge our momentary relation to the world on the basis of our knowledge of the love of God and on the basis of what we derive from this knowledge, namely, that every child of God possesses a significance greater than the world which God directs in accordance with his final purpose, i.e., our salvation.[21]

It was remarked above that for Ritschl faith in providence was a *thoroughly existential* attitude, which establishes yet another unmistakable similarity between his thought and that of Herrmann's pupil, Bultmann. For both of them, such faith can be entertained only from within the standpoint of *subjective inwardness*, within which the believer works out *his own* interpretation of how God acts towards *him* in and through worldly events and phenomena. Both vehemently deny that faith in providence has anything to do with an *objectively constructed* interpretation of human history or affairs; although Ritschl rejects the materialists' denial of the miraculous on deterministic grounds, like Bultmann he is strongly disinclined to derive God's providential action from allegedly *miraculous happenings* in the space-time continuum. The most striking similarity between their views comes out in their shared teaching on how the man of faith interprets his relation to worldly events, which is described by Bultmann in a celebrated short passage:

> In faith I can understand an accident with which I meet as a gracious gift of God or as His punishment, or as His chastisement. On the other hand, I can understand the same accident *as a link in the chain of the natural course of events.*[22]

Not only does this statement demonstrate that Bultmann, like Ritschl before him, wishes to prevent a head-on collision between Christianity and the natural sciences, but shows that both of them regard providential faith as *a way of looking at* worldly events, good and evil, welcome and unwelcome, which continually enquires of their meaning in the light of God's love, promise, and purpose. A further statement of Bultmann brings this out with great clarity:

> The credal belief in God as creator is not a guarantee given in advance by means of which I am permitted to understand any event as wrought by God. The understanding of God as

creator is genuine only when I understand myself here and now as the creature of God.[23]

Here is another point at which Ritschl's thought, transmitted to modernity by disciples like Herrmann, functioned as a source for the German theology of the last few decades, a remark which applies with equal force to Ritschl's discussion of patience and humility below.

The next two items in the Christian's *Lebensführung* are *patience* and *humility*. Patience in the Christian's lifestyle is derived from a certain unavoidable theological *agnosticism*, indicated by Paul in his statement of Romans 11: 33 that the judgements and ways of God are *unsearchable*,[24] which implies, in Ritschl's view, that the Christian's knowledge of God's saving purpose 'does not imply an antecedent knowledge of the special methods by which God guides to salvation particular bodies of men or particular individuals'. Such reverent agnosticism therefore 'implies that we can hardly comprehend the application of God's saving will *to our own destiny*, or its intertwining with the history of particular groups of men or of the whole of humanity'.[25] It is faith in providence that produces this patience which accepts deserved evils as divine punishments and also as education, undeserved evils as tests, or, perhaps at the same time, as the honour of martyrdom.[26] As such, it is a distinctively Christian virtue, not to be confused, say, with Stoic apathy:

> The consciousness of reconciliation with God places the assurance of personal worth firm above all the special motives which arise from the world; and therefore the pain which springs from their oppressive action can be subordinated to the joy which, in our feeling of self, denotes the incomparable worth of Divine sonship.[27]

Guided by this, he expounds those New Testament statements that the Christian can *glory* in the afflictions and persecutions which he undergoes for Christ's sake (James 1: 2; Romans 5: 3), and that the Christian must 'rejoice in suffering'. But truly Christian patience in no wise derives from emotional subjectivism, for it possesses revelatory and doctrinal bases (e.g. reconciliation with God and faith in providence). Although patience in origin 'is fundamentally always a determination of the will',[28] when firmly established it 'may take the form of a quality of feeling' within the character-formation process of the Christian man. As such, it can be defined as *that organ by which the man of faith grasps, comprehends or overcomes the stream of worldly events which confronts him in day-to-day existence.* There are clear parallels in his treatment of *humility* which, it is not incorrect to say, is also a *feeling-tone* of the self enabling the Christian to grasp and come to grips with the everyday stream of mundane events. Like patience, it possesses adequate credal-revelatory bases: apart from the wide range of Old Testament evidences, there are the paramount historical facts of 'Jesus' self-abasement in obedience even unto death' and 'His resolve to fulfil His moral vocation'.[29] If we keep these historico-dogmatic roots in view, there is no objection to saying that 'humility . . . will be subjective religion itself' and that 'humility is the Christian religion in the form of religious virtue'.[30] Humility possesses important God-ward and man-ward relations; for success and happiness, every bit as much as oppression and suffering, possess acute dangers for the Christian soul, in tempting it towards independence from God and dependence on the world:

> To sustain patience in the absence of success, and humility in its abundance, is a quite specific test of Christian piety.

But it possesses also important man-ward implications. There is the clear New Testament teaching that Christian humility implies *modesty* towards other men, which is a 'principle of respect for other persons', implying the recognition that each person has a place in God's system of things.[31] It is almost humorous to notice that he cannot refrain, in selecting examples of humility and modesty, from portraying theological opponents and *bêtes noires* in an unfortunate light. Humility, he insists, should involve

> a hesitation to regard our religious and moral convictions, however well intended, as God's cause or to defend them as such.

Theologians lacking in humility are 'insolent and arrogant people', because 'they profess as universal ends which are really particular'. The biblical understanding of humility was perverted in the monasticism characteristic of the High Middle Ages, which failed to grasp that true humility can only be exercised in 'all the different experiences of life', not in the cloister, where the world-renouncing monk believes that he alone has genuinely humbled himself before God through his abstinence. A pernicious falsification takes place if

> humility towards God is taken to mean that one should place himself, like a corpse, at the disposal of the Superiors of an Order.[32]

He similarly castigates pietism's and Calvinism's doctrine that humility before God is attainable only through the *sectarian* renunciation of social joys and rejection of aesthetic recreation.

His teaching on *prayer* (the final element in the Christian's lifestyle) is well known, controversial, and, in the opinion of certain unsympathetic commentators, the key to understanding his defective teaching on Christian existence. For generations the impression has been widespread that Ritschl attempted *to reduce all prayer to thanksgiving*, and an unbiased re-reading of his texts makes it hard to contradict this. He is extremely critical of petitionary prayer and, to be sure, there is value in what he has to say in the first instance of the tendency to identify Christian prayer with petition. Justifiably, he deplores prayers which 'call upon God to vindicate our rights and slay our foes', or are directed 'to every conceivable blessing, such as trouble the minds of the heathen'.[33] He points to Pauline statements like Philippians 4: 6 and 1 Thessalonians 5: 16–18 in order to reach the conclusion that

> for the Christian Church *thanksgiving as an acknowledgement of God stands higher than petition* . . . (and) is not one species of prayer alongside of petition, but rather the general form of prayer, while petition is merely a modification of thanksgiving to God.[34]

There follows what has been called the ruthless and exhaustive reduction of *all prayer* to thanksgiving, when he attempts to formulate a 'rule of prayer' for Christianity. Such a rule enjoins us that

> in our joyful assurance of peace with God arising from recon-ciliation, we should give thanks to God *in every case and under*

all circumstances, and only ask something when thanking Him at the same time.[35]

The crucially revealing phrase here is 'in every case and under all circumstances' – God should be praised *whatever is the case, no matter what happens*, in the social and natural orders. Hence the dogmatic importance of the saying in 1 John 5: 14, 15, 'That God hears if we pray according to His will, so that we immediately experience the fulfilment of our prayer'. But, since we might possibly petition for blessings contrary to the divine will, we ought only to petition in the perfect readiness to rest our soul in the expressed contrary will of God. If so, we see that 'prayer is the expression of humility and patience, and the means of confirming oneself in those virtues'.[36] This structure of prayer 'denotes that transformation of prayer back into *the voiceless feeling of humility and patience*'. It is noteworthy that a double reduction is being effected here: first, all prayer is reduced to thanksgiving; second, thanksgiving is further reduced to the adoption and cultivation of *two existential attitudes to life* (humility and patience). This is defined in the *Unterricht* with formal precision:

> Prayer, whether as thanksgiving or as petition, is the conscious and intentional exercise both of faith in God's providence and of humility. It is also, as thanksgiving, the proof of patience and, as petition, the means of gaining or strengthening patience.[37]

It is precisely at this point that Ritschl's teaching has evoked the sharpest of criticism, consisting of the view that, despite his disclaimers to the contrary, and his indisputable use of the most traditional language of Christian spirituality, his real meaning really tends in the direction of some kind of *stoicism*. Predictably, the incisive Orr was troubled by all of this,[38] and seized upon Ritschl's celebrated dictum, 'that all things, evil included, are working for the believer's good'. He warns us to beware of Ritschl's real meaning; we must not be misled into thinking that the world proceeds otherwise than according to ordinary natural laws, or that providence can 'shape events' to meet the specific need of individuals, especially in response to their prayers. Orr directs our attention sharply to Ritschl's famous statement, already noted, that 'the supremacy of the believer over the world is ideal, not empirical'. If this means anything, it does *not* mean that God providentially adopts circumstances to his case, but rather, from the man-ward side, the believer, in exercising faith, by some 'spiritual alchemy' is enabled to use even the evils of the world to good account, to use them as means for spiritual ends, or for a proof of his independence of the world. Strong evidence for this line of thought exists in Ritschl's warning that we *cannot* 'by our prayers and counsels, exercise *an influence on* the Divine dispensations'.[39] Orr's conclusion is therefore that Ritschl's complete doctrine of providence can be exhaustively reduced to the proposition that 'the world is constituted for the ends of the spiritual life, and, with humility and patience, may be used by us for these ends'. If so, there is some ground for the classic, if harsh, judgement of Leonhard Stählin:

> If providence neither reaches out beyond the actual course of things, nor can intervene therein, it has *no other content than that very course itself*: so that when a man trusts in providence, he has no more guarantee for his personal security than when he trusts to the actual existent order of things.[40]

Even the generally sympathetic Garvie was troubled by Ritschl's doctrine. It was one of the great merits of Garvie's work on Ritschl that he drew the attention of the theological profession to the broad and deep influence on Ritschl's entire system of the latter's 'speculative construction of the idea of the eternity of God', which we discussed in Chapter II. While Garvie finds the origins of Ritschl's reduction of all prayer to thanksgiving partly in his antipathy to certain pietistic excesses, and partly in his hostility to prayer conceived as a magical charm worked by man on God, he insists that it is also rooted in Ritschl's understanding of God's eternity not only as adherence to his promise, but also *fixity in his method of fulfilment*, which results in a limitation and impoverishment of God's fatherly providence, which comes to mean, in Ritschl's system, little more than *acceptance of whatever God may choose to send us*. Human desires and aspirations, expressed in prayer, are quite ruled out of court by a grotesquely heavy emphasis on submission to the divine will, which completely obliterates any inkling of a certain legitimate liberty and independence *coram deo*.[41] It is instructive to be reminded that it was precisely at this point that Herrmann, the greatest of Ritschl's disciples, broke with the teaching of the master. The point is so important that we ought to ponder Herrmann's actual words from *The Communion of the Christian with God*.[42] He argues that in Christian prayer there should be united two essential elements in the spiritual life: first, the 'heart-felt desire to receive special help from God' (virtually excluded by Ritschl), and, second, 'the humble (i.e., joyful) submission to God's will'. He comments:

> It is fruitless to try to bring about this union by merely saying to a soul that it may indeed ask God for a definite gift, but it must also be always ready to find the gift denied. If we make such an attempt we should either make the prayer heartless, or we should pretend a resignation that was utter hypocrisy. On the other hand, in the prayer of faith this union follows of itself; for faith does not see in God an indefinite power that holds both good and ill fortune in its hand, and which may perhaps be influenced by men's stormy asking. Our faith sets us rather before a God whose help is certain.

Were we to follow, as Christians, the kind of prayerful ideal set before us by Ritschl, and divest ourselves of all petitionary activity before God, we would, in Herrmann's words, 'imagine a God who has a kind of love for the human ideal, but has no sympathy for our needs'. We conclude then that Ritschl's account of prayer is not merely defective but revealingly so, that in the last analysis he was working with a highly speculative notion of a timelessly 'eternal' God, who could hardly be conceived of as *intimately involved in*, or as in any material sense *intervening in*, that stream of mundane events in which the believer finds himself. Accordingly, it is hard totally to withhold sympathy from those who have judged that his teaching on prayer does corroborate somewhat the Barthian judgement that for Ritschl the 'Christian life' at its heart involves an *anthropozentrische Lebensphilosophie* (anthropocentric philosophy of life), whereby the Christian, by dwelling on the 'thought of God', or by intramentally entertaining the notion of his reconciliation with God, is enabled (in his own words) to 'take the sting from suffering', depriving it of its power to divert him from realizing his ideal being. Indeed, at one point in his texts he comes within a hairsbreadth of teaching that this is so:

> This is the distinctive test of reconciliation with God, that one also becomes reconciled with the course of events that God brings to us, *no matter how hard* a blow these events deal us.[43]

Finally, it is illuminating to put to Ritschl's position a criticism derived from the falsification controversy of post-war philosophical theology. To Ritschl's all-important claims on behalf of faith in providence, patience, humility and prayer, we could put a question derived from Anthony Flew's analysis of theistic assertions:[44] what would have to occur or to have occurred in the world to undermine faith in providence, to erode away patience and humility, and to make redundant that practice of prayer whose object is to consolidate and increase all three? It seems that Ritschl's answer would necessarily be that no conceivable worldly event or state of affairs could do these things. In that case, his position would be vulnerable to Flew's charge that since faith in God is contradicted *by nothing at all* in the stream of worldly events, it does not make *any material assertion whatever about worldly reality*. (It does seem, though, that a position like Herrmann's would not be so vulnerable.) If so, we can see plainly why the perceptive Orr seized upon Ritschl's revealing dictum that 'the supremacy of the believer over the world is ideal, not empirical', and why the hostile Stählin refused to draw any distinction, on Ritschl's own grounds, between 'trusting in providence' and 'trusting to the actual existent order of things'!

We continue by focusing attention on that aspect of Ritschl's teaching on the Christian's lifestyle which has, probably, evoked the most hostility and, more than any other, furnished his opponents with material for the construction of a damaging stereotype – namely, the 'civil vocation' of the Christian. To be fair to him, there can be no doubt that the hostile barrage directed against his unfortunate, latter-day identification of 'Christian existence' with 'life in our civic vocation' sadly diverted attention away from his suggestive and valuable teaching about the *ethical vocation* demanded of every Christian. Earlier, we expounded his view that in Christianity a qualitative perfection was attainable by all, in which each human life becomes an

integrated and coherent whole, determined partly in response to
a given set of particular conditions of life, and linked teleologically to the Kingdom of God. Such a viewpoint is crystallized
in his assertion that each and every one of us has, if we can find
it, an 'ethical vocation'. Such views, welcomed without qualification generations ago by unbiased interpreters like Garvie[45] and
Mozley,[46] significantly anticipated the insights of modern
Christian personalism and existentialism. And those familiar with
certain strands in modern Catholic theology will clearly perceive
parallels with Catholic thought's stress on the 'lay apostolate',
with its insistence that each Christian has in the world, according
to his gifts and capabilities, and in the light of his historical
situation, a delimited and definite task to fulfil, a concrete
mission to accomplish before God. In Hefner's luminous phrase,
Ritschl *meant* to emphasize the significance of Christianity for
the concrete realities of human existence. It would be a pity if his
stress on civil vocation were to obscure and divert attention away
from all of this. But criticisms of his position cannot be indefinitely
postponed, and we must now examine his excessively close
identification of the Christian life with activity in a civil vocation.
In all fairness, it ought to be recorded that he himself effected this
identification because he *believed* it to be necessarily involved in
the message of the Lutheran Reformation, and so introduced his
discussion with a reference to the teaching of the Augsburg
Confession.[47] When he insisted on the obligation laid on each of
us to work out our salvation in our *place of work*, he *sincerely
believed* that he was but maintaining the Reformers' repudiation
of the medieval depreciation of the married state, and the
monastic teaching that full perfection is attainable only through
the abandonment of worldly vocation and trade, in favour of life
in the cloister. Then again, he *believed* sincerely that the identification was implied by his vision of the Kingdom of God, as that
dimension within which Christ's disciples were bringing to bear a
transforming influence upon *every* department and dimension of
the State, education, trade, commerce, public service and international relations:

> Our special calling, in fact, is seen to be the field of moral action
> to which we are summoned, because we appropriate it as sub-

ordinate to the universal final end of the good, or as an integral part of the Kingdom of God.[48]

In other words, Ritschl was terrified of the social consequences of otherworldly quietism and monasticism in an age which was harshly critical of the ethical pretensions of Christianity, and the operation of these motives should be recognized in that identification for which calumny has been brought upon his head. These qualifications having been made, we attend to his attempt to confine Christian existence to the area of one's calling:

Moral action in our calling is, therefore, the form in which our life-work as a totality is produced as our contribution to the Kingdom of God, and in which, at the same time, the ideal of spiritual personality as a whole in its own order is reached.[49]

In the performance of our vocation

we produce our personal contribution to the common weal of the Kingdom of God.

There follows the sentence in which he did not hesitate to draw the grimly logical conclusion from all of this, which has been much quoted and has given much offence:

Accordingly, fidelity to one's vocation is at the same time following the example of Christ.

With astounding honesty, he goes on to argue that vocational fidelity (equated with following Christ's example), 'does not exclude personal interest in its success or the acquiring of property' (!), although he adds hastily that attention to the vocation's communal ends prevents these latter motives from serving sheer selfishness. As a disciple of Luther, Ritschl was naturally concerned with the believer's redemption from a neurotic and destructive fear that his nonfulfilment of an infinite moral law meant for him wretched imperfection of life and therefore a separation from blessedness. Therefore, he writes, typically:

The conception of moral perfection in the Christian life ought on no account to be associated with the idea of a fruitless search for actual sinlessness of conduct in all the details of life.[50]

Rather, and following Christ's example, he ought to hit upon a *Lebenswerk*, a rounded, internally interconnected and coherent 'whole', to which Ritschl applies the title *Beruf* (vocation, calling), co-extensive with his civil 'vocation'. And the Christian thus really and truly fulfils the moral law in this special vocation (or, as he is fond of putting it, he fulfils 'the universal in the particular'):

> Each individual acts morally when he fulfils the universal law in his special vocation, or in that combination of vocations which he is able to unite in his conduct of life.[51]

Thus, 'goodness of life' is conditioned by and concentrated into one's calling, and this in itself delivers one from that neurotic and destructive fear which is an ingredient of many alternative systems of Christian ethics:

> The fact that good action is conditioned by one's calling invalidates the *apparent* obligation we are under at each moment of time to do good action in every possible direction.

But is Ritschl here implying that faithful discharge of vocational responsibilities is completely and exhaustively, in Christian terms, the fulfilment of all righteousness? (We recall that Brunner, as noted earlier, accused him of *substituting* the idea of *Beruf* for the Kantian central conception of *Law*.) Not quite, although at points he comes perilously close to doing so. For example, at one point he declares, dangerously, that his doctrine of vocation

> excludes moral necessity to expend good action on such ends as do not fit into the individual vocation.

And the quite unprecedented importance he attaches to vocational fidelity and performance comes out in the following celebrated statement from the *Unterricht*:

> Since it is in his own particular ethical vocation that each one is to work at the common task of the Kingdom of God and fulfil the universal moral law, *most of the moral duties are thereby determined in advance*. Thus the duties of one's vocation are the ordinary duties of love.[52]

Nevertheless, he shrinks from making an exhaustive identification in so far as he concedes that there are also 'extraordinary duties of love', which he describes in this way:

> Such good action, however, as is incumbent, but is not directly determined thus (i.e. by our vocation), may be viewed as obligatory, on condition that by a judgment of duty *it can be construed analogously to our vocation*, that is, provided that after consideration of all the circumstances one is called to discharge it *as an extraordinary duty of love*.

But talk of such extraordinary duties 'analogous to our vocation or those of our calling' is singularly difficult to understand. One clue to its meaning is his desire to liberate Christians from the intolerable obligation to obey a moral law limitless in scope, and to perform a series of numerically unlimited 'good works', an obligation quite incompatible with the *consciousness* of realizing Christian perfection. Another is his unshakable view of the Kingdom as God's and man's supreme end, which convinced him that only action directed towards that end merits the title of Christian action, so that the moral law, from the standpoint of the Christian life, cannot be any form of *codification*. Rather, the moral law

> as the system of those dispensations, intentions, and actions which follow necessarily from the *all-embracing end of the Kingdom of God* and from the subjective motive of universal love, *cannot be codified* so as to decide, in each possible case of morally good action, that such action is necessary.[53]

Christianity therefore necessarily needs the notion of a moral 'judgement', guided by particular circumstances, and conditioned by the special virtues of conscientiousness, wisdom and circumspection.[54] Christian morality, properly speaking, is directed more to the formation of a proper moral *disposition* than to the multiplication of 'good works'. It follows that in a material sense the Christian *determines* for himself the moral law:

> Out of the moral disposition which in the field of a special vocation takes shape in action for the highest end, we have to evolve those principles by which we regulate particular groups of moral action, and in harmony therewith, form particular

judgements of duty affirming that it is necessary in a given case to realise the final end of the good. Under these circumstances and in this form the individual, *out of his freedom, produces the moral law, or lives in the life of freedom.*[55]

In other words, *our vocation is a moral academy in which our moral training is received and in which our moral sensibilities are nurtured and developed.* For example, in a note to the text of the *Unterricht* he explains that it is in vocational activity that *conscientiousness* in general is conceived and developed:

> Because the duty of one's vocation is the regular and ordinary form of the duty of love, its fulfilment is rightfully recognized as a part of Christian perfection. For the determination of the duties belonging to one's vocation, the virtue of conscientiousness which corresponds to the vocation is, in the formula of the authoritarian conscience, the ordinarily sufficient subjective standard. Hence conscientiousness seems to extend also to the judgement as to whether one is called to *the performance of certain extraordinary duties of love.*[56]

It is, moreover, in his vocation that the Christian has experience of deciding which ends tend towards the final end of the Kingdom of God, which he as an individual is 'called' to pursue above all others, thus enabling him to posit analogous ends for moral striving in extravocational areas. Another factor determining Ritschl's meaning is his repudiation of the view that perfection is attainable in *solitude*, whether that of monasticism or of sectarian quietism. Only 'in moral *relations* can the believer . . . become a whole in his own right', he writes, 'for the ethical development of the individual will is utterly inconceivable apart from social interaction *with other persons.*'[57] Work is a social interpersonal context within which patience under affliction is developed.[58] Finally, vocational labour establishes man's lordship over nature in order to maintain and serve the *physical* aspect of human existence.[59] In the Christian's wholehearted devotion to vocational activity there is involved a special 'feeling of self', deriving from release from the harsh demands of an unfulfillable, statutory moral law and from inner freedom from the world, leading to a feeling of blessedness in the knowledge that through his activity he is incorporated into the Kingdom of God.

But even the most fair-minded of Ritschl's interpreters cannot ignore the damning common factor of all the stereotypes – *his identification of Christian destiny with vocational fidelity and activity*, which evoked formidable and by no means unjustified hostility, which eventually assisted materially in the rather contemptuous dismissal of his theology. Clearly, most of the criticisms laid against his position here cluster around or are derived from one overarching charge: namely, that *he apparently did not perceive the extent to which the social, economic and vocational structure of the West was determined by secular, impersonal and even ungodly forces and factors, an insight which gathered tremendous momentum throughout his own nineteenth century.* That he did not see this, it is alleged, is a sign of quite incredible insensitivity. To judge by his published works, he apparently possessed no inkling whatever of the kind of nineteenth-century reflections and discussions eventually to be published in 1904–5 in Max Weber's *Die protestantische Ethik und der Geist des Kapitalismus*,[60] to a brief consideration of which we now turn. Weber pointed out that in the *milieu* of modern Protestantism, the German term *Beruf* and the English term *Calling* unmistakably suggest the notion of 'a task set by God', in the sense of 'a life-task, a definite field in which to work'.[61] After indulging in a philological analysis of the terms,[62] he concluded that like the meaning of the word, the idea is new, *a product of the Reformation.*[63] This is not to deny that both the Middle Ages and late Hellenistic antiquity knew something of the positive value of routine worldly activity. Yet one thing was unquestionably new, the valuation of the fulfilment of duty in worldly affairs as the *highest* form which moral activity could assume. In Weber's judgement, one central dogma of all the Protestant denominations is that the sole way of living acceptably *coram deo* is not to surpass worldly morality in monastic asceticism, but exclusively through the fulfilment of the obligations imposed upon the individual by his position in the world, by his *calling*. So far as Luther's own doctrine was concerned, this was rooted in anti-Catholic, antimonastic polemic,[64] which led him to contrast most sharply the monk's 'selfish withdrawal from temporal obligations' with the Christian's labour in a calling as the outward expression of brotherly love. Weber only has contempt for

Luther's justification of this viewpoint – namely, that 'the division of labour forces every individual to work for others' – which forms a grotesquely naïve contrast to George Adam Smith's economic realism:

> It is not from the benevolence of the butcher, the brewer, or the baker that we expect our dinner, but from their regard to their own interest. We address ourselves, not to their humanity, but to their self-love; and never talk to them of our own necessities, but of their advantages.[65]

It stands also in the sharpest contrast to the viewpoint of a theologian like Pascal, who in certain moods could only understand worldly activity in terms of vanity or low cunning! At any rate, one effect of the emergence of the European Protestant Churches was that, in comparison with the viewpoint of Catholicism, the moral worth and the religious sanction of organized worldly labour in a *Beruf* was hugely increased.[66] Luther, indeed, claimed biblical authority for his concept of the calling, and Weber concedes that the overall tendency of the Old Testament was that of *traditionalism*, expressed in the phrase, 'Everyone should abide by his living and let the godless run after gain.' Fundamental for understanding civic vocations in the New Testament is *primitive eschatology* leading to *social traditionalism*: since the Second Coming of the Lord was imminently looked for, there was no alternative for anyone but to abide in the station and worldly vocation in which he had been found by the call of the Lord, and labour as before; thus, he would not be a burden to the brethren as the object of charity, and it would only be for a little while.[67] Such scriptural positions were, in Weber's view, crucial for Luther's final standpoint on worldly callings. Luther was already a *traditionalist* before 1517, and in his development from 1518 to 1530 became even more so, because of two crucial historical factors – his bitter conflict with radical, revolutionary fanatics and iconoclasts (like Thomas Münzer), and the *Bauernkrieg* of 1524–6. His nasty experiences here, says Weber, meant that for him the objective historical order of things in which the individual has been placed by God becomes for Luther more and more *a direct manifestation of the divine will*.[68] His ongoing reflections on the theology of providence and predestination hardened his conservatism, which resulted in his identifying absolute obedience to God's will with absolute acceptance of the *status quo*. His final traditionalistic socio-economic conservatism insisted that the individual should abide once for all in the station and calling in which *God had placed him*, and should restrain his worldly activity within the limits imposed by his established station in life. And the tendency in the later Luther to define the True Church in terms of pure, crystallized doctrine was, in Weber's judgement, sufficient to impede radically new developments in the area of social ethics. Weber indicates a two-sidedness in Luther's doctrine of the calling: first, the calling is something which man *just has to* accept as a divine ordinance; second, work in the calling is *the* task set by God to the individual. Of the two aspects, primitive, orthodox Lutheranism stressed the former at the expense of the latter. In fairness to Ritschl, he clearly tried to develop the positive content of the latter while saying little explicitly about the former (but of course, the latter presupposes the former).

Clearly there is truth in Weber's thesis, as there is also scope for disagreement with him by Reformation historians, economic historians, systematic theologians, and the like. But that is here strictly speaking beside the point. For what is very much to the point is the total absence of evidence in Ritschl that *he was aware of contemporary reflections on Reformation social theory and ethics* in the second half of the nineteenth century, and his naïve and insensitive identification of Christian existence with non-optional vocational activity as if the text of the Augsburg Confession were timelessly infallible. There are, in Weber, two passages[69] devoted to philological and historical analysis of the term *Beruf* in the biblical and Indo-European languages, and in the history of religion, in the light of ascertaining if the concept will bear the doctrinal weight which Lutherans wish to place upon it. But in Ritschl we find no such thing. There is not a shred of evidence that he was aware of Matthias Schneckenburger's important 1855 work, *Vergleichende Darstellung der lutherischen und reformierten Lehrbegriffe*,[70] or of Gustav Schmoller's slightly later 'Geschichte der Nationalökonomischen Ansichten in Deutschland während der Reformationszeit',[71] both of which would, minimally, have made him distinctly nervous of identifying Christian existence with naturally determined vocations in their sixteenth-century Lutheran sense! (Weber also significantly points out that the considerable literature generated by the celebration of Luther's four hundredth anniversary in 1883 – to which Ritschl, as we shall see below, made a distinguished contribution[72] – 'made no definite contribution to this particular problem' of the *Beruf*.[73]) Weber's classic is famous for having demonstrated a close connection between, on the one hand, the Protestant desire for assurance of salvation, and, on the other, the empirical satisfaction of this in success in trade, business and vocation, which enabled him to insist that certain types of Protestant ethic must be regarded as *one* of the causes of modern capitalism. His analysis is not irrelevant to latter-day Lutheran developments: when Ritschl states, as noted earlier, that vocational vigour (equated with following Christ's example) 'does not exclude personal interest in its success or the acquiring of property', he comes dangerously and insensitively close to affirming that vocational success, and the personal affluence derived therefrom, constitute the principal indicators of reconciliation with God through Christ. Such insensitivity was to be, in the long term, very expensive from the point of view of his reputation! It permitted Barth to accuse Ritschl of teaching that the Kingdom of God can only be striven for within *naturally determined* communities and not outside them, and Brunner to find him guilty of teaching the *divine legitimization of the movement of history* as such. In the view of them both, this legitimization had calamitous consequences for both theology and Church, which became not merely insensitive but even hostile to radical developments in social ethics involving grave criticism of the economic and social patterns in the West. Lecturing in 1957 on nineteenth-century Protestant theology, Barth criticized it thus:

> How confused was the position of the evangelical Church in regard to changing world views! How long did it take the Church to become concerned about social questions, to take socialism seriously, and with how much spiritual dilettantism was this finally done! How naively did the Church subscribe

to political conservatism in the first half of the century and in the second half to the preservation of the liberal bourgeoisie, the growing nationalism and militarism![74]

All of which enables us to deal with the universally quoted pejorative label applied to Ritschl, 'bourgeois'. Not only did this denote, as Tillich frequently observed, that vigorous, independent, anti-authoritarian, disciplined, world-dominating *type* of personality attracted by Ritschl's theology, but also that social and economic *class* which could have 'vocations', while the working-class proletariat only had 'jobs'. For it required financial independence from the world, and concomitant educational opportunity and choice, to be able to hear and respond to a 'call' towards a 'lifework'. A recent writer, having explained that in the New Testament the word *KLESIS* (calling, vocation) always refers to God's invitation to man to the life of faith within the *EKKLESIA*, points out that in the period of secularization beginning after the Reformation, the idea of vocation *was itself secularized*, so that today people speak readily about someone having a vocation to be a schoolmaster or doctor – though hardly a dustman or a bus-conductor – *without any reference to the call of God in Christ*.[75] Not only did Ritschl not apparently see also that it was only members of the bourgeoisie who could *switch vocations* (with academics becoming high civil servants, lawyers members of the legislature, and theologians diocesan bishops, and vice versa), but he was apparently unaware of that nineteenth-century industrial experience which gave rise to world-wide clamour for far-reaching industrial and economic reform – namely, the experience of daily labour as a mechanical, boring, frustrating and dehumanizing activity, *the context of man's alienation not merely from the world but from his true, genuine destiny.*

This clamour, later to be theoretically articulated by Marx and Engels, can be described as fundamentally incompatible with Ritschl's insistence that man's ultimate standing *coram deo 'depends on* the goodness and the rounded completeness of the life-work he achieves in his moral vocation'. It is no wonder then that Barth rejected Ritschl's *entire reinterpretation of Christianity*, because of the latter's affirmation that where there is no reconciliation in the sense of the *Behauptung des Lebensideals* (realiza-

tion of life's ideal) through loyalty to and activity in one's profession, *there is no justification either!*[76] Not that he was any dyed-
in-the-wool conservative, as his courageous, polemical opposition
to his theological age demonstrates. Hefner has demonstrated
how Ritschl entertained a vision of a new theology to satisfy the
needs of his age, and to a large extent realized this vision in his
work; but Hefner concedes that this did not include a rejection
of much tradition, nor much social and political change.[77] He
judges that Ritschl's call for obedience within society's vocations
had a conservative thrust, and that nowhere does he hint that
nineteenth-century vocational structure might be shattered by
changes in society and replaced by something fundamentally
different or better. While he was not uncritical of his own society
and did not divinize it, Hefner concedes that he apparently had
no inkling of any alternative societal form in which God's Kingdom might be served. Hefner argues that it is ironic that, despite
Ritschl's attempt to marry religion and ethics, and his vision of
the Kingdom penetrating and transforming the world, all of these
were eventually to be undercut by a stiff commitment to his contemporary vocational structure. In an age when there were strong
pleas for democracy and social justice, and when conditions
among the working-class population were miserable, Ritschl's
stress on the high religious possibilities of vocational obedience
must have seemed ironic to those outside the middle and upper
classes! Hefner's (reluctant) conclusion is that in spite of Ritschl's
impressive theological achievement, he was almost totally captive
to his own élitist social class, and that his awareness of the tran-
sience of contemporary metaphysics was not matched by a sense
of the impermanence of societal forms.[78] And if we try to check
Hefner's conclusions against Ritschl's texts, we find that the
former is all too right. For example, we find Ritschl affirming that

> the right ethical disposition (i.e., of the Christian) includes
> necessarily a disposition to uphold the law, and in the com-
> munity of laws we customarily presuppose such a disposition
> on the part of every individual.[79]

And despite the immense and important controversy that had
raged in post-Reformation Europe over the correct interpretation
of Romans 13: 1–7, he, as though the controversy had never

taken place, unswervingly heads for the traditionalist and conservative position:

> The state is acknowledged as God's ordering, and obedience to juridical authority is prescribed as a religious duty.[80]

We must now deal with a criticism which derives not so much from social and political ethics as from philosophical ethics. It was argued in Chapter II that Ritschl is correctly interpreted as a theologian who strove to make Christianity independent of natural theology. It was the philosophically acute Orr who brilliantly perceived a similar striving in the area of *natural ethics*.[81] Orr justifiably complains that Ritschl's doctrine of the Kingdom, the supreme ethical motive of Christians, is somewhat *abstract* and *skeletal*: it requires to be fleshed out, to be given material significance, from the complex of duties in *ordinary* Christian morality. To make the same point another way, Ritschl's rather abstract ethical principle, 'Love your neighbour, and faithfully discharge the duties of your station', needs to be given positive content from our knowledge of *ordinary* moral duties and relations, grounded in *nature* and the *ordinary* moral consciousness, so that 'doing God's will on earth' may be pictured concretely. Grace, regardless of Ritschl's aversion to the idea, presupposes nature (as the second creation presupposes the first), and no adequate account may be given of God's end for man unless man's relations, duties and responsibilities, rooted in man's consciousness as a moral creature, are taken into account. The Kingdom of God, even as a religious conception, has a natural background, and cannot properly be elucidated apart from the help of a philosophical analysis of man's nature and powers, undertaken from a Christian standpoint. Just as we argued in Chapter II[82] that Ritschl, by abandoning the maxim that 'grace presupposes nature', cannot be acquitted of the charge of bequeathing to the twentieth century that disastrous divorce of faith from reason which has bedevilled much modern theology, so he cannot but be regarded as a pioneer of a 'Christian ethics' wishing to declare its independence from natural or philosophical ethics, or an ethics of grace wishing to be free of an ethics of nature. Yet from this declaration many of his problems flow. On the basis of natural ethical reflection there normally occurs a discrimination between *types* of vocation: the natural, serious-thinking man normally draws a distinction between the 'vocation' of the nurse and that of gambling hall proprietors, between that of social workers and that of concentration camp guards. These extreme examples establish a point. If we wish to establish criteria enabling us to draw such distinctions, we shall not derive an iota of assistance from the writings of Ritschl, for he plainly teaches that *naturally-given* vocational roles prescribe the great bulk of our duties in advance, so that *naturally-allocated* vocational practice, principle and precept overflow into our natural, non-vocational existence, informing and cultivating it, giving it content and direction. Further pursuit of this line of thought would take us far afield into a complex and polemical region of such importance that we are obliged to say at least a few words about it here: namely, *the relation of German thought to the notion of Natural Law*.[83] It was Ernst Troeltsch who convincingly expounded the view that if we really want to understand Western society and its history, we ought to realize that the difference between 'Western' thinking, characteristic of Britain, America and France on the one hand, and German and Swiss thinking on the other, is that the former accepts and the latter rejects the notion of Natural Law. It is beyond our scope here to enquire about the truth or falsity of Troeltsch's theory, although it may be remarked in passing that many intimately familiar with German history and literature tend towards a qualified acceptance of it, not least because of its great explanatory potential. But if Troeltsch's theory were true, certain interesting things would follow. We would be enabled to understand, for instance, why Ritschl, an eminent representative of German thought, found himself unable to identify and describe human duties on the basis of Orr's 'natural philosophical analysis of man's nature and powers, as springing from man's rational endowment and powers' (i.e., *Natural Law*), and was obliged to do so on the basis of (in Troeltsch's terms) some 'dogma' or other. Self-evidently, the 'dogma' in question is the teaching of Luther and the Confession of Augsburg that the Christian forms his lifestyle within that vocation in which, by God's providential ordinance, he finds himself. This in turn illumines the way in which the nineteenth-century German bourgeoisie highly evaluated their vocations. Not only was the content of their lives determined by their vocational commitment, but the significance of their individual lives stemmed from their positions within a vast hierarchical vocational superstructure. If so, it is hard to shout down those who have wished to reach the harsh judgement that in their doctrine of vocation, theologians of Ritschl's ilk were not so much interpreting the New Testament for modernity, as expounding a Lutheran dogma in the light of German non-acceptance of Natural Law. The long-term repercussions of nineteenth-century German vocational theory are deeply disturbing. As one modern interpreter of Troeltsch's theory, anything but unsympathetic to German culture, described it succinctly:

> In Hitler's Germany, the ordinary 'decent' individual who did what his society expected of him found himself in the German army; the doctrinaire devotee of Natural Law found himself in a concentration camp.[84]

If so, there may, indeed, be something in the charge that Ritschl helped to fashion a *Kulturprotestantismus* which encouraged adherence to the dictum, 'My country, right or wrong'![85]

Before closing this chapter, it is only fair to deal swiftly with three related points, if only to leave the reader with a broader perspective within which Ritschl's contribution may be justly evaluated – the relationship between Christianity and vocation, Ritschl as a thinker singularly sensitive to the criticisms of ethical rationalism, and his view of the nature and establishment of the Kingdom of God. On the subject of vocation, now that the heyday of neo-orthodox anti-Ritschl hostility is past, we can survey the subject more dispassionately, and perceive that the Reformation's stress on the Christian significance of secular work as God's service, in Van Harvey's words, *introduced a dynamic factor into Western society*.[86] In modern times the Lutheran view (reinterpreted and reaffirmed by Ritschl) met sharp opposition in Marx's argument that labour in capitalistic theory was regarded by the employer as simply an expendable means of production, a viewpoint which evoked such different responses as Christian Socialism in Europe, the American Social Gospel movement, and the social writings of several popes. Subsequently, says Harvey, theologians and moralists have devoted an extraordinary amount of effort to interpreting vocation from a Christian standpoint in their writings on the State, the rights and duties of labour and management, marriage, war, and related issues. It can therefore be argued that Ritschl's contribution constitutes a significant episode in an ongoing debate going back to the Reformation and beyond, even if this is judged as having fermented discussion partly or mainly through disagreement. It is a debate which has influenced Roman Catholic theology, particularly, and predictably, in its German forms. Karl Rahner, for example, speaks of the Christian's vocation in terms of the recognition by an individual that a specific career or *Lebensmode* (mode of life) corresponds to God's will for him and is the *Lebenswerk* within which he can attain to his eternal salvation, even if the career is one that is disagreeable, since one may have a duty to do what one finds difficult.[87] While arguing, as a Catholic, that the term *Beruf* refers primarily to a call to the priesthood or religious life, he nevertheless maintains that the further theological exploration of vocation blends into that of the cognition of *particular* obligations, distinct from that of *general* ethical norms, that only limit the field of what is right without being able to define it, which takes us into the problem of *individual* or *existential* ethics. It is remarkable that Rahner's terminology, 'particular obligations' as contrasted with 'general norms', parallels Ritschl's distinction between the 'universal moral law' and 'special ethical vocation' (or the 'rounded wholeness of a person's life's work'). For Christian theology, an existential ethics is not merely necessary but unavoidable, since a person's moral behaviour is by no means but an 'instance' of a general, essential moral norm, but the 'realization' (*Behauptung*) of himself in his individuality, and the necessity for the systematic investigation of this *must* issue in an existential ethics.[88] The way in which a man must fully realize himself (*sich behaupten*) is intimated to himself alone and is not adequately covered by general norms, so that so-called existential ethics necessarily complements essential ethics (although we must avoid the error of 'situation ethics', which substitutes existential for essential ethics). In this context, 'situation' refers to that historical point created by the individual, by his *unique* personality and personal relationships, and the kind of reflection about *general ethical norms* of which he is capable, from which his concrete moral behaviour flows. Given the fulfilment of these conditions, within and behind the 'situation' of the individual, *a concrete call of God is legitimately presented to the individual*. This short section, expounding Rahner on vocation, has been included for two important reasons. First, the *similarities* in the discussions of Ritschl and Rahner are sufficient to show that the former's work on vocation is neither hopelessly dated nor impossibly tied to the preconceptions and social ideals of the late nineteenth century. Second, the *dissimilarities* between the two may be even more significant: they consist of Rahner's careful and proper emphasis on 'general norms', 'essential ethics', and the like, an emphasis on Natural Law, which as Orr rightly pointed out, *was completely lacking in Ritschl's account*. It highlights once more the tragic extent to which he erred in going on to identify, without proper qualification, the uniquely personal, situational, existential, ethical lifestyle of the individual with that individual's civic vocation as determined by his birth within a social or economic group. It was an identification that he did not need to make, and one which overshadowed and obscured the contribution he *meant* to make. In terms of theological reputation and influence, it was to be an expensive mistake.

Second, a word must now be said about a topic much alluded to in preceding pages, about Ritschl as a thinker extraordinarily sensitive, like many of his religious contemporaries, to the attacks of *ethical rationalism*. Such rationalism was rooted in that criticism of religion carried out during the period of the European Enlightenment. It is a remarkable fact that most educated people, when they hear of the Enlightenment 'criticism of religion', tend to confine this to those logical epistemological and conceptual critiques of theism composed by Hume and Kant, or the kind of argument to be found in Hume's essay on miracles. This is to overlook what Claude Welch calls 'the deep and pervasive moralism' of the Enlightenment's rationalism.[89] This rationalism had deeper roots in post-Reformation European history, and clearly it would be difficult to explain its genesis apart from two historical factors – the European Reformation itself and the Thirty Years' War of 1618–48. For the Reformation, which evoked the Counter-Reformation, apart from presiding over the occurrence of European disunity, generated much *odium theologicum at ecclesiasticum*, fanaticism, intolerance and persecution; the Thirty Years' War, following on the heels of the Reformation, with its bloodshed and fratricide, was altogether too much for seventeenth-century man, bringing about what Arnold Toynbee has called the 'Seventeenth-century Revulsion from Religious Fanaticism' and the 'Seventeenth-century Reaction in the West Against Religious Intolerance'.[90] Accordingly, the aim of the eighteenth century was a non-ecclesiastical Natural Religion which abhorred all appeal to passion, sentiment and fanaticism in religious matters. Inherent in Enlightenment ethical rationalism was the vigorous complaint that, *despite the high ethical tone and the huge moral claims of Christianity, empirical Western religion had lamentably failed to fulfil these claims.* Indeed, David Hume could go much further; commenting on the *practical* motives behind Hume's sceptical onslaught upon religion, Norman Kemp Smith tells us that in Hume's view religion had in the main a malign influence, was preposterous in any form, irrational and superstitious, encouraging man to live an artificial life, and to indulge in, above all else, fanaticism.[91] It is only against the background of such rationalism that we can appreciate Kant's morally-based theology, with its conviction that henceforward religion must be not only compatible with moral seriousness, but be itself, in root and branch, *the product of it.* It is of fundamental importance to grasp that the classic German theologians of the nineteenth century *all wrote with extreme sensitivity to such rationalism.* This may be beautifully illustrated from Schleiermacher's *Reden* (1799), where he, addressing himself to the contemporary 'cultured despisers' of religion, gave expression to such sensitivity thus:

> You see how immediately this beautiful modesty, this friendly, attractive forbearance springs from the nature of religion. How unjustly, therefore, do you reproach religion with loving persecution, with being malignant, with overturning society, and making blood flow like water. Blame those who corrupt religion, who flood it with an army of formulas and definitions, and seek to cast it into the fetters of a so-called system.[92]

Noteworthy is Schleiermacher's claim that the inevitable outcome of *genuine* religion is 'beautiful modesty' and 'friendly, attractive forbearance'. In other words, that *authentic* religion may be recognized in its *necessary* realization of certain *personal ethical ideals*, which at once clearly distinguishes it from those falsely pernicious forms of it which are systematically exposed in the *Reden*. Schleiermacher's important claim, that *genuine religion necessarily manifests itself in a realized 'ideal of life'*, formulated in the teeth of harsh criticisms of European ethical rationalists, becomes *normative* for Schleiermacher's successors in the mainstream of nineteenth-century German theology. Of none of them is this truer than of Ritschl. It is arguable that it is his agreement with Schleiermacher's claim, that was hardly questioned at all by his theological contemporaries, that underlies his alleged 'moralism', his attempt to transpose objective dogmas into their subjective behavioural correlates, his claim that Reformed theology had never satisfactorily linked religion and ethics, justification and reconciliation, faith and conduct; his reiterated plea that Christianity, far from being primarily a dogmatic, organizational or ecclesiastical phenomenon (generating *odium theologicum*), is essentially a new lifestyle (*Lebensführung*) or the *Behauptung eines Lebensideals* (achievement of an 'ideal of life'). If this line of argument were plausible, it would make a considerable difference to our assessment of one of the main, if not *the* main criticism of Barth: namely, with Ritschl reconciliation means the realized ideal of human life, that it was this result and it alone in which he was interested, and that morally it consists of activity in one's vocation and in *the development of personal virtue*.[93] What is deeply disturbing are the deductions drawn from this judgement by the Barthian school: if Ritschl and his disciples concentrated upon the achievement of a Christian *Lebensideal* they were *ipso facto* indifferent to God, their theology was a heavily disguised anthropology to be described as anthropocentric rather than theocentric, they spoke about man rather than God and more often than not confused the two, and the rest of it. What is truly astounding in the Barthian critique is the total absence of any sympathetic historical elucidation of those formidable *moral* factors operative in the West to which European thinkers from Kant to Ritschl were highly sensitive, *in the light of the ethical*

claims of the New Testament itself! We ought therefore to be
extremely cautious of conventional, but suspect, hostile talk of the
adherence of post-Enlightenment religious thought to *idealism*, in
so far, as we have seen, such idealism was neither wholly nor
mainly epistemological, but rather *ethical* in character, aimed at
refuting the charge that religious fervour is demonstrably incompatible with the highest possible development of personal ethical
ideals. Two recent commentators, Philip Hefner and David Lotz,
have persuasively argued that Ritschl's thought can only be
properly understood against the background of the late nineteenth-century resurgence of anti-religious and anti-Protestant
polemic.[94] Lotz mentions contemporaries such as Jacob Burckhardt, Paul de Lagarde and Friedrich Nietzsche, as examples of
anti-Protestant polemicists. Noteworthy is Burckhardt's view of
the Reformation as essentially negative, anti-ascetic and undisciplined.[95] His judgement was that the Reformation was an act
of unrestrained destruction perpetrated against everything sanc-
tioned by age and authority.[96] The Reformers themselves were
nothing better than grasping confiscators of church properties
and endowments, the ecclesiastical counterparts of the Spanish
conquistadors. We should not underestimate the influence of such
views for, in Lotz's judgement, Burckhardt is representative of a
climate of opinion in the latter nineteenth century. Ritschl's
academic colleague, Lagarde, directed his attack on the doctrine
of justification by faith which, in his eyes, possessed only polemical
significance, and represented a relapse of Paul into Judaism.[97]
It followed that the main results of the Reformation were
essentially negative – the mindless disunification of Germany and
the philistine relinquishment of religious authority to the secular
German princes. Burckhardt spelled out what he saw as the
antinomian consequences of justification by faith, the Reformation as the faith of all who would like 'not to have to do something any more'; through the sixteenth-century polemic over predestination, justification, good works, and the like, *all of ethics
got out into the high seas.* Lotz demonstrates that Ritschl's reinterpretation of central Reformation motifs is invulnerable to
charges of this kind, due to his heavy stress on the 'Christian's
God-given freedom for loving service to the world in obedience

to his Lord'.[98] His noteworthy attempt to interpret Ritschl's Reformation *Festrede* of 1883 as a point-by-point attempt to refute the kind of polemic produced by Lagarde is impressively persuasive.[99] Lotz's final judgement is that we shall not properly understand Ritschl's thought, unreflectively characterized as 'moralistic', unless we grasp the following aspect of his *Zeitgeist*: to the modern mind the very notion of justification and reconciliation was increasingly anathema, since it presumably threatened personal freedom and seemed to undercut the need for a moral reordering of society.[100] Hefner's line is not dissimilar, stressing Ritschl's version of the Lutheran understanding of justification as teaching that God liberates man to live freely *in* the world, through his vocation, without reliance upon artificial props whether in the form of an ecclesiastically controlled State or a repressive sacralized social order.[101] The Reformation proclamation of Christian freedom committed the Christian to working for the righteousness and justice of society at every level, and valued every worldly occupation and institution in its own right, without demanding that it be 'Christian'. It may well be, argues Hefner, that Ritschl's sensitivity to anti-Protestant propaganda contributed to his unyielding insistence that Christian faith supports vocational obedience to the established order.

Third, and finally, we offer a few comments on Ritschl's view of the nature and mode of establishment of the Kingdom of God, with the preliminary observation that behind this notion also there lies sensitivity to ethical rationalism. Most of the secondary literature on Ritschl indicates his precursors in the history of modern teaching on the Kingdom. Most of it correctly pays some attention to the work of Schleiermacher, but some of it, of which the most notable example is Norman Perrin's *The Kingdom of God in the Teaching of Jesus*, does not even mention two of the most significant precursors, Immanuel Kant and Richard Rothe.[102] This section of the chapter is included in an effort to fill that gap created especially by the puzzling omission of Rothe's pioneering work. Kant made the notion of the Kingdom of God central to his reinterpretation of Christianity in his *Religion Within the Limits of Reason Alone*, affirming the necessity for a so-called 'ecclesiastical faith' (highly suspect for moral reasons during the Enlightenment) to flow over into 'pure religious faith', a moral faith, expressing a morally good disposition, which is aimed at gaining a *public foothold*. When this happens, says Kant, we have reason to say that 'the Kingdom of God is come unto us'.[103] Within this process of transition from merely ecclesiastical faith to moral faith there lies (invisibly) 'as in a seed which is self-developing and in due time self-fertilizing, the whole, which one day is to illumine and to rule the world'. Schleiermacher also made the Kingdom central to his understanding of Christianity in the *Glaubenslehre*, insisting that in God's final purpose it is the Kingdom which is, strictly speaking, the object of the divine care, a Kingdom within which each disciple has his 'vocation', i.e., his appointed activity.[104] But in point of fact, a much more immediate, and illuminating, stimulus to Ritschl's reflections on the Kingdom is to be found in the work of his contemporary Richard Rothe (1799–1867), whom Ritschl encountered during his brief sojourn as a student at Heidelberg.[105] It was Rothe's work on Christian ethics, combined with that on Church–State relationships, which impressed Ritschl most lastingly, particularly his conclusion that in redemption a *response* is demanded from man in the form of absolute surrender to God in a life which commits itself to the moral purpose of the world, a life made possible only through the gift of Christian freedom. The scope of the Christian life is co-extensive with the scope of the State itself, and those 'orders' of which the State consists, civic and public life, the vocations of trade or scholarship, institutions like Church and family. The end of Christianity is no less than the *Christianization* of civil society, which can come about only by the Christian as he exists and strives within the nexus of a whole set of natural relations. Rothe never doubted that this demand flowed from the vocation of the Founder of Christianity to found the Kingdom of God. Such a view led him to indulge in a radical review of the relationship of Church to State. He completely abhorred the notions that the Church is an end in itself rather than a means, and that the Church and Kingdom are identical. On the contrary, since it is the Kingdom which is God's final end, the Church can only logically be the means or instrument for the realization of

God's desire, which is the Kingdom of God upon earth. In other words, the *final end* of Christ's life and work was not the Church, but a Christian *world*, to be striven for in the first instance by the Christianization of the State. In his important *Die Anfänge Der christlichen Kirche* of 1837, Rothe interestingly sketches how the original, primitive understanding of the Church (as *means*) was gradually overlaid and obscured by the Cyprianic and post-Cyprianic view of the Church as *end-in-itself*, the intrinsically valuable divine society with its exclusive hierarchical government, its law, its dogmatic system, all of which led, imperceptibly perhaps, but perfectly logically, to the papalism of the Roman theocracy. One disastrous consequence was that a powerfully organized Church, turned in upon itself in order to consolidate its own legal system and define the role of its own officials, felt obliged to assert its independence by struggling against the State. Such a development involved clericalism, which is incompatible with the obligation of Christians to transform the State through their *occupations* in the common life. Rothe was adamant that equally incompatible was sectarian pietism, with its disastrous withdrawal of Christians from the common, civic and public sectors of the State. It is only against such a background of ideas that we can understand some of Rothe's more paradoxical statements, such as 'Not more Church, but less', or that 'the chief task of believers today must be to free Christ from the Church'! It was no wonder then that he was in no way alarmed by pessimistic mid-century talk of the decline or disappearance of the Church, since he understood that the Church referred to in such talk is the Church engrossed in retaining or extending its position and power, or the authority which it has won over the State and its own members. Rather, he looked forward to the day (and evidence exists that occasionally he felt this not to be far away) when through its ethical penetration of civil society by its members Church and State would coalesce. Accordingly, during the last decade or so of his life, he helped to found and entered enthusiastically into the activities of the Baden *Protestantenverein* (German Protestant Alliance), a union of all shades of theological opinion devoted to winning back those alienated from the faith, to defining a significant role for the laity in Church and State, to understanding the culture and thought-forms of modernity, to striving for religious liberty together with parochial autonomy and creativity.

Within this understanding of the history of Christianity there is, according to Rothe, one event of such gigantic importance that we can view it as the dawning of a historical *KAIROS* – the Reformation. Here we find the proclamation that faith has to do with the world (rather than exclusively with the Church), and that the highest service to Christ can be fulfilled in the common round, in the family, in the service of one's fellows in public and civic office. Not that he was uncritical of the Reformation – it erred gravely in resuscitating against the Hildebrandine doctrine of the visible Church, the Augustine notion of the invisible Church; the term 'invisible Church' is a contradiction in terms; the whole point about the Church, as founded by Christ to be the means to the final end of the Kingdom, is that it ought to be visibly active, vibrantly transforming the common life of the community. Two final points about Rothe are relevant. The first is that his moral seriousness and his emphasis on the this-worldly Kingdom were quite compatible with a highly supernaturalistic eschatology, a vision of the final return of Christ with all his saints prior to the purification and renewal of the creation. The second is that, in Barth's opinion, in the ethical pietism of Rothe 'one can see heralded the monergism of the Kingdom of God as Herrmann Kutter saw it, lay-Christian activism as understood by Leonhard Ragaz, and the religious socialism of our day'.[106] It is against the background of such a framework of ideas that Ritschl's teaching on the Kingdom must be understood – a network of Christian ideas born partly of a lively sensitivity to ethical rationalism. A brief comparison of the views of Ritschl with those of Rothe enables us to perceive more clearly the overall shape of the former's thought. There is the same high estimate of the significance of the Reformation, with the weight placed on 'holy worldliness' expressed in vocation. There is the same 'liberal-Protestant' shape to the history of Christianity as 'fallen', characteristic also of the viewpoints of 'liberals' like Rudolf Sohm and Harnack. There is a similar abhorrence of otherworldly ascetic sectarian pietism. There is in Rothe's ecclesiology the clue to much in Ritschl's: for the latter also abhorred the identification of Church and Kingdom; no one stressed more than he that Jesus brought the Church into being to work and pray for the Kingdom, to exist teleologically, for a purpose beyond itself. This in turn throws valuable light on a much-overlooked aspect of Ritschl's teaching. We have already noted his antipathy to the notion that 'the coming of the Kingdom' approximates somehow to the worldly successes of the *ecclesia militans*, to that position of power, prestige and influence won by the Church in legal struggles with the State, with the signing of concordats and the like, victories which, for Ritschl, have not only little to do with the coming of the Kingdom, but with the Christian religion itself. His repudiation of such notions is very important indeed, for it means that he refused to adopt, despite allegations to the contrary, an *organizational* or *institutional* view of the Kingdom. We need only recall his puzzling statement that the Christian's lordship over the world and his activity in and for the Kingdom are 'ideal not empirical', and place it beside his central affirmation that amongst the effects of Christ's lordship we must reckon the transformation through the principle of love of the public conscience, the entrenchment of this in public institutions, and the progressive liberation of the human mind from the dominion of nature, to conclude that he is referring to the Kingdom of God in Gospel terms – symbolically, *as a mustard-seed or as a little leaven in the dough*. It is impossible to find in his writings explicit references to the Kingdom as some kind of this-worldly empire, institution or organization, like the League of Nations, the United Nations, or the like. This is not altered by the facts that some latter-day American 'Ritschlians', especially disciples of the Social Gospel pioneers Gladden and Rauschenbusch, tended to identify the Kingdom with, say, the geographical spread of American civilization, culture and Christianity, over the raw 'nature' of the untamed West, or that certain American Christian ethicists of the 1920s and 1930s looked for the transforming christianization of the raw jungle of post-war American political, social and industrial life. This is *not* Ritschl, and great care must be exercised not to regard him through the eyes of latter-day 'disciples', some of whom in America had clearly never read him! Enormous care must also be taken over *the alleged rate of growth of the Kingdom*. It cannot be denied that Ritschl, like most of his contemporaries, was affected by the optimistic, progressivistic, and utopian *Zeitgeist* of the late nineteenth century, and that one reason for the appeal of his system at the turn of the century was that it struck harmonious chords in the optimistic and utopian ethos of the day. But this must not divert attention from the fact that we find him in his texts to be quite agnostic and very reticent about the empirical and temporal circumstances of the Kingdom's growth and consummation. For the close-knit christological texture of his system firmly excluded any notion in contradiction with his central doctrinal viewpoint, that entry into the Kingdom is *exclusively* contingent upon the believer's acceptance of justification by God in Christ, which liberates and energizes him for reconciling activity in the Kingdom. This brings us to a related point: great scepticism ought to be directed towards any insinuation that the 'Ritschlian' doctrine implies that in some way the growth and consummation of the Kingdom *depends mainly upon* the expenditure of merely human effort. For Ritschl, in the last analysis, the Kingdom is rooted in the work of God. But, of course, his entire account of Christianity was from the outset intended to be, for the first time, one which gave a meaningful place to the human *will* in the dispensation of God, which for the first time since the Reformation satisfactorily correlated God's gift with God's *demand*, the Christian faith with the Christian *life*. It follows that human deciding, willing and striving naturally *cannot be separated* from the fulfilment of the will of God in his Kingdom.

This brings us to our final word about Ritschl on the subject. We have just noted that Rothe's heavy ethical emphasis was compatible with a strongly supranaturalistic eschatology. It is enlightening to enquire about how Ritschl compares in this respect. Such a comparison meets a special difficulty in the shape of a widespread stereotyped impression that he *de-eschatologized* Christianity's teaching on the Kingdom, in removing from New Testament teaching those otherworldly and apocalyptic features of it in favour of an exclusively intramundane, immanentist, progressivist doctrine attractive to his nineteenth-century *Zeitgeist*. Accordingly, it is alleged, it required the publication in 1892 of *Die Predigt Jesu vom Reich Gottes* by his son-in-law, Johannes Weiss, and of Albert Schweitzer's *Die Leben Jesu Forschung von*

Reimarus zu Wrede in 1906, to demonstrate that Ritschl's 'Kingdom' had precious little to do with the Kingdom preached by Jesus, a Kingdom pictured in apocalyptic imagery as the sudden, catastrophic irruption of God into history. But such a simplistic story simply will not do. It is impossible to deny that Ritschl was culpable in ignoring the apocalyptic-eschatological setting of Jesus' teaching on the Kingdom; but it is unfair to overlook the extent to which, especially in *Rechtfertigung und Versöhnung* II, he was expounding one side of the dominical teaching on the Kingdom. We could translate this point into the terminology of twentieth-century research into the Kingdom by saying that he stressed a *realized* type of eschatology to the near-exclusion of a *futurist* one, or that he quite failed to appreciate the tension between present and future in Jesus' teaching on the Kingdom, or that he failed to see the Kingdom as simultaneously and paradoxically present *and* future. But this is categorically not to say that he did not see the problem, a conclusion rendered impossible by paragraph 77 of the *Unterricht*, where he summarized much that had appeared in the second volume of his major work. The Last Judgement was modelled by Christ and the apostles on Old Testament expectations, through which they came to expect the Judgement as an observable, mundane event, following which Christ would assume his final Lordship of the Kingdom of God on earth, a reign which was to be inaugurated by the resurrection of believers and the *PAROUSIA* of Christ. Ritschl comments:

> This form of future expectation has not maintained itself in the Church, though it is still held in sectarian circles. The hope cherished in the Church *gives up the expectation that this earth will be the scene of Christ's dominion*, while it holds fast the practical truths of the divine judgement and the separation of the blessed and the lost, as well as the final attainment of the highest good in the case of the former. Since a consistent eschatological theory cannot be gained from the data of the New Testament, the hints of the New Testament as to the condition of the blessed and the lost lie beyond the possibility of a clear presentation. The important thing, however, is not the satisfying of curiosity but the assurance that no one is

blessed except in union with all the blessed in the Kingdom of God.[107]

It is true that certain of Ritschl's early commentators (e.g., Orr)[108] complained that his system lacked a detailed, systematic section devoted to eschatology, which is undeniable: but none of them denied that references to it were scattered abundantly throughout his system, or alleged that he attempted to *de-eschatologize* the Christian faith. But actually it was hardly on-going New Testament scholarship of the Weiss-Schweitzer type only, or mainly, which engendered disillusionment with the 'Ritschlian' teaching on the Kingdom of God. It was rather the outbreak of World War I and its ghastly aftermath which made Europeans bitterly cynical towards *any* theory whatsoever tinged with progressivism or utopianism. And from the standpoint of historical theology, it was the lessons which the early Barth drew prophetically from the war and its causes that all but pushed Ritschl's doctrine of the Kingdom into oblivion, where it remained during the frightful years of the Weimar Republic, the Third Reich, and World War II.

NOTES TO CHAPTER VI

1 *Protestant Theology*, pp. 655–8.
2 *The Mediator*, pp. 134–5.
3 *Perspectives on 19th and 20th Century Protestant Theology*, p. 218.
4 *Jesus – God and Man*, p. 45.
5 *The Protestant Ethic and the Spirit of Capitalism*, London 1930, p. 187.
6 *Instruction*, para. 46; cf. para. 13, n. 32.
7 See, e.g., *J. & R.* III, p. 646.
8 For what follows, see *J. & R.* III, para. 67, and *Instructions*, paras. 48 f.
9 *J. & R.* III, p. 651, italics mine.
10 *Instruction*, para. 48.
11 *J. & R.* III, p. 502.
12 *Instruction*, para. 50, italics mine.
13 ibid., para. 48.
14 *J. & R.* III, p. 665, italics mine.
15 ibid.
16 *Faith and the Vitalities of History*, pp. 12 f.
17 ibid., p. 13; for the interpretative significance and function of the term *Lebensführung* in Ritschl, op. cit., pp. 54 f.
18 See *Instruction*, para. 51, and *J. & R.* III, pp. 614–25.

19 *J. & R.* III, p. 617.
20 ibid., p. 618, italics mine.
21 *Instruction*, para. 51; cf. *J. & R.* III, p. 625.
22 *Jesus Christ and Mythology*, London 1960, p. 62, italics mine.
23 ibid., p. 63.
24 *J. & R.* III, p. 625.
25 ibid., p. 636, italics mine.
26 *Instruction*, para. 53.
27 *J. & R.* III, p. 629.
28 *Instruction*, loc. cit.; cf. *J. & R.* III, p. 637.
29 *J. & R.* III, p. 635.
30 ibid., p. 637.
31 *Instruction*, para. 52.
32 It is excessively harsh statements like this one which have prompted critics like Tillich to characterize Ritschl's theology as attractive to strong, active, independent, self-disciplined, world-dominating, anti-authoritarian, bourgeois personalities.
33 *J. & R.* III, p. 645.
34 ibid., p. 644.
35 ibid., italics mine.
36 ibid., p. 646.
37 *Instruction*, para. 54.
38 For what follows, see Orr, op. cit., pp. 176–8.
39 *J. & R.* III, p. 626, italics mine.
40 *Kant, Lotze and Ritschl*, p. 232, italics mine.
41 Garvie, op. cit., pp. 376–7 and 354–5.
42 See the reissued version, London 1972, para. 31, 'Prayer and Willing Resignation', and para. 32, 'Prayer for Earthly Blessings', pp. 337–41.
43 *Geschichte des Pietismus* I, p. 40, italics mine.
44 *New Essays in Philosophical Theology*, London 1955, pp. 96 f., and my discussion of this in *Theology and Metaphysics* III, 17 f.
45 Garvie, op. cit., p. 359.
46 Mozley, op. cit., p. 233.
47 *J. & R.* III, p. 665.
48 ibid., p. 666; cf. ibid., p. 466.
49 ibid., p. 668; cf. p. 669 and *Instruction*, para. 57.
50 *J. & R.* III, p. 665.
51 ibid., p. 666.
52 *Instruction*, para. 70.
53 *J. & R.* III, p. 514, italics mine.
54 ibid., p. 515.
55 ibid., pp. 666–7, italics mine.
56 *Instruction*, n. 185, italics mine.
57 ibid., para. 64, italics mine.
58 *J. & R.* III, pp. 630–1.
59 ibid., p. 612.
60 ET by Talcott Parsons, *The Protestant Ethic and the Spirit of Capitalism*, London 1930 and later, especially chapter III, 'Luther's Conception of the Calling: Task of the Investigation', pp. 79–92.
61 op. cit., p. 79.
62 ibid., pp. 205–6.

63 ibid., p. 80.
64 ibid., p. 81.
65 *Wealth of Nations*, book I, ch. II, cited by Weber.
66 *The Protestant Ethic*, p. 83.
67 ibid., p. 84.
68 ibid., p. 85.
69 ibid., pp. 204–6 and 207–11.
70 Grüder Verlag, Stuttgart 1855.
71 *Zeitschrift für Staatswissenschaft*, XVI, 1860.
72 See *infra*, p. 255.
73 *The Protestant Ethic*, p. 214.
74 From 'Evangelical Theology in the Nineteenth Century', *The Humanity of God*, London 1961, pp. 27–8.
75 *A Dictionary of Christian Theology*, pp. 358–9.
76 See *supra*, p. 220.
77 Introduction to *Three Essays*, p. 37.
78 ibid., p. 38.
79 *Instruction*, para. 60.
80 ibid., para. 61.
81 For what follows, see Orr, op. cit., pp. 119–20 and 179.
82 See *supra*, p. 67.
83 See Ernst Troeltsch, 'The Ideas of Natural Law and Humanity in World Politics', in Otto Gierke's *Natural Law and the Theory of Society 1500–1800*, translated by Ernest Barker, vol. i, Cambridge 1934, pp. 201–22; for a discussion of Troeltsch's theory, see Ian Henderson, *Can Two Walk Together? The Quest for a Secular Morality*, London 1948, ch. II, 'Natural Law', and ch. III, 'My Station'.
84 Ian Henderson, op. cit., p. 87.
85 See *supra*, p. 221.
86 See the article 'Vocation' in *A Handbook of Theological Termas*, New York 1964, pp. 249–51.
87 *Concise Theological Dictionary*, pp. 483–4.
88 ibid., pp. 160–1.
89 *Protestant Thought in the Nineteenth Century*, vol. i, p. 34.
90 *An Historian's Approach to Religion*, London 1956, pp. 151 f. and 251 f.
91 N. Kemp Smith, 'Hume's Views Regarding Religion in General', from the introduction to *Dialogues Concerning Natural Religion*, Oxford 1935, pp. 11–31.
92 *Speeches*, pp. 54–5.
93 *Protestant Theology*, p. 657.
94 Hefner, Introduction to *Three Essays*, pp. 33 f., and Lotz, *Ritschl and Luther*, 'The Vindication of Protestantism', pp. 162 f.
95 Lotz, op. cit., p. 162.
96 ibid., p. 163.
97 ibid., p. 165.
98 ibid., pp. 166–7.
99 ibid., pp. 167–8; Lotz's translation of Ritschl's *Festrede* is included as an appendix to his *Ritschl and Luther*, pp. 187–202.
100 ibid., p. 169.
101 Introduction to *Three Essays*, p. 34.
102 *The Kingdom of God in the Teaching of Jesus*, London 1963, pp. 13 f.;

the succession of scholars briefly discussed by Perrin are Schleiermacher, Ritschl, Weiss, Dalman and Schweitzer.
103 *Religion Within the Limits of Reason Alone*, New York 1960, p. 113.
104 *The Christian Faith*, para. 164, especially p. 725.
105 English-speaking readers may conveniently consult, e.g., Lichtenberger, op. cit., pp. 492–526, Pfleiderer, op. cit., pp. 148–53, Barth,
Protestant Theology, ch. XXIII, pp. 597–606.
106 Barth, op. cit., p. 598.
107 *Instruction*, para. 77.
108 Orr, op. cit., pp. 179–81.

CHAPTER VII

Ritschl's Theology: Prospect and Retrospect

Perhaps in the preceding pages enough has been said of Ritschl's thought to demonstrate that it possesses much of interest, relevance and enduring vitality. Now that the period of excessive, partly undeserved and impoverishing hostility towards the nineteenth century is over, those who have cultivated even a passing acquaintance with the recent literature on the period are convinced that in the next few decades we are going to hear a great deal more of its theological ideas, viewed from new perspectives and under fresh aspects. If this happens, and there is every reason to believe that it will, sound ongoing theological work will be enriched in two ways. First, an immeasurable mass of theological raw materials would be made available. Second, invaluable assistance for understanding a highly confused contemporary theological situation in the light of its rediscovered past would be rendered to the perplexed and the confused. The first of these is indicated in the title of this chapter by 'prospect' and the second by 'retrospect', each of which will be dealt with in turn in the remainder of these conclusions. Under the heading of 'prospect', there will be explored those areas of Ritschl's work which qualify as worthy of further examination in the immediate and near future. Under the heading of 'retrospect' the question will be explored of those ways in which a sound understanding of his system illumines the systematic theology of the past several generations and enables us to see, hopefully, a hitherto unnoticed or discounted unity between the religious thought of the nineteenth century and that of the twentieth.

To deal first with promisingly fruitful areas of Ritschl's achievement, it is argued that the first one is that of *theological hermeneutics*. It is impossible to undertake even a cursory study of Ritschl's system without encountering the fact that he attempted to re-interpret the Christian tradition in the light of a set of pre-suppositions which he derived from an encounter with the cultural *Zeitgeist* of the second half of the nineteenth century – the critical and moral philosophy of the *Aufklärung*, the philosophy of Lotze, the disillusionment with Hegelian idealism, impatience with Christianity regarded as a form of mystical pietism, the rise of sophisticated forms of positivism and naturalism, biblical criticism, incipient secularization, methodological empiricism, and diverse forms of anti-religious and anti-Protestant polemic. It hardly needs saying that a few generations ago, during the heyday of Barthian orthodoxy, the operation of such interpretative presuppositions served quite simply to condemn such theology and consign it to near-oblivion. Barth himself, surveying in 1957 nineteenth-century Protestant theology and the reaction of himself and his colleagues to it, judged that such theology 'went overboard – and this was its weakness – insofar as confrontation with the contemporary age was its decisive and primary concern'.[1] The trouble was, said the mature Barth, that theology never failed to react, whether approvingly or disapprovingly, critically or uncritically, to impulses from outside, at times even with extreme nervousness. The disastrous upshot was that nineteenth-century theology ascribed normative character to the ideas of its environment. The latter-day consequences were reductions and simplifications, forgetfulness and carelessness, leading to theological impoverishment, triviality and error. But, the question must be put, could nineteenth-century theologians have done otherwise? Barth's view was that they could – they could have ignored 'the favours or disfavours of this world, confronted it with the results of theological research *carried out for its own sake*'.[2] For they failed to realize that respectable dogmatics could be good apologetics. On this, three comments must be made. First, while conceding the monumental importance of Barth's own *Kirchliche Dogmatik*, the potential ghastly dangers implicit in Barth's prescription must not be overlooked. For his invitation to '*theological research carried out for its own sake*', accepted glibly by those much less able and gifted than himself, and quite differently motivated, may be, and unquestionably has been an invitation to theological triviality, irrelevance and naïvety! Second, it may be disastrously mistaken to believe that Barth and his colleagues, despite their loud and persistent disclaimers to the contrary, did not work with hermeneutical presuppositions, perhaps in some cases all the more insidious because unacknowledged and unexamined. It was greatly to Paul Tillich's credit that he perceived and formulated this:

> Barth's greatness is that he corrects himself again and again in the light of the 'situation' and that he strenuously tries not to become his own follower. Yet he does not realise that in doing so he ceases to be merely a kerygmatic theologian.[3]

To put this in concrete, historical terms, it would be crassly anti-rational to maintain that the magnetism exercised by Barth's system in its day was independent of presuppositions derived from his analysis of the *Zeitgeist* – the nihilism, despair, guilt and pessimism characteristic of the post-war Weimar republic, the formidable onslaught on metaphysical and ethical language characteristic of the inter-war period, and the ghastly conflation of Christian faith and National-Socialist ideology and religion as carried out in the Third Reich and Second World War. In other words, Barth's theology, perhaps more critically than uncritically, also *never failed to react* to impulses from outside, a fact in which its greatness resided. And Bultmann had Barth unquestionably in mind when he affirmed:

> The demand that the interpreter must silence his subjectivity and extinguish his individuality, in order to attain to an objective knowledge is . . . the most absurd one that can be imagined.[4]

Third, the huge interest which sprang up around the theological programmes of both Tillich and Bultmann in the post-war period demonstrates that the hermeneutical issue cannot be dealt with simply by sweeping aside that nineteenth-century tradition represented by Ritschl and by consigning it for several generations to theological near-oblivion. For when Tillich spoke a generation ago of theology's task as having to relate the 'kerygma' to the 'situation', and of the theologian's responsibility of 'correlating' kerygmatic answers with human questions,[5] he was re-admitting the hermeneutical question in a form which was anathema to the neo-orthodox into the centre of our North

Atlantic theological stage. But Bultmann's postwar theological programme did the same in a much more notoriously outspoken way: his talk of modern man's acute difficulties in 'understanding' the Gospel, his affirmation that talk of a 'presuppositionless' interpretation was meaningless, his sensitivity to the epistemological implications of altered world-views and cosmologies, his openness to existentialism's ability to assist in the articulation of a *Vorverständnis* without which the Gospel would remain unintelligible for modernity, all of this reintroduced hermeneutical issues into the heart of theological discussions in such a way as to make them unavoidable for contemporary workers in most branches of theology. For Bultmann as for Tillich the central and unavoidable problem for systematic theology was the relation between, on the one hand, contemporary man as determined by his situation within the *Zeitgeist*, and, on the other, the kerygma, a fiercely difficult, not to say intractable problem which will be with us so long as theology survives. Yet who can doubt that the classic systematic theologies of the nineteenth century represent rich source-books for the *analysis* of such a problem? Certainly the recent Ritschl Renaissance has shown this to be so in his case. For it is quite impossible to read and assess Ritschl without making a set of hermeneutical judgements. All talk, for instance, of Ritschl's 'distorting' biblical and confessional sources through the operation of his alien 'nineteenth-century presuppositions' and the like, is quite meaningless in the absence of prior scientific reflection on hermeneutical issues, on exactly what is meant by the 'objectivity' of the sources, on any interplay (if any) which *is* allowable between the 'subjective' interests or intentions of the interpreter and the materials which he is handling, on the crucial, central question of whether there is available to us a pure, 'undistorted', normatively objective account of Christianity in every way unaffected by human presuppositions, and the like. Philip Hefner has placed Ritschl within a long European tradition (consisting of thinkers like Schleiermacher, Dilthey, Heidegger, Gadamer, Ebeling and Ricouer) which holds that man does not merely *use* the historical method, but rather *is* a historical being, an insight which has gone hand in hand with a close phenomenological analysis of man's psychic and intellectual processes as he is caught up in the historical process of assessment and dialogue, a phenomenological analysis which has attained a high level of sophisticated description.[6] Hefner's judgement is that although Ritschl's efforts along this line must attract considerable criticism (his attempt to analyse the dynamics of human life is partly vitiated by his concentration on his own lifestyle as the source for these), 'his concentration on the psychic life of man, as the arena within which the encounter with revelation was to be charted, gave a formal impetus for full-scale phenomenological work and encouraged his followers to do what he did not do' (we shall see what Hefner means by this last phrase when below we probe the relationship between Ritschl and Bultmann). In trying to reach an estimate of Ritschl's contribution, David Mueller remarks that we must recognize the fruitful way in which he incorporated the subjective pole represented by the faith of the community and the individual within his system.[7] In stressing God's historic revelation in Christ, the objective pole, Ritschl was doubtless trying to remedy a deficiency in Schleiermacher, but 'his development of the subjective pole was consciously indebted to him', so that 'in a sense one must see Ritschl attempting to revivify the rich understanding of faith and the life of faith set forth powerfully in Luther and Schleiermacher'. Mueller reaches a conclusion startlingly similar to Hefner's when he judges that the impetus that Ritschl's theological method gave to the development of more anthropological and existential methodologies in the twentieth century in W. Herrmann, Bultmann and others has not yet been fully acknowledged or investigated (as noted, we shall return to this area below). Mueller further remarks, not without justification, that Ritschl's modern ethical and existential bent may well prove to be more suggestive for contemporary theological work than the individualistic, romantic and 'mystical' approach of Schleiermacher, or the excessively individualistic trend introduced into theology by Kierkegaard. It hardly needs to be added that nothing said above implies a blanket approval of Ritschl's interpretation of Christianity. It is simply being argued that his system deserves careful contemporary examination for the light which it casts on the hermeneutical issues which must engross contemporary theologians.

The second promisingly fruitful area of Ritschl's work which deserves re-examination and re-evaluation, is that constituted by *the Kingdom of God, social ethics and eschatology*. When one recalls the pejorative caricature of Ritschl as the superficial exponent of the Kingdom of God as a this-worldly, ethicizing organization, it is now astounding to consider the way in which more reflective recent theology has, in disillusionment with various recent theological trends, begun to look back beyond these to the work of someone who, perhaps more than anyone in the Christian tradition, wrestled with the problem of significantly relating the Kingdom of God and human action to the fabric of Christianity. Here we must recall briefly what was noted in the previous chapter – that it cannot be denied, in the light of Weiss-Schweitzer and later criticisms, that Ritschl did stress a 'realized' type of eschatology somewhat to the detriment of a 'futurist' one, and that the historical lessons which the early Barth drew from the occurrence of World War I, cumulatively articulated by dialectical theology and finding a welcome response in the European disillusionment with all forms of optimistic utopian progressivism, served to banish the 'Ritschlian' teaching on the Kingdom into near-oblivion. In criticizing the subsequent and violent 'eschatologization' of Christianity by Barthian theology, it would be unfair to discount a certain notable contribution to social ethics by Karl Barth throughout his long career – his prophetic analysis of that nineteenth-century European capitalistic rapacity whose outcome was World War I, his description of those miserable social and economic conditions which helped to evoke the Russian Revolution, his courageous Christian stand against Nazi totalitarianism and anti-semitism, his exposure of what he took to be the appalling consequences of the Lutheran doctrine of the Two Kingdoms, his sympathetic plea for a compassionate Christian understanding of the Marxist societies of Eastern Europe. Nevertheless, it is equally impossible to overlook that 'certain coldness' of Christianity to civilization advocated by Barth in the *Römerbrief* – the persistent questioning of and protesting against all merely human efforts and achievements, the constant rather negative contrasting of 'this world' with 'the world to come', the rather chilly judgement of everything penultimate in the light of the ultimate, the continual referral of everything worldly to that world to come whose sole author and

giver is God. No doubt there was a time when the world needed
to have just this word spoken to it, but it just could not endure
as the sole basis for a social ethic, and hence indefinitely fend off
a certain theological disillusionment. And Bultmann's later and
alternative claim that 'objectivist' eschatological statements (taken
as referring to objective, worldly history) were mythological, and
his proposal that they should now be understood as referring to
the life-span of the existing, individual Christian (i.e., should be
demythologized), could not indefinitely fend off either (on the
grounds of excessive individualism) a certain impatience which
has become apparent in recent theology. It is against such a
historical backdrop, it is argued, that we may understand the
desire to look once again at the teaching of Ritschl on the
Kingdom. Hence it is Hefner again who quotes Norman Metzler's
use, supported by Wolfhart Pannenberg, of the phrase 'the
Ritschl-Weiss historical nexus', whose value is enduring and
whose real implications are just now being fully unfolded by the
current 'eschatological' school of theology, which includes
Pannenberg, Carl Braaten, and Jürgen Moltmann.[8] The new
understanding of Ritschl within this context is summarized
admirably by Hefner as follows:

> The suggestion is that Ritschl and his tradition were correct,
> that the Kingdom of God in the New Testament and in
> Christian dogmatics *is* both eschatological and ethical, but not
> in the precise way Ritschl set forth. That is, the Kingdom is not
> to be conceived, as Ritschl did, as a reality which is to be
> realized in and through man's concrete ethical actions, actions
> which thus fulfil both God's highest good and man's, offering
> self-fulfilment for both God and man. Rather, the Kingdom is
> a future reality realized only by God, but which proleptically
> gives shape to present action, even though it is a future reality
> to be consummated. This is so because man lives under the
> impact of that coming Kingdom which was also present in
> Jesus through his resurrection.

Hefner concludes that Ritschl's insights on the kingdom as a
central, if not all-embracing, issue for Christian faith is another
example of the fruitfulness which his theology has had for
succeeding generations. It is now being recognized that there is

close similarity between Ritschl's eschatology and that of modern existentialist theologians. Of this Hefner remarks that the interiorizing of eschatology by the existentialist theologians is not far from Ritschl's ethicizing of it. Earlier Mueller had remarked that one can argue that existentialism's realized eschatology is actually not much different from Ritschl's.[9] But Mueller proceeds to argue that Ritschl's is actually superior, for 'it is clear that his conception of the Church and the Kingdom of God provided him at least with the possibility of transcending the tendency towards an excessively individualistic ethic', a teleological dimension of this thought 'almost wholly absent in Christian existentialism'. Indeed, he goes further – the strong eschatological-teleological element in Ritschl's theological thinking on Kingdom and Church established its superiority over that of Herrmann, Harnack, Barth and Bultmann, and accounts for the impact made on contemporary theological work by the reflections of Jürgen Moltmann:

> The fact that the discussion of the future and the Christian hope evident in the theology of Moltmann and others is making such an impression currently is evidence that the teleological dimension of Ritschl's thought – with all its deficiencies – was not taken with sufficient seriousness by his successors.[10]

The third promisingly fruitful area of Ritschl's work that clearly deserves reconsideration is that of *the possibility, viability and methodology of systematic theology*. There cannot be many in contemporary theological circles who would deny that currently there is a dismaying and disconcerting lack of systematic theology (or theologies). It is not that there is a lack of scientific theological work, but rather that a variety of theologians appear to be working separately on a wide variety of theological problems, reaching sets of results which are essentially unrelated to each other. If we look to Germany, the traditional home of modern systematic theology, we find, oddly, a vacuum *vis-à-vis* systematic theology there. It is not the case that German theologians are less productive than formerly, but rather that theologians such as Moltmann and Pannenberg have not as yet produced their reflections in traditional German systematic form. (A. D. Galloway, writing in 1973, tells us that some of Pannenberg's ideas are still in an

undeveloped condition, and remarks that he is currently engaged
in working out the basic theory of knowledge underlying his
system.)[11] Naturally, there is scope for speculation about the
causes of this vacuum, as there is room for disagreement about
its desirability or undesirability. It might be, for instance, that
we are moving into a period where we shall witness the emergence
of new theological styles of writing. On the other hand, it must
be admitted that Tillich's 'system' evoked at least one implacably
hostile critique,[12] rooted in the sharp contrast between 'Gospel'
and 'system'. While not denying that theology might greatly
benefit from the emergence of fresh styles or that Tillich's eccentric style of system-building has understandably alienated many
theological enquirers, it is probable that a significant vacuum in
the systematic area may not only be dangerous but seriously impoverishing. This is easily demonstrated from familiarity with the
vast influence and fruitfulness in the remote and recent past of
works such as Calvin's *Institutes*, Schleiermacher's *Glaubenslehre*,
Ritschl's *Justification and Reconciliation*, Herrmann's *The Communion of the Christian With God*, Barth's *Church Dogmatics*, and
Bultmann's *Theology of the New Testament*. One has only to
contemplate the religious, social and political influence exerted
by some of these works (e.g. Calvin's), the way in which some of
them (e.g. Schleiermacher's) functioned as textbooks for generations, the way in which all of them centralized and concentrated
discussions on an international scale, functioned catalytically in
evoking significant disagreement, further reflection and so research, supplied the continuity necessary for the development of
a 'school' (e.g. the Ritschlian school) spanning several generations, and so on. In the light of a sober look at such considerations, one can only be dismayed by any large or prolonged
vacuum brought about by the temporary demise of systematic
theology. If one reaches this conclusion, it immediately becomes
urgent to enquire why and how the classic systematic theologies
exercised the functions and acquired the great authority which
they did. And this enquiry cannot be made apart from the in-
depth study of an actual systematic theology, such as, typically,
Ritschl's *Justification and Reconciliation*. We have hopefully
learned enough of that in order to grasp something of the
influence and authority which it wielded during several genera-

tions. Liberated as we are from Barth's discredited judgement that 'Ritschl has the significance of an episode in more recent theology, and not, indeed not, that of an epoch',[13] we are able to listen to the preferable judgement of Hefner:

> (Ritschl) spoke a word to his own age that was so appropriate and so in resonance with his contemporaries in Germany that despite its weaknesses it became the dominant theology of his generation. It has proven fruitful up to this day in several major areas of theological concern, even though parts of it have been rejected or permitted to remain dormant.[14]

Mueller concurs:

> Perhaps no theologian of the nineteenth century experienced so significant a period of dominant influence upon Protestant theology and the life of the Church . . . as did Albrecht Ritschl.[15]

Mueller proceeds to argue that an examination of the major emphases of Ritschl's theology makes it evident that we are confronted with a theological programme of considerable dimensions. He continues:

> In the period between his death in 1889 and the present, perhaps only Barth and Bultmann have exerted so decisive an influence upon theological construction as he did in his own lifetime and thereafter.[16]

And David Lotz reminds us of von Harnack's description of Ritschl as 'the last of the Lutheran church fathers', and speaks of 'the growing recognition, in the wake . . . of dialectical theology, that the great liberal theologians of the later nineteenth and early twentieth centuries, among whom Ritschl was certainly pre-eminent, have continued relevance for present-day theological endeavours'.[17] But we will not grasp the attraction of and the fascination with Ritschl's theology over a period of fifty years unless we see that, like Schleiermacher before him, he gathered up into a close-knit systematic unity his historical analysis of the Christian tradition with what appeared to him to be the main elements of West European culture – the dangerous collapse of Hegelian idealism, its replacement by forms of materialism and naturalism, the emergence of a new interest in Kant, the attacks of ethical naturalism and the consequent demand for a Christian social ethic, the growth of critical empiricism, and advances in the study of the Bible. Unless we grasp this, we fail to account for the huge internal authority of his theological system for his day and the pervasive influence of the school which bore his name. In other words, the striking influence wielded by Ritschl's new theological construction derived from the fact that from his encounter with the culture of his day he produced a strikingly relevant analysis of the forces and factors which powerfully moved and intimately concerned very many of his West European contemporaries. Had he not done so, it would be impossible to explain not only the enthusiasm of his disciples and adherents but also the energy expended by his critics upon him. This casts considerable light on the viability of systematic theology. For to read Ritschl's system and to perceive its inner and outer dynamic impels us to ask whether a systematic theologian could produce a comparable system for the last quarter of the twentieth century, which would exhibit creative features analogous to those features of Ritschl's which, whether by enthusiastic agreement or unyielding disagreement, catalytically produced such a rich corpus of theological literature and centralized theological discussion for a couple of generations? Or, it may be asked, is such a theological system no longer viable for our time? If not, might this be so because West European culture no longer possesses a unity in anything like the sense in which it was unified in the second half of the nineteenth century? Might it be argued that West European culture is today so splintered and inchoate that the scientific theologian is unable to produce a consensus in the light of which to reinterpret and reassemble his theological raw materials? If so, is this reflected in the rather splintered and inchoate appearance of theological science at the present time? Or, on the other hand, could it not rather be the case that the rather sickly appearance of systematic theology is due to the disconcerting but inexplicable lack of a latter-day Schleiermacher who, by sheer creative genius, is able to blend together the rather disparate, inchoate and apparently mutually incompatible ingredients of our culture into a hermeneutically viable whole, which would enable a new theological generation to reinterpret the materials of the tradition in a new and hopefully striking way? It is submitted that these are desperately pressing questions for our day. But they cannot be tackled without a sound grasp of the systematic theologies of the recent past, of which Ritschl's, we can now see, was a notably striking example. To summarize the argument bluntly: it is no use talking about systematic theology unless one knows what one is talking about!

Having examined briefly the *prospect*, from different viewpoints, of Ritschl's theological construction, it is now time to consider the light which it casts upon recent theology in *retrospect*. Hopefully enough has just been said to indicate that the contemporary theological scene is extremely complex and potentially confusing. It must be said that viable ways forward can only be suggested in the light of a sound appreciation of a present which is itself firmly rooted in a recent and not-so-recent past. For many movements and developments have combined and blended in myriad ways to produce the contemporary almost intolerably confusing situation. We might describe this in terms of one striking difference between theology and, say, the natural sciences. Whereas the contemporary student of one of the sciences is under practically no obligation to trace the main developments in his subject from the middle of the sixteenth century, the contemporary theological enquirer who refuses or fails to do so may find himself gravely misinformed and hopelessly trapped in confusion. Of the many reasons for this one is that theology is and necessarily always has been thoroughly *anthropological* in nature – it has always probed the nature of man, his understanding of himself and his fellows, and his relationship to his environment. For this reason, while new developments have brought about shifts, and sometimes large shifts, in perspective and emphasis, it is hard to conceive of a 'new' development which would involve a complete repudiation of past doctrines in anything like the way in which, for example, new discoveries in physics have involved physicists in the repudiation or *absolute rethinking* of the physics of previous generations. To put this differently, there are indeed discontinuities in the development of theology – but these have to be viewed in dialectical tension with those indispensable continuities which, indeed, go to define and constitute the subject. To put this yet another way, theology is a thoroughly *historical* discipline, in the sense that in every generation its practitioners must enter into creative dialogue with *the tradition* (no one understood this better or practised it more faithfully than Ritschl). Naturally, in selecting those elements which have gone to produce the contemporary scene, care must be exercised to avoid narrowness or bias. While we are here legitimately examining developments within German theology, it would be unbalanced and unfair to underestimate the contribution of (mainly) Anglo-Saxon contributions, such as post-analytic philosophical theology, and the like. But our concern here is with systematic theology, and it is impossible to evade the conclusion that Germany's contribution has been quite preeminent. And within the German-speaking contribution since, say, 1919, two figures tower over all others, those of Barth and Bultmann. Moreover, many other (and rather lesser) contributions, both European and American, tend to be derived from one or other, or both, of these two, while others are significant for the extent to which they diverge from one, or both, of them. (This can be perceived in many ways. One very striking example is the fact that one of the constitutive confessions of the contemporary German Evangelical-Lutheran Churches is the Barth-inspired Confession of Barmen of May 1934, denying the existence of revelations 'subsidiary to' God's Word in Scripture, and repudiating all 'natural' theology – a nice example of the continued operation of 'Barthianism' in ecclesiastical and academic thought and life.)[18]

The truth of the matter is that the work of these two has not yet been fully evaluated – the work of them both is far too recent. It is vital for the future of systematic theology that they be not misunderstood. Yet the strong probability is that they *are* being misunderstood, if the work of both is not being positively related to its roots in the thought of the nineteenth century. If this is so, one generally accepted model of the relationship between nineteenth-century German systematic theology and that of the twentieth century might be more or less false – that one which incorporates an *abrupt discontinuity* between the two, initiated with the publication of the first edition of Barth's *Römerbrief* in 1919. The conclusion not uncommonly drawn from this is that the theologies of the two periods are *fundamentally different* to the extent that we may, so to speak, draw a line under most of the theological productions up until 1914 and make a fresh beginning from 1919 onwards. And, of course, they *are* different, and it would not only be unscholarly but foolish to overlook just how different they are.[19] But the point is that in recent decades we have heard *so much* of these differences that the over-emphasis on them has become almost grotesque. That is, the discontinuities have been so heavily underlined that important continuities have been pushed into the background and lost sight of. The result is historical impoverishment and a distorted intellectual perspective. But happily some recent researches have appeared, as noted throughout these pages, which have begun, in a tentative way, to redress the historical balance. What follows here is offered in the hope that it will contribute to this process. It is submitted therefore that a different model for understanding the relation between nineteenth- and twentieth-century theology is required. It is further submitted that this model must incorporate the firm strands of continuity that really exist, say, between the thought of Ritschl and that of Barth, and that of Ritschl and that of Bultmann. If such continuity could be established, many interesting results would flow from it. One of the most significant would be that we would be enabled to view the evolution of German systematic theology from Kant onwards under a new unified aspect, without, naturally, discounting overmuch significant breaks or discontinuities. Another important one would be that we should have to overhaul somewhat that account of the 'rise and fall of Ritschl's theology' which was given in Chapter I and elsewhere. More particularly, we should have to rethink carefully the traditional opinions about the 'abrupt decline' of Ritschl's leading ideas in the period beginning in 1919, leading to a more or less complete 'demise'. Depending on the strength of the various continuities established, we might be forced to the conclusion that certain Ritschlian fundamental principles and insights continued to operate, in reinterpreted and therefore concealed form, to be sure, throughout the 1920s, and that in the new anthropological turn which Bultmann's theology took after 1927 a certain refurbishment of certain of Ritschl's methodological principles and leading ideas may be perceived. But this is to hypothesize and anticipate, and must depend on yet another critical glance at Ritschl's system. It would be unrealistic not to anticipate resistance, not to say hostility, to proposals for a significant shift in historical perspective within such an important area. And, indeed, one can sympathize with those who wonder how it was that such a 'distorted' historical perspective established itself during several generations. Nevertheless, it must be insisted that, in the light of the evidence, it can happen. For one thing, when we recall what was said above about the definitively and intrinsically *historical* and *anthropological* nature of theological science, it is hard to resist the conclusion that we ought, *a priori*, to feel dubious of proposals leading to such a 'new' beginning in theological reflection that its immediate precedents may be abandoned almost absolutely. For another, it may be urged *a priori* that if theological historians in recent decades have felt obliged to re-examine and re-evaluate Schleiermacher, Baur, Strauss and Troeltsch, the reasons for doing so probably apply equally cogently to Ritschl. Moreover, it may be worth recalling that at least one recent writer has ascribed to Barth's vision of turn-of-the-century theology the term *myopic* – implying that the most dependable assessment of the achievements of an era is rarely achieved by the immediately succeeding one. As has often been remarked, it would be unwise to judge the Victorians by the picture painted by Lytton Strachey in 1918! Having said that, it is time to turn to the subject of Ritschl's theology under two aspects: first, under that of an enquiry into various strands of continuity between his thought and that of Barth, and, second, under that of an attempt to establish various even more significant overlaps between Ritschl's work and the achievement of Bultmann.

In our investigation of continuities between Ritschl and Barth, we shall adopt the following method: first, we shall enumerate rather general ones which have been identified by various writers on our period of modern systematic theology; second, we shall list rather more specific ones which we encountered within our examination of Ritschl's texts in preceding chapters. An interesting point of departure is some remarks, already noted, made by Dr Garvie as long ago as 1899, when he applied three interpretative terms to Ritschl's theological system – *bibliospheric, Christo-*

centric and *pistobasic.*[20] With regard to the first of these, Garvie is critical: he objects to the rather 'arbitrary' manner in which Ritschl used New Testament evidence, and to Ritschl's tendency to assert his 'theological independence' over against the 'authority' of Scripture. Nevertheless, in Garvie's opinion there is nothing in Ritschl's attitude to the Scriptures necessarily to forbid an advance *to a fuller recognition of their significance and value for Christian faith.* So far, therefore, as the bibliospheric character of Ritschl's system is concerned, Garvie's conclusion is that 'Ritschlianism stands on the path of *necessary and desirable Christian progress*'. In other words, the momentum within Ritschl's system is towards a very much more *bibliospheric* theology, of the kind now associated with the Barthian system. With regard to his second term, *Christocentric*, Garvie is again critical: for one thing, the evangelical testimony and apostolic interpretation of the Person and Work of Christ need to be more fully utilized by Ritschl. For another, the speculative idea of the Kingdom of God must be brought into subordination to the historical fact of the Person and Work of Christ by him. In other words, the image of Christ is less distinct and vivid in the theology of Ritschl than it might be. Nevertheless, in Garvie's opinion, 'the importance which it does certainly attach to the Person and Work of Christ proves that it is *already moving* along the lines of a sound and healthy development, and is, therefore, *not incapable of such correction as seems desirable*'. In other words, the dynamic within Ritschl's system is towards a very much more christocentric theology, of the kind perhaps that we saw emerging in the theology of the Barthian school. With regard to his third descriptive term, *pistobasic*, Garvie is once more critical of Ritschl: while he welcomes Ritschl's emphasis on the religious consciousness of salvation through Christ, he is less enthusiastic about its content and scope. He judges that excessive stress has been placed on the feeling of dominion over the world at the expense of a new religious relation to God through Christ, and on the excessively *practical* satisfaction yielded by Christianity at the expense of *intellectual* benefits. He therefore argues for a certain intellectualization of the Ritschlian religious consciousness, so that salvation 'meets the questions of the mind and the longings of the heart, as well as the needs of the will for liberation and development'. Nevertheless, progress in these matters is possible, and these limitations ought not to be allowed to obscure the valuable place given to the experimental character of Christian theology by Ritschl, who is right in insisting that theology has to deal with the religious consciousness, not with truth realized in abstraction, but with truth realized in life. It is submitted that it is impossible to make sense of Garvie's words, that Ritschl's thought is 'pointing in the right direction', that it stands 'on the path of Christian progress', that it is 'moving along the right lines', that it is capable of the appropriate improvement, supplementation, correction and the like, without concluding that it is *pointing towards* a more bibliospheric, christocentric and pistobasic version of Christianity, or a more 'orthodox' (or 'neo-orthodox'?) type, not dissimilar to that type represented by Barthian theology in the twentieth century, even if such theology was to move eventually to a onesidedly extreme pistobasic and bibliospheric position. It is also hard to contemplate Garvie's judgements without being reminded of Ferdinand Kattenbusch's 1934 assessment, already noted above, that Barth's early theology can be interpreted as bringing the best of Ritschl to fulfilment.

If we now turn from Garvie to H. R. Mackintosh, writing in the heyday of Barthianism (1936), and revealing clearly his preference for Barth over Ritschl, it is interesting to note that nevertheless he is careful to identify continuity between the two. Mackintosh, in discussing the theological work of Ernst Troeltsch, makes the point that Ritschl was charged by the *Religionsgeschichtliche-schule* with ignoring, in his restatement of Christianity, the new facts brought to light by the scientific study of religions. In fact, Ritschl had isolated Christianity and dealt with it almost as if there were no other religion in the world. Mackintosh comments:

> Indeed, the brilliant scholars who led the way in elucidating the Hellenistic background of the New Testament might be said to have done their work in spite of Ritschl rather than under his influence.[21]

Two brief comments need to be made about this. First, if Troeltsch's judgement is correct, then the strictures of later dialectical theologians against liberal theology's attempt to subsume Christianity under the genus of religion – as only one of many instantiations of it – hardly apply to the bibliospheric and pistobasic Ritschl. Second, if Mackintosh is right here (and there are no sound grounds for doubting it), then the Barthian's rather tedious reiteration of the expression 'the Schleiermacher-Ritschl-Troeltsch line of development' is both unscholarly and untenable. We cannot but be reminded of Horst Stephan's famous judgement that Ritschl's emphasis on the Church as the theologian's starting-point led to theology's isolation from cultural matters,[22] and that the isolation in which Ritschl had interpreted Christianity, the Bible and the Reformation was dangerous. At another point, Mackintosh pays handsome tribute to Ritschl for his valuable stress on the self-sufficiency of faith and on the liberating power of God's revelation in Christ. Mackintosh correctly remarks that Ritschl and his disciples gave life, variety and freshness to the dogmatic field for a whole generation, and in virtue of their sustained contention that Christian faith is its own sufficient basis, that theology must rest entirely on the revelation of God in Christ and that systematic doctrine exists to further the practical work of the Church, they were widely felt to be liberators of the theological mind. These are, for the generally hostile Mackintosh, generous words, and on their basis he proceeds to formulate the following striking judgement:

> It is now some years since Ritschl's great successor, Karl Barth, stepped into the arena; and that Barth is definitely a more Christian thinker than Ritschl no one, I should suppose, can doubt who takes revelation seriously. *But in declared intention and programme the two theologians are much nearer to each other than has often been supposed.* The difference may, perhaps, be shortly put thus: that Ritschl undertakes to furnish a theology inspired throughout by Scripture, but too often fails to keep his promise, whereas Barth is set upon thinking out something that will deserve to be called a 'Theology of the Word of God', and has so far proceeded with a consistency and power which is engaging the attention of the whole Christian Church. *It is in performance, not in chosen aim, that the two men stand so far apart.*[23]

It ought not to be overlooked how closely Mackintosh's judgement corresponds to and corroborates that of Garvie just dealt with above.

If we turn from Mackintosh to his colleague, John Baillie, we find him identifying two strands of continuity between Ritschl and Barth. At one point he discusses Barth's firm insistence that no knowledge of God exists in the world save in the hearts of regenerate Christians. On this insistence he comments:

> He [Barth] stands, *as did Ritschl and Herrmann in previous generations*, in the tradition of that Lutheran christocentrism which made Christ the Mediator no less of knowledge than of salvation; the christocentrism which denies that except in His Incarnation in Jesus of Nazareth God has ever spoken to man at all; the christocentrism which seizes eagerly on the New Testament declaration that 'neither knoweth any man the Father, save the Son, and he to whomsoever the Son will reveal him', and understands that to mean not merely God's fatherliness but His very reality was made known to men through Jesus alone.[24]

And at another point Baillie fastens upon a second strand of continuity in the doctrines of the Fall and the *Imago Dei*.[25] Baillie's judgement is that the doctrines of Barth are rooted in Ritschl's teaching in *Justification and Reconciliation* III. Barth insists that the image of God impressed upon man at creation is, in Baillie's terminology, an *archaeological* fact, in the sense that there is now no trace in human nature of its having existed. How then can we talk of it in the absence of empirical evidence? The typically Barthian answer is that the knowledge of the original *imago dei* is reserved exclusively for those in whose natures God's image has been recreated through Christ – 'and given in and with that recreation'. (We could put this slightly differently by quoting Barth's insistence that christology *must* precede all anthropology, that there is no valid knowledge of properly constituted human nature which is not derived from the Person of Christ.) Baillie interestingly points to the source of such teaching in Ritschl's *Justification and Reconciliation* III, and quotes the following sentence:

The doctrinal statements in the Confessions, too, regarding the original state of man, have no other significance than that of antedating the Christian ideal of life.[26]

Baillie does not mention the fact, but on the same page of Ritschl there is further evidence that his work may be the source of Barth's unshakable insistence upon christology's absolute precedence over anthropology. For example, Ritschl writes:

If . . . in the Christian religion Jesus Christ is the standard of His believers' view of the world and estimate of self, then in Dogmatics His Person must be regarded as the ground of knowledge to be used *in the definition of every doctrine*.

If so, he continues:

Even the dogmatic doctrine of man must not be filled up by adducing elements from the Biblical creation-document, but by that spiritual and moral conception of man which is revealed in the life-course of Jesus, and in His intention to found the Kingdom of God.[27]

The 'Ritschlian' roots of certain Barthian leading ideas seem here to be proved beyond all reasonable doubt.

If we now turn from Baillie in order to consider the 'early' Bultmann, it is illuminating to consider some words from his 1924 paper, 'Liberal Theology and the Latest Theological Movement',[28] already mentioned in an earlier chapter. In engaging in criticism of liberal theology, Bultmann at the outset is at great pains to explain that

the attack against the so-called liberal theology is not to be understood as the repudiation of its own past, but as a discussion with that past. The new movement is not a revival of orthodoxy, but rather a carefully reasoned consideration of the consequences which have resulted from the situation brought about by liberal theology. It is no accident that the latest movement originated not from within orthodoxy but out of liberal theology. Barth was a student at Marburg, Gogarten at Heidelberg, Thurneysen at both.[29]

Commenting upon Bultmann's *interpretation* of recent events (for there are no grounds for assuming Barth's agreement with it), the editor of the English version of *Glauben u. Verstehen* I, Robert W. Funk, comments:

> In associating himself with Barth and Friedrich Gogarten, Bultmann joins in the attack on the so-called liberal theology (i.e. on the Ritschlian theology, broadly speaking), but he takes care to observe that dialectical theology *is the immediate and grateful progeny of liberal theology.*[30]

Several lines later he mentions Bultmann's later fateful divergence from Barth, and it is easy to read between Bultmann's lines a distinct nervousness lest he be understood as being party to cutting all lines of continuity with the theology of the later nineteenth century. (In the second half of this chapter we shall perceive with great clarity the grounds of Bultmann's nervousness.) If we now turn to consider the view of Tillich, we find that the main line of continuity from Ritschl to Barth is construed by him as *anti-mysticism*. At one point, Tillich deals with Barth's attack upon Troeltsch's notion of the religious *a priori* and his claim that the *imago dei* is totally effaced in man. Tillich comments:

> This immediately involved him in an attack on mysticism, *following here the line of Ritschl and Harnack.*[31]

And in *Systematic Theology* I he says much the same thing:

> It is unfortunate that those in the Kant-Ritschl line and those in the neo-orthodox schools in theology have pointed only to the possible and actual abuses of the mystical approach without acknowledging its world historical function . . .[32]

And elsewhere he describes the continuity thus:

> The meaning of mysticism has been misinterpreted by Protestant theology *which began with Ritschl and is still alive in Barthian theology.*[33]

(We shall return to this matter briefly below when we consider how Ritschl's antimetaphysical stance anticipated modern 'theologies of the Word of God'.)

We need not linger unduly over the case of Wolfhart Pannenberg, whose views on the matter have already been fully noted. To recapitulate swiftly, Pannenberg sees two Ritschl-Barth strands of continuity in the antimetaphysical stance of them both and in a certain christological emphasis. First, he affirms that Barth's opposition to programmatic apologetics as well as all 'natural theology' is in many respects an extension and radicalization of the battle position set up by Ritschl.[34] Second, the correlation of the Work and Person of Christ (and the correlative firm refusal to separate them) in christology since Schleiermacher has been substantially due to Ritschl, a situation which has happily prevailed in modern theology, a proposition which, says Pannenberg, is verifiable by reference to the works of Paul Althaus and Karl Barth. In this section of our study of Ritschl-Barth affinities it only remains for us to consider very briefly those strands of continuity identified by contemporary workers in the Ritschl field. Philip Hefner does not in fact add materially to what we have already learned, but does corroborate the judgements of earlier scholars in the field. First, we note Hefner's statement, echoing a point made by Bultmann, that in Europe, the generation that was to overthrow Ritschlianism was largely trained by Ritschlians.[35] Hefner's opinion is that three of Ritschl's most important and most strenuously argued assertions provide formal resources for his twentieth-century Barthian antagonists.[36] They are Ritschl's insistence that theology must base itself on the revelation of God in Jesus Christ as portrayed in the New Testament (what developed into Barth's so-called Christomonism), Ritschl's adamant rejection of any 'natural' theology or philosophical statement of the Christian faith, and his correlative argument that the theologian must irrevocably take his stand within the community of believers. (Hefner mentions subsidiary strands of continuity, including the appropriation of Luther and the other principal Reformers for dogmatic resources, a rejection of Schleiermacher's emphasis upon feeling as a main theological resource, a rejection of historical positivism, and a rejection of romanticism, mysticism and aestheticism in theology.) So far as the alleged Christomonistic continuity is concerned, Lotz concurs. He describes it in this way: 'Ritschl's starting point (reminiscent of Barth's approach!) is a biblical theology of the Name, i.e. as employed in Scripture.'[37] Elsewhere Lotz, with total justification, remarks:

It is quite remarkable that Karl Barth should say little or nothing in his survey of nineteenth-century theology about Ritschl's rejection of natural theology and Ritschl's christocentrism. H. Richard Niebuhr, by contrast, in his brief treatment of Ritschl in *The Meaning of Revelation* . . . is much fairer in his appraisal of Ritschl's achievement.[38]

So far as Ritschl's central methodological emphasis on the *Gemeinde* as the area out of which and for which theology is done, it is worth at this point noting Mueller's judgement:

> Barth's *Church Dogmatics* no doubt was influenced by Ritschl's concentration upon the Church and may be seen as a fruitful development of that emphasis.[39]

Within this area of establishing Ritschl-Barth continuity, Hefner makes a point of huge significance when he anticipates a crucial potential objection that might be raised by those sympathetically committed to Barth's judgements. For might it not be objected that since Ritschl and Barth were both dogmatic theologians in the German-speaking tradition, clearly they would both be obliged to deal with common themes – God, christology, ecclesiology, soteriology, and the like? It might be argued that *apparent* continuities were more or less *fortuitous* similarities of interest. Hefner comments:

> In these areas of commonality, it is not a question of isolated points of agreement; rather, we are dealing with issues which Ritschl and the Barthians alike made central to their programmatic efforts to renew dogmatics in their respective generations.

Hefner adds a point upon which there can be no possibility of disagreement, namely that for some dialectical theologians, these elements were mediated through Wilhelm Herrmann, a close friend and disciple of Ritschl, who was a respected teacher of both Barth and Bultmann. Hefner's overall conclusion in the matter is perhaps best set down in his own words:

> Perhaps the fundamental bond (i.e., between Ritschl and Barth) is their common effort to build a theology exclusively upon the distinctive revelation in the New Testament of Jesus

and their common effort to maintain this position polemically against other options in their times.

He adds, with ample justification, that the Ritschl-Barth areas of commonality are today being widely felt to be highly restrictive, a sign perhaps that in the theology of the immediate future they might be abandoned in the programmatic attempt to deal with late twentieth-century secularization and unbelief.

If we now turn briefly from Hefner to Mueller, we find that the latter not only corroborates much of what we have just learned, but adds to the list of overlaps. For example, he speculates convincingly that the theocentric epistemology of Barth may well have originated in Ritschl:

> We observed . . . that Ritschl held it to be axiomatic that all of our knowledge of God derives from his self-manifestation in history alone. The dictum so beloved of neo-orthodoxy – 'Through God alone can God be known' – could well have its origins in Ritschl's viewpoint.[40]

In the same place he refers to Ritschl as one of the leading critics of speculative and philosophical approaches in the doctrine of God, and hence the implacable foe of natural theology, words which apply equally appropriately to Barth and which recall the judgement of Pannenberg. He also locates further sources of Barth in Ritschl within the doctrine of sin. Mueller correctly observes that Ritschl breaks with the older dogmatics which dealt with man's fall and sin *prior to* christology and soteriology; in contrast, Ritschl unfolds the doctrine of sin in connection with the doctrine of reconciliation. Mueller observes:

> In this he anticipates the procedure of Martin Kähler, Karl Barth, and others, *but Barth indicates no indebtedness to Ritschl.*[41]

We recall that two of the influences upon the thinking of the young Barth had been the Christian Socialists, Leonhard Ragaz and Herrmann Kutter, who materially influenced early twentieth-century reflections on the sinful influences of the world and its institutions upon the development of human nature (Ritschl's 'Kingdom of Sin'). In the same tradition stand Rauschenbusch and Reinhold Niebuhr. Mueller comments:

> But all of them surely learned much from Ritschl, who spoke
> with prophetic power at this point.[42]

Again, Mueller takes up Ritschl's objections, dealt with in an
earlier chapter, to the dogmatic notion of an 'infinity of sin'. His
commentary is as follows:

> In a manner that anticipates a position of Karl Barth's,
> Ritschl warns against absolutizing the power of sin. 'Sin, as a
> product of the limited powers of all men, is yet limited, finite,
> and quite transparent to God's judgement.'[43]

Yet again, on a different line, in discussing Ritschl's view of
Christ's precedence over the community in the eternity of the
divine love, foreknowledge and will, Mueller observes:

> Following the lead of a certain wing of Reformed theology and
> *anticipating the outline of Karl Barth's christocentric doctrine of
> election*, Ritschl reasons that Jesus Christ is the eternal object
> of the Father's love.[44]

And towards the end of his work, Mueller includes a section
devoted to 'the key to Ritschl'. One proposal considered there is
that this is to be found in christology, about which Mueller
observes:

> Our discussion of Ritschl's theology has made his Christo-
> centrism evident and this has led some to find in it the unifying
> principle of the whole. No natural knowledge of God is
> possible; all knowledge of God derives from his revelation of
> himself in Jesus Christ.[45]

Finally, it is worth noting that Mueller is vividly aware of the
problem involved in arguing that, very mysteriously, someone of
the stature and gifts of Karl Barth seemed unaware of, or was
unwilling to concede the existence of, those strands of continuity
enumerated above. Mueller comments:

> Contemporaries of the early Barth saw more lines of continuity
> between his thought and the theology of the nineteenth century
> and Ritschl in particular than he himself observed or admitted.
> This is due, no doubt, in part to a kind of myopia which often

afflicts prophetic figures like Barth in the throes of establishing new theological frontiers – something that we noted Barth himself admits. Our own historical distance from the events surrounding the attack of the dialectical theologians on Ritschl and his successors makes possible more balanced estimates of his contribution.[46]

We are now in a position to draw our discussion of the Ritschl-Barth continuity to a close by briefly recalling a few significant points within our study of Ritschl's texts in earlier chapters, where we located possible sources of twentieth-century Barthian theology. First, in Chapter II, in discussing Ritschl's epistemology of religion, we felt obliged to judge that he stands within the long tradition which includes Tertullian, Occam, Pascal, Luther, Kierkegaard and Barth, emphasizing the gulf which yawns between the God of Christianity and the God referred to in the profane reasonings of philosophers and men of science. In the same chapter attention was paid to Ritschl's attack on mystical pietism, where we found incontrovertible evidence that by opposing such pietism's alleged individualism, ahistoricality and otherworldliness, Ritschl's own theological dynamic was towards modern christocentric and bibliocentric theologies of the Word of God and towards *Gemeindetheologien*, a thrust which moved Tillich to speak of the Ritschl-Harnack-Barth antimystical tendency in modern Protestant theology. Then again, in our discussion of christology, we noted that Barth was willing to concede that Ritschl had played a significant and substantial role (if, in Barth's judgement, an inadequate one) in the evolution of a christologically-oriented Christian theology, over against the rationalistic unitarian Deism of the *Aufklärung*. Within the context of our discussion of Ritschl on sin, we observed that Ritschl anticipated early twentieth-century theology by insisting that man only comes to a proper knowledge of his sin through the preaching of the Church, which enables him to compare his life with that of Christ, and his achievement with God's and man's highest good, the Kingdom of God. And finally, within the context of Ritschl's ethical teaching on the vocation of the Christian, we found ourselves concluding that just as he had anticipated and prepared the ground for dialectical theology by divorcing supernatural from natural theology, so had he, analogously, striven to establish the autonomy of 'Christian ethics' from philosophical ethics, 'supernatural' from 'natural' ethics, the ethics of grace from the ethics of nature. In this exploration of the so-called Ritschl-Barth overlap, it only remains for us to comment as precisely as possible upon what is being affirmed here. It hardly needs saying that no attempt is being made to suggest that Barth was some kind of neo-Ritschlian or that dialectical theology was some kind of refurbished Ritschlianism expressed in misleadingly different terminology. The differences between the two systems are far too wide for any such wild suggestion! Nor must we discount the influences on Barth's system from distinctly non-Ritschlian sources – from the theologies of the Reformers, the thought of Kierkegaard, of Overbeck and Dostoievski. All of these, blended by the prophetic and creative genius of the man himself, contributed to the construction of a system singularly different from that of Ritschl. Having conceded that, more must now be affirmed. Certainly, we must affirm that we have heard and read in recent decades so much of this side of Barth that other sides of him have been concealed from us. Certainly, we affirm that Barth learned much more within his early Ritschlian theological matrix than he or his followers were able or willing to concede. Certainly, we affirm most strongly that Barth and his co-workers were standing, more than has been realized or admitted until recently, upon the shoulders of a man whose name, in the words of Harnack, they vilified. Certainly, we affirm with Bultmann and others, that Ritschlian 'liberal theology' fathered dialectical theology, and that according to sound genetic principles we cannot understand the make-up of an 'immediate and grateful progeny' without an intimate understanding of the parent. And certainly we affirm that grave misunderstanding of Barth's contribution will result if we do not try to root many of its characteristics in the system which immediately preceded it. On reflection, in plotting the Ritschl-Barth relation, it appears that we must note carefully two moves made by the early Barth. First, we must observe how he, in the luminous phrase of Pannenberg, 'extended and radicalized' many of the themes and emphases which Ritschl had made central to his thought. These themes, as noted above, can be described as bibliospheric, christocentric, pistobasic, community-centred, anti-apologetic, antimystical, and the rest. All of these were there, it must be insisted, at least *in nuce*, in that theology in which Barth was nurtured. But, it is now being realized, that extension and radicalization were excessive, so that they have evoked a strong reaction. Second, we must note the systematic, not to say ruthless, way in which Barth strove to eliminate from theology those 'subjective' and 'idealistic' elements allegedly derived from Ritschl's nineteenth-century *Zeitgeist*, especially those involved in the so-called Kant-Lotze description of the human predicament resolvable only by recourse to 'the Christian religion'. Not, indeed, that we must imagine for one moment that the wide appeal exercised by Barth's massive restatement of the Christian faith had nothing to do with his highly abnormal, not to say horrific and nihilistic *Zeitgeist* of the Weimar Republic and the Third Reich, or that it was due simply to Barth's miraculous rediscovery of the 'original meaning' of the Bible! Indeed, the alarming elimination of the subjective theological pole eventually caused considerable disquiet, not to say disillusionment, both of which were clearly expressed in the later (i.e., post-1927) theology of Bultmann, who was eventually to be accused, very significantly, and not at all unjustifiably, by Barth himself, of having become *all over again* some kind of neo-Ritschlian! Two brief historical points need to be made. The first is that if what we have said above (about the reaction evoked by Barth's elimination of the Ritschlian stress on 'subjectivity') is plausible, then the statement that after 1920 Ritschl's theology underwent a (more or less complete) *demise* needs to be highly qualified. One qualification would have to be that if such a demise occurred, it did so partly in name only. The second is that if we wish to explore the evolution of German systematic theology after 1927 we must be assiduous in seeking for the concealed operation of trends from Ritschl's thought in extended, reinterpreted, concealed and indirect forms.

We turn now to the second half of our study in order to explore the alleged Ritschl-Bultmann and Ritschl-existentialism overlap affirmed to be of crucial importance for the correct understanding of recent theology. Before we commence, a brief word about Bultmann's historical matrix needs to be said. Among the *cogno-*

scenti it has always been generally admitted that Bultmann is perhaps the most complex of modern theologians, that his fascinatingly many-sided thought is possibly the most mosaic-like of any, and that its sources are not only manifold, spanning considerable periods of intellectual history, but also interrelated in a singularly complex manner.[47] In reading Bultmann one must ponder at point after point whether behind the text lies Heidegger, or Strauss, or Baur, or Dilthey, or Erich Auerbach, or Graf Yorck von Wartenburg, or Herrmann, or someone else! As has often been remarked, in the light of the great fuss made by Bultmann about clear 'understanding', the title of Barth's celebrated paper, 'Rudolf Bultmann – An Attempt to Understand Him', was intended by Barth to be ironically humorous! It was for reasons such as this that it was argued at the beginning of the chapter that Bultmann's thought (like Barth's) has not yet been properly understood and evaluated, and the probability is that it is being misunderstood if not properly rooted in antecedent theological and philosophical systems. In this connection, it is probably true that even those with only a slight acquaintance with Bultmann's thought are aware that it is intricately related to both dialectical theology and to Heidegger's philosophy, even if they are unable to describe exactly what these relations are. The pity is that too many are unaware of intricate linkages between his thought and other important movements no longer at the centre of theological interest. It is against this background that we can appreciate, for example, Roger A. Johnson's recent book, *The Origins of Demythologizing: Philosophy and Historiography in the Theology of Rudolf Bultmann*.[48] One of the many virtues of this is that it makes it abundantly clear that Bultmann's work is rooted not only, for example, in the historiography of the *Aufklärung* but also in the neo-Kantian epistemology of Paul Natorp and Hermann Cohen, and in the neo-Kantian Lutheranism of Wilhelm Herrmann. It has been long recognized that the 'Ritschlianism' of Bultmann was mediated to him by Herrmann at Marburg, but Johnson's book is notable for its analysis of this mediation in considerable technical detail. Any detailed account of an intricate Ritschl-Herrmann-Bultmann development in modern theology is beyond the scope of this work, and it would be ungrateful to complain of Johnson that he has not penetrated beyond Herrmann to the latter's sources in Ritschl. Nevertheless, there is one important group of cognate terms which so closely links up the thought of all three that a word had better be said about it here – 'objectifying', 'objectification' and 'deobjectifying'. For instance, in the case of Bultmann, the point is made that the term 'demythologizing' could be accurately replaced by 'deobjectifying'; 'demythologizing' would 'be to eliminate any attribute of God or man which might be construed as "objective" in contrast with "existential" '.[49] One of the deplorable attributes of myth according to Bultmann is that it is *objectivierend* (objectifying).[50] For Bultmann, 'objectifying reason' (and its products) represent a 'threat to being', because it is the potential enemy of the realization of individuality.[51] According to Bultmann, Johnson affirms:

> God may not be integrated into a system of 'earthly objects through a structure of causal lawfulness', nor may God be identified with some comprehensive 'general law' or 'principle', nor may the deed of God be considered from 'the point of view of happenings ordered by law'.[52]

Beside this we may place the following celebrated statement by Bultmann:

> Faith can be only the affirmation of God's action upon us, the answer to His word directed to us. For if the realization of our own existence is involved in faith and if our existence is grounded in God and is non-existent outside God, then to apprehend our existence means to apprehend God. But if God is not universal law, nor a principle, nor anything objectively given, obviously we can know his reality only because he speaks to us, only because he acts upon us.[53]

In other words, it is unconditionally invalid, theologically speaking, to conceive either of God or the self as 'objective', in the sense that they are 'located' in or 'belong to' an objectively given world, rather than the world of personal being, an affirmation made *by Bultmann and Herrmann alike*.[54] We are by now well on the way towards Bultmann's 'use of objectifying as synonymous with inauthentic self-understanding or sin'.[55] It is quite clear then that so far as the connection between Ritschl's thought and that of Bultmann is concerned, Ritschl's most distinguished disciple, Herrmann, is *the* link. But what exactly of Ritschl's distinctive thought did Herrmann mediate to Bultmann? There can be no doubt that this was a movement in thought which, as we discovered earlier, lay right at the heart of Ritschl's theological method, from what we called earlier[56] the objective-metaphysical mode to the subjective-existential. This was based, we discovered, upon Ritschl's view that modern theology's greatest enemy was that form of *objectivism* which speaks of sin, guilt, justification and reconciliation as processes which occur in a dimension which does not significantly impinge upon human consciousness (for which we borrowed Karl Rahner's modern term 'extrinsicism'), an objectivism the systematic reversal of which throughout his system by Ritschl marks him out, in the view of Wrzecionko and others, as one of the most significant anticipators of modern existentialist theologies. It was for such a reason that we argued earlier that by 'deobjectifying' the discourse of Christianity Ritschl could also be regarded as indulging in embryonic demythologizing. We shall return to this matter shortly when we list those doctrinal themes which we discovered were deobjectified by him, but it is as well to keep this term in mind as we proceed further, for it refers to a method which is almost all-pervasive within Ritschl's theological work as a whole.

We proceed now, adhering to that method followed in the treatment of Barth, to indicate rather general strands of continuity from Ritschl to Bultmann, as they have been identified by various writers on our period, before listing the more specific ones which we encountered in our examination of Ritschl's texts. Dr James Brown, for instance, in examining the subject-object relation in modern systematic theology,[57] has identified a recurrence of Ritschl's value-theory in modern existentialism. He writes:

The vogue of philosophies of value has somewhat receded in recent times. But it is possible to trace the vestigial survival of the term 'value' in new derivatives from the Heideggerian *Sorge*. 'Concern' is a key word, for example, in the theological vocabulary of Tillich. 'Theology deals with what concerns us inescapably, ultimately, unconditionally . . . without the element of ultimate concern no assertion is a theological one.'[58]

Put more simply, Brown is saying that what is of value for the soul is that which concerns the self ultimately. Helmut Gollwitzer, not dissimilarly, fastens upon the entire value-judgement theory as *the* most distinctive theme which Ritschl has bequeathed to modern theology.[59] Having remarked that contemporary existentialist theology stands in the backwash of the acceptance of a Kantian approach by Ritschl (mediated to it by W. Herrmann), Gollwitzer continues:

> Albrecht Ritschl distinguishes religious judgements (=value-judgements) and theoretical judgements as exclusive of every subjective interest and constitutive for science. Both, however, are intended by Ritschl (contrary to the ruder distinction imputed to him between judgements of value and judgements of being) as 'judgements of being'. In the judgements of religion the highest subjective interest is included.[60]

According to Gollwitzer, those who have *existentialized the talk of God* since Kant include Ritschl, Kierkegaard, Dilthey, Herrmann, Buber, Ebner, Jaspers and Heidegger. But Gollwitzer very perceptively identifies another significant extension of Ritschl's value-theory into modern existentialist theology. When existentialist theologians typically reject speaking of God as he is 'in himself' (for which they appeal naturally to Luther), they are taking their stand in the tradition of Ritschl's distinction between disinterested judgements of being on the one hand and judgements of being combined with interested judgements of value on the other hand. It was precisely the acceptance of this Lutheran-Ritschlian distinction that caused Friedrich Gogarten in 1929 to attack Barth's *Christliche Dogmatik im Entwurf*, an event which marks Gogarten's fateful departure out of the dialectical camp for membership of the existentialist group of which Bultmann was the main inspiration.[61]

Several thinkers, as observed earlier, seize upon a solid strand of Ritschl-Bultmann continuity in the area of christology. Wolfhart Pannenberg, for example, in defending those who have employed a christological procedure 'from below upwards' (i.e., starting with the historical Jesus), remarks that in the nineteenth century Ritschl was the first to build his christology on the question about the divinity of the historical man Jesus. Pannenberg continues:

> In this he has been followed not only by the narrower circle of the Ritschlian school up to Wilhelm Herrmann, but also by Werner Elert, Paul Althaus, Emil Brunner, Carl Heinz Ratschow and others among contemporary Protestant dogmaticians, and, of course, by Friedrich Gogarten and others, e.g., Gerhard Ebeling, *who stand close to Bultmann*.[62]

Indeed, Pannenberg judges, Ritschl's christology is actually superior to those of Bultmann and Tillich, who are guilty of over-emphasizing soteriology at the expense of christology:

> With the exception of Kant, Schleiermacher, Bultmann and Tillich, one has not thought consciously from the perspective of a soteriological interest at the expense of the actual reality of Jesus of Nazareth. *Even Ritschl did not want that.*[63]

John Macquarrie has taken much the same christological line in this area of Ritschl-existentialism overlap. In a discussion of Melancthon's celebrated dictum that 'to know Christ is to know his benefits', he remarks:

> It is true that both Luther and Melancthon retreated from their bolder sallies into existential theology, but they did begin a way of thinking about the person of Christ that has persisted in Lutheranism and may be seen in new forms in *Ritschl in the nineteenth century and in Bultmann in the twentieth.*[64]

Elsewhere, Macquarrie analyses in depth what is involved in this christological overlap. He ponders Bultmann's outright rejection of every attempt to *objectify* God. The New Testament pronouncements of Jesus' divinity are not, in Bultmann's view, about his nature, but seek to give expression to his *significance* (for us). Macquarrie makes the following observation:

> Of course, Bultmann is not saying anything very novel here. In the nineteenth century Albrecht Ritschl was saying something similar when he taught that a christological pronouncement is a value-judgement and 'not a judgement which belongs to the sphere of disinterested scientific knowledge'.[65]

Macquarrie further argues that Bultmann's doctrine that a

christological pronouncement is simultaneously a pronouncement about oneself is *exactly* what Ritschl calls a value-judgement. It expresses what Bultmann calls a self-understanding (*Selbstverständnis*). Macquarrie's view, hardly to be quarrelled with, is that in the use of 'God' as a value word, we find the source of existential and pragmatic interpretations of dogma.[66] Macquarrie pursues the subject into the important question of how Bultmann is to be classified, and quotes the opinion, already noted briefly, of Karl Barth:

Is he [i.e. Bultmann] a rationalist, or an apologist, or a disinterested historian? Or is he a philosopher or theologian? Barth concludes that the best description is to say that Bultmann is simply a Lutheran, with Herrmann, Ritschl, Melancthon and Luther himself behind him.

Macquarrie is here quoting from Barth's notable 'Rudolf Bultmann – An Attempt to Understand Him', and if we turn to the text of that we find Barth corroborating what was said earlier about a certain definite Ritschl-Herrmann-Bultmann development in modern theology. In stressing Bultmann's distinctively Lutheran background, he comments:

All I want is to understand Bultmann as best I can. After all, he learnt his theology from Wilhelm Herrmann, and he is fond of quoting him. In justice to Bultmann, we must remember all he could have learnt and probably did learn from Herrmann long before he ever heard of Heidegger. I am referring to his constant simplification of the Christian message, his emphasis on its ethical and anthropological aspects.[67]

And with reference to Herrmann's intellectual antecedents, Barth remarks:

It was surely Herrmann who maintained the genuine Lutheran tradition, albeit a narrow one. It is just these elements in his theology which have influenced Bultmann so much. And, as everyone knows, there were two other theologians who stood behind Herrmann, Tholuck, the theologian of the heart, and Ritschl, dry-as-dust.

In this attempt to describe rather general strands in the Ritschl-

Bultmann continuity, it only remains for us to glance briefly at
the opinions of Mueller, Hefner and Lotz, many of which have
already been alluded to in earlier chapters. The former two are
agreed that an incontrovertible overlap can be seen in the area of
eschatology. We noted Hefner's opinion that the interiorizing of
eschatology by the existentialist theologians is not far from
Ritschl's ethicizing of it and Mueller's that one can argue that
existentialist theology's realized eschatology is actually not much
different from Ritschl's. Mueller adds something more explicit:

> He (Ritschl) concedes that the primitive Church anticipated an
> imminent Parousia, but argues – *anticipating later demytholo-*
> *gizers* – that this expectation was even for the early Church a
> part of the 'shell' and not the 'kernel' of their teaching. He
> continues: 'And there the matter will rest, for that anticipation
> has not acted prejudicially on any of the positive social duties
> which follow from Christianity'.[68]

In other words, Ritschl, followed by Bultmann, 'demythologized'
or 'deobjectified' the biblical eschatology by reinterpreting its
significance for 'ethical lifestyle' or 'human existence' respectively.
To return to Hefner, we have already mentioned his main conclusion in this matter (in which he follows the well-researched
Wrzecionko), that Ritschl's preoccupation with self-consciousness
was of great significance for later theological existentialism as
represented by Gogarten and Bultmann. This preoccupation, says
Hefner, was particularly mediated to them through Herrmann,
and it provided an antecedent thrust towards their existentialist
orientation.[69] But David Mueller has perceptively located all
kinds of interesting areas where Ritschl can be said to have paved
the way for and inspired Bultmann and his colleagues. For
example, while agreeing with a broad spectrum of Ritschl
scholarship that it is the 'deobjectifying' method which links the
two most intimately together, he affirms, very significantly, that
the other side of this particular coin is an objectionable *subjectiv-*
ism shared by them both.

This is a topic of considerable importance and deserves a
careful examination. Mueller begins his exploration of this
accusation by commenting:

> The restriction (by Ritschl) of all knowledge of and discourse

about God to the way in which he is perceived by man is determinative of the bent of much Lutheran theology from Luther to Bultmann, and is simultaneously the source of certain strengths and weaknesses of both Lutheranism and modern theological existentialism.[70]

The disciples of Ritschl, in Mueller's view, have had to pay a very heavy price for adopting his epistemology:

The application of his epistemology led his successors and especially twentieth-century existentialists to regard God as nothing but a symbol descriptive of certain dimensions of human experience.[71]

He puts this slightly differently:

Ritschl and even more his successors tend towards a theological subjectivism that calls in question the objective reality of God and turns faith in upon itself.

But this is a theological tendency, Mueller argues with much justification, that goes back to Schleiermacher, and can be seen recurring in Ritschl in his claim that the subject-matter of theology is the investigation of the religious consciousness of the apostolic community of faith. Like Schleiermacher before him, he weakens the revelatory pole in his thought by restricting theology to an investigation of man's religious and ethical response to God's revelation. Mueller's own conclusion, which we must note to be pejorative and not above criticism, is as follows:

It seems, therefore, that there is a steady movement towards theological subjectivism in Ritschl's own development that issues ultimately in the loss of transcendence and agnosticism in twentieth-century existentialism.

Mueller identifies a cognate Ritschl-Bultmann overlap in the fact that they both utilize, as we discovered in Chapter III, an existential *Vorverständnis* as a hermeneutical key for unlocking the genuine meaning of Christianity:

Long before Bultmann and his followers, he (Ritschl) insisted that man's asking about God involves a certain preunderstanding concerning the nature of revelation and human existence.[72]

Just like Bultmann and his disciples, Ritschl holds that human existence is profoundly problematic:

> Man's existence in the world is threatened because of the spirit-nature split within man and because of an indifferent and hostile world.

If man is alleged to be capable of 'knowing himself' prior to or independently of talk of God's revelation, then this can only mean to be conscious of the dilemma deriving from the spirit-nature dichotomy. In Mueller's judgement, the consequences of Ritschl's adoption of an existential *Vorverständnis* are that only that is of value in the revelation of God which speaks to the dilemma raised by human existence in the world, and that all God-talk is restricted to what is of value to the community of faith and the individual believer within it. The kinds of criticism which this kind of thing inevitably evokes apply equally, in Mueller's judgement, to Ritschl and Bultmann:

> By proceeding with this theological method, Ritschl makes himself vulnerable to the kind of criticism later directed against Bultmann's hermeneutic. Ritschl also utilizes a particular pre-understanding – not really so different from Bultmann's – which requires that the New Testament be interpreted as though its concern was always to resolve the question of human existence. In this way both Ritschl and Bultmann are often guilty of making it appear that God is of value only insofar as he answers man's problem. God is forced to fit the mould of man's preunderstanding and therefore his sovereignty and freedom are denied from the start.[73]

We must be very careful in assessing Mueller's pejorative judgement here. It has been quoted in full in order to make one crucial point only – the valid one that two very similar theological methodologies have evoked almost identical criticisms, thus corroborating what we have already argued concerning a significant Ritschl-Bultmann overlap. Nevertheless, it is arguable that Mueller's choice of critical language does not sufficiently guard him against the grave criticisms levelled against neo-orthodoxy by, say, Tillich. For if God's revelation does not correlate *in some way* with man's understanding of his own predicament, it is hard to resist the conclusion that the message must be thrown at those in the situation – thrown like a stone.[74] If it is alleged that God is not in *some* significant sense the answer to the question implied in the human situation, then it is obligatory to refute the assertion that man cannot receive answers to questions he has never asked, and that the Christian message consists of truths which have fallen into the human situation like strange bodies from a strange world![75] Nor can it be allowed that the use of a Ritschl-Bultmann preunderstanding of some sort implies *necessarily* that God's sovereignty and freedom are denied from the start. For we have already noted above (Chapter III) that to press this may be to overlook the careful distinction drawn by Ritschl (in which he was stoutly defended by John Baillie) between the *ratio cognoscendi* and the *ratio essendi,* or to ignore Tillich's fundamental point that while God in his *abysmal* nature is quite independent of man, he may be dependent on the way in which man receives his manifestation.[76] On the other hand, to be fair to Mueller, there are clear signs that he is somewhat unhappy towards the end of his book with the starkly uncompromising neo-orthodox critique of Ritschl. He is well aware, in the light of his reasonable assessments of Ritschl's work in the main corpus of his book, that a hostile dismissal of Ritschl's theology as anthropocentric or anthropological (i.e., *merely* serving human needs) is far from inevitable. He is properly aware that the description could begin (as Ritschl meant it to start) from the point of God's *will* or *purpose* or *intention*:

> The fact that God intends man to fulfil his destiny as spirit within the Kingdom of God is therefore not the sign of an anthropocentric theology, but rather of a theology that accentuates God's loving will. God does not realize his glory apart from man, but in the process of bringing humanity to its fulfilment in the Kingdom of God. Thus what might appear to be a man-centred theology *from the human perspective* is, in fact, a theocentric or Christocentric theology when viewed, as it were, in the light of God's ultimate purpose for mankind in the Kingdom of God.

There are no easy solutions to these problems. The fundamentally and inalienably bi-polar structure of all Christian theology cannot easily be got rid of, and just as a given theologian may, indeed, through hypersensitivity to his intellectual *milieu*, reduce or misinterpret the kerygmatic-biblical materials, his critic may find himself through his own criticisms caught up in irrelevance, not to say triviality, through fanatical or onesided commitment to the so-called sources of revelation. It is excruciatingly difficult to make up one's mind about Ritschl's interpretation of doctrine after doctrine of those which make up the totality of Christianity. An excellent example of this difficulty is to be found in assessing Ritschl's understanding of *sin*, where one finds oneself wondering if, despite loyalty to those striving to get Ritschl a fair hearing, his traditional critics have right on their side in accusing him of excessive openness to his optimistic nineteenth-century *Zeitgeist* to the point of being unable to do justice both to the biblical records and to Christian experience. In spite of Ritschl's impressive reinterpretation of sin for his contemporaries, it is hard to deny that he allows his 'idealistic' hermeneutic to obscure and dilute much of what Scripture has to say here. As Mueller says, rather too much stress is laid on the spirit/nature (or spirit/world) aspect of man's predicament at the expense of the Bible's man/God aspect.[77] Mueller interestingly suggests that this is perhaps why Ritschl finds it impossible to speak of man's radical alienation from God in the manner of the Old Testament, the teaching of Jesus, the apostle Paul, and the Reformation. Relevant here also perhaps is his definition of sin as 'ignorance' and his radical restriction of the 'Wrath of God'. But his stress here, in Mueller's view, also has christological implications; Jesus appears more as revealer than as redeemer, since his saving activity is not required to effect a radical cure. In this context, David Lotz goes further: he argues strongly that Ritschl, despite his vast contribution to modern Luther scholarship plotted by no one more adequately than Lotz himself, in the last analysis failed to grasp Luther's profound teaching on how the Christian's daily existence is constituted and nurtured by his *contemporary* encounter with God in his preached word, a word which simultaneously crushes and exalts, condemns and justifies, accuses and forgives. In Lotz's words, Ritschl must be faulted

for neglecting to ascertain the precise manner in which Luther
comprehends this experience from the perspective of the theology
of the cross, in the light of the Word of the cross.[78]

Ritschl quite overlooked that

> Luther repeatedly maintained that God's free pardon of the
> sinner . . . does not take the form of insight or enlightenment
> or memory or even historical perception, which, once attained,
> continues in effect without interruption.

He failed to perceive that for Luther

> rather it is an event which ever again *occurs* through the faith
> which comes by hearing, in the course of the ongoing proclama-
> tion of the Word.

Lotz puts the same point in slightly different form:

> The Christ who once came to sinners on the plane of history
> still comes today in the Word of promise, and, when that
> gracious coming is personally received in faith, all the posses-
> sions and benefits of Christ accrue to the believer.

(It must be added that this seminal insight of Luther, focused in
the concept 'contemporaneity' which was recovered for the
modern period by Kierkegaard, was appropriated by all of the
pioneering dialectical theologians – Bultmann included – and
that to the present day it is one of those factors which sharply
distinguishes all 'theologies of the Word of God' from that of
Ritschl and his disciples.)

We turn now to list briefly a selection of those significant points
from our exposition of Ritschl's texts in earlier chapters, which
we identified as possible sources of or inspiration for twentieth-
century theologies of human existence. For example, in our
analysis of Ritschl's religious epistemology we attached importance to his phenomenological analysis of *consciousness*, leading
to his stress on man's feeling or awareness of himself as a being
who, although a part of nature, nevertheless transcends nature,
and is called to be lord of nature. We argued that this anticipated
in remarkable fashion modern existentialism's teaching that man
is aware of himself as *Dasein*, transcending the dimension of

Vorhandenheit. We urged also that Ritschl's conviction that 'metaphysics' typically ignores man's self-consciousness as spirit remarkably parallels modern existentialism's hostility (articulated in various forms since Kierkegaard) towards the comprehension of human being under universals. In expounding Ritschl's conception of God, we noted the quite fundamental position within his system of 'feeling' (e.g., man 'feels' himself a creature of spirit, or 'feels' grievously the need of God), and argued that this locates him within a phenomenological tradition rooted in the work of Schleiermacher (with his all-pervasive stress on *Gefühl*), and that Ritschl's work in this area significantly anticipated and inspired those phenomenological analyses as are presupposed by modern theological existentialists like Gogarten and Bultmann. Again, in our epistemological excursions, we noted the spirit/nature contradiction as a hermeneutical key (Ritschl's 'general conception' of religion), and insisted upon the point, not now to be seriously contested, that this closely parallels and anticipates Bultmann's explicit use of an anthropological *Vorverständnis* as an interpretative tool for uncovering the basic structure of the Christian faith. In elaborating this similarity, we compared Ritschl's spirit/nature dichotomy with Bultmann's authentic/inauthentic one; we identified an unmistakable similarity in the fashion in which both regard man as problematically related to the 'objective world', and in which they both insist that although, indeed, in Christian faith man is liberated 'from' the world he is nonetheless freed in order to live properly 'in' the world, in Ritschl's case in God-given freedom and 'vocational lifestyle', in Bultmann's in the authentic life of faith, freed from care and nurtured by 'worldly encounters'. In this context, it is perhaps worth reproducing one of the most famous sentences of Ritschl's system, which occurs towards the end of an important discussion of the place of ascetism and monasticism in Christianity:

> Thus there attaches to Christianity only so much world-negation as belongs to world-mastery.[79]

Mueller has summarized it all very succinctly indeed:

> Both Bultmann's conception of inauthentic existence marked by man's enslavement to the world and to powers less than

God and of authentic existence characterized by man's realization of true selfhood through faith have antecedents in Ritschl
and in the idealism that influenced both.[80]

We noted Bultmann's telling confession that within the area of
modern scriptural hermeneutics *the* two interpreters who had a
real affinity with his own aims and methods were Adolf Schlatter
and Albrecht Ritschl. In exploring Ritschl's conception of 'the
World', we identified another anticipation of theological existentialism in his teaching on 'inauthentic' existence as being sunk in
or determined by 'the World', understood as contemporary impersonal social structures, to be contrasted with 'authentic'
existence, compounded out of possibilities whose source transcends 'the World'. In examining Ritschl's exposition of the
doctrine of sin, we observed his constant effort (clearly seen in
his subjective-existential theory of sin and suffering) to relate
theological doctrines, themes and affirmations to the states of the
religious consciousness and to various episodes of religious experience (which we dubbed 'anti-extrinsicist'). In pondering his
doctrine of justification, we suggested that it could be characterized by a set of notable correlations – of justification with reconciliation, of the objective with the subjective, of gift with task, of
Christian doctrine with Christian *Lebensführung*, which bear
comparison with Bultmann's fundamental methodological insistence that the Christian *indicative* must ever be correlated with
or must issue in the Christian *imperative*. Within a christological
context, we encountered Ritschl's treatment of the *Imitatio
Christi*, noting his rejection of any slavishly direct copying of
Christ's lifestyle, on the grounds that this might obscure or deny
that each individual is called to assume a unique Christian identity in the world, to make a unique contribution to God's kingdom, to fashion a unique lifestyle, as each individual is historically
and temporally unique and the task of life is 'given' to each –
views which, we argued, located him firmly within those traditions
which were blended into modern Christian theologies of existence. In describing his doctrine of the lifestyle of the Christian,
we called attention to its clear 'existentialist' anticipations – to
its insistence that every Christian existent is a qualitative 'whole'
in his own right, transcending the natural and social orders,

choosing and moulding his own lifestyle in response to what
Ritschl called the *given* particular 'conditions of life', a lifestyle
which must be manifested in a specific, concrete, worldly 'calling'.
And finally, in the context of his discussion of Christian perfection
and ethics, we noticed that, in the light of his affirmation that
each Christian must, in a sense, 'fashion for himself' the moral
law in accordance with these particular, given, 'conditions of life',
he might well be regarded as a notable precursor of 'existential
ethics' in a Christian context.

In conclusion, we list as briefly as possible several themes and
doctrines which, we discovered in our reading of Ritschl's texts,
were 'deobjectified' by him. We need hardly add that, in the light
of what was said about Roger Johnson's thesis, such deobjectifying must be regarded as the anticipation of that 'existentializa-
tion' (Gollwitzer) or 'demythologization' (Bultmann) characteristic of modern theological existentialism. First, we recall that he
carried out a thoroughgoing deobjectification of certain of the
divine attributes: God's 'eternity' was understood as the unchanging or continual aim of God *towards man*; his 'omnipotence' and 'omniscience' were defined in relation to *human*
hopes, needs and aspirations. It is noteworthy that Ritschl's
procedure here evoked the same kind of criticism that was to be
levelled against Bultmann's several generations later – namely,
that it inevitably produces a kind of disconcerting dualism:
between, on the one hand, the dimension of personal existents
and, on the other, the natural and social (i.e., impersonal) world;
or, between the area dealt with by religion and that covered by
the natural and social sciences. In reinterpreting Ritschl's doctrine
of sin, we found ourselves bound to describe it as 'existential-
experiential' – we noted his insistence that we *must* experience it
in the practical estrangement of the will from God, and that such
experiential awareness must be sharply contrasted with an ontological, speculative or theoretical knowledge of sin, or of a sinfulness which would fall outside of human experience. In elucidating
Ritschl's anthropology, we observed that in his treatment of
original sin, he rejected on epistemological grounds any notion
of the self as some kind of imperceptible but abiding substratum
or principle, described by him as 'metaphysical' or 'neo-platonic'

– alternatively, he adopts a view of the self as empirical, historical, temporal, intentional, volitional, transitional, not at all so different from that conception of the self presupposed by more than one kind of theological existentialism.[81] Also in the context of original sin, we could not but note the startling similarity between Ritschl's doctrine of the kingdom of sin and Bultmann's exposition of original sin as set forth in his *Theology of the New Testament* I, where, we concluded, it was impossible to avoid the conclusion that Bultmann is expounding a quite Ritschlian view of sinfulness, as a cumulative process which leads to the extension and consolidation of evil as a social factor. We observed in the same context how Ritschl radically deobjectified the relation of sin to suffering – affirming that the judgement that suffering and pain are consequential upon sin is a personal and individual one, that only the existent may make *upon his own* existence from within the circle *of his own* subjectivity and religious self-consciousness. The corollary of this was the contentious rejection of any speculative, objective, ontological theory automatically correlating suffering-states with antecedent wrongdoing in the 'external' historical and social order. Again, in a christological context, we observed Ritschl's attempt to deobjectify or existentialize the *Vocatio Christi*, by insisting that the vocational obedience of Christ must find its subjective correlate in, or issue in, the vocational activity and destiny *of every Christian believer*. From the particular ethical vocation of Christ there is to be derived the affirmation that all genuine human existence is *essentially vocational*. In the same context, we noted the radical deobjectification of Christ's work in its effect on general human sinfulness: we noted Ritschl's sharp distinction between 'general' and 'special'; the 'generally efficacious' death of Christ must have a 'special' subjective correlate in the life of the community and of the individual Christian believer; a 'general' justification does not necessarily come to grips with 'special' vices; a 'general' or 'common' salvation must be so existentially appropriated that it comes to grips with and deals with a 'special' depravity. It hardly needs to be added that such soteriological propositions both presuppose and expound Ritschl's 'existential' conception of human life as special, unique, individual, concrete, historical and temporal. In the same christological and soteriological context, we observed his attempt to deobjectify or existentialize Christ's Victory over Satan – maximally, this myth embodies Christ's spiritual conflict with the untruthfulness and wickedness of his *human contemporaries*; it symbolizes, at the most, the loathsome calumny which is the most characteristic 'mark of Satan' in the *merely human* adversaries of Christ. Or, conversely, the myth symbolizes that fidelity, forbearance and patience with which Christ faced the most intense suffering which his vocational obedience and activity evoked from 'the World'. And finally, we could not but note the thorough deobjectification of *faith* – for Ritschl, faith can be described as essentially experiential and existential. It can only be exercised from within the circle of the believer's *own* religious self-consciousness and directed towards the nexus of his *own* experiences. Faith, for Ritschl and Bultmann alike, is not an objective theory comprehending or connecting 'external' events or affairs in the 'objective' world; rather, for both of them, it is 'a way of looking at' worldly events, considered as good or evil, pleasurable or painful, predictable or unexpected, in the light of God's promise and providence, continually asking the meaning of such events *in relation to the spiritual life of the believer*, in relation, that is, to God's blessing or admonition, reward or punishment, encouragement or testing. Therefore, quite appropriately in the light of his teaching, Ritschl can speak of faith as a 'feeling' or 'tone of feeling' with which the Christian believer faces and deals with that stream of historical worldly events which is his temporal environment. It is on grounds such as these that the principal argument of this chapter is put forward – that the theological system of Albrecht Ritschl represents a most significant anticipation and inspiration of more than one type of German systematic theology in the twentieth century.

NOTES TO CHAPTER VII

1 See *The Humanity of God*, pp. 18 f.
2 ibid., p. 20, italics mine.
3 *Systematic Theology* I, p. 5.
4 From 'The Problem of Hermeneutics', in *Essays: Philosophical and Theological*, p. 255; cf. Bultmann's 'Is exegesis without presuppositions possible?', *Existence and Faith*, London 1961, pp. 289–96.

5 Tillich, op. cit., pp. 67 f.
6 See his introduction to *Three Essays*, pp. 41–5.
7 *An Introduction to the Theology of Albrecht Ritschl*, pp. 159 f.
8 Hefner, op. cit., pp. 45–7; with this cf. these words from Allan D. Galloway's *Wolfhart Pannenberg*, p. 12, which cast light on Ritschl's achievement: 'Ever since the first generation of Christians, the problem of interpreting the teaching of Jesus about the coming Kingdom of God has been the central problem of Christian theology . . . Every great theologian has always recalled us to it, and Pannenberg has done this in a very bold manner.'
9 Mueller, op. cit., pp. 160–1.
10 *The Theology of Hope*, London 1967.
11 Galloway, op. cit., p. 12.
12 Kenneth Hamilton, *The System and the Gospel*, London 1963.
13 *Protestant Theology*, p. 654.
14 Hefner, op. cit., p. 47.
15 Mueller, op. cit., p. 15.
16 ibid., p. 159.
17 Lotz, op. cit., p. 15.
18 Article 2 of the VELKD (Vereinigte Evangelische-Lutherische Kirche Deutschlands): 'The United Church, joining through its member churches and along with other evangelical churches of Germany in a federation of confessional churches, preserves and promotes that fellowship which came into being in the struggle for the Confession and which was witnessed to in the Confessional Synod of Barmen in 1934. The repudiations voiced there, interpreted in the light of the Lutheran Confession, remain authoritative for the practice of the Church.'
19 For the differences see, e.g., *Revelation and Theology: An Analysis of the Barth-Harnack Correspondence of 1923*, ed. by H. M. Rumscheidt, Cambridge 1972; *Karl Barth: An Introduction to his early theology 1910–1931*, by T. F. Torrance, London 1962; *Karl Barth's Struggle with Anthropocentric Theology*, by D. N. Snyder, 's Gravenhage 1966, pp. 63–78.
20 For Garvie's discussion, see op. cit., pp. 380 f.
21 *Types of Modern Theology*, pp. 182–3.
22 Quoted by Hefner in op. cit., p. 26; see also the discussion in Mueller, op. cit., pp. 149–50; Horst Stephan's critical assessment of Ritschl's theology is to be found in his paper 'Albrecht Ritschl und die Gegenwart', *Zeitschrift für Theologie u. Kirche*, 1935; with the line taken here on the distinctive divergence of Troeltsch from Ritschl, we may compare the following words of T. F. Torrance – speaking of the year 1910 in Barth's career, Torrance remarks: 'By this time he had come to look upon himself as sharing to some extent in the dominant theological trend led by the younger followers of Albrecht Ritschl, yet not without growing alienation particularly in view of the *dénouement* of this school in the *Religionsphilosophie* of Ernst Troeltsch', op. cit., p. 16. For this entire matter, see Hans-Georg Drescher, 'Ernst Troeltsch's intellectual development', *Ernst Troeltsch and the Future of Theology*, ed. by J. P. Clayton, Cambridge 1976, pp. 3–32.
23 Mackintosh, op. cit., pp. 172–3, italics mine.
24 *Our Knowledge of God*, pp. 17–18.

25 ibid., pp. 21–4.
26 *J. & R.* III, p. 331, quoted by Baillie, op. cit., p. 24 n.l.
27 Ritschl, ibid., italics mine.
28 *Faith and Understanding*, pp. 28–52.
29 ibid., p. 28.
30 ibid., p. 30, italics mine.
31 *Perspectives on 19th and 20th Century Protestant Theology*, p. 241, italics mine.
32 p. 156.
33 *A History of Christian Thought*, London 1968, p. 136, italics mine.
34 *Basic Questions in Theology* II, p. 121.
35 ibid., p. 36.
36 For Hefner's discussion, see ibid., pp. 40–41, 'Resources for Dialectical Theology'.
37 Lotz, op. cit., p. 42.
38 ibid., p. 184, n. 85.
39 Mueller, op. cit., p. 162.
40 ibid., p. 51.
41 ibid., p. 64, italics mine.
42 ibid., p. 73.
43 ibid., p. 76, quoting *J. & R.* III, p. 369.
44 ibid., p. 59, italics mine.
45 ibid., p. 158.
46 ibid., p. 149.
47 See, e.g., my *Theology and Metaphysics*, London 1970, I. 17, where I argued that the attempt to grasp even Bultmann's antimetaphysical tendencies involves understanding his positive relation to Lutheranism, neo-Kantianism, Ritschlianism and Barthianism.
48 Leiden 1974.
49 ibid., pp. 8–9; cf. H. P. Owen, *Revelation and Existence*, Cardiff 1957, p. 5, and my *Faith and Philosophy*, p. 163, where I suggested 'deobjectify', 'existentialize' and 'de-generalize' as viable translations of Bultmann's *entmythologisieren*. But I would now concede to critics, particularly the late Ian Henderson, that these might well obscure the positive connections between Bultmann's deliberately-chosen terminology and the work of Eichhorn, Gabler and D. F. Strauss.
50 Johnson, ibid., p. 15.
51 ibid., p. 80.
52 ibid., pp. 179–80, quoting from Bultmann's 'Welchen Sinn hat es, von Gott zu Reden?', *Glauben u. Verstehen* I, ET *Faith and Understanding*, pp. 53–65.
53 ibid., p. 63.
54 Johnson, op. cit., p. 194.
55 ibid., p. 184.
56 See, e.g., *supra*, pp. 149 f.
57 *Subject and Object in Modern Theology*, Croall Lectures for 1953, London 1955, pp. 197 f.
58 ibid., p. 197, quoting Tillich's *The Protestant Era*, p. 98.
59 See his *The Existence of God as Confessed by Faith*, London 1965, Part One, 4, 'Existentializing of the Talk of God Since Kant', pp. 67–78.
60 ibid., p. 74.

61 ibid., pp. 206–7; Gogarten's critique is to be found in *Theol. Rundschau*, new series, 1929/1, pp. 60–80; see also James D. Smart, *The Divided Mind of Modern Theology, 1908–1933*, Philadelphia 1967, *passim*, especially pp. 174 f.
62 *Jesus – God and Man*, pp. 36–7, italics mine.
63 ibid., p. 48, italics mine.
64 *Existentialism*, London 1973, pp. 31–2, italics mine.
65 *The Scope of Demythologizing*, p. 117, quoting *J. & R.* III, p. 398.
66 ibid., p. 123.
67 *Kerygma and Myth* II, p. 123.
68 Mueller, op. cit., p. 143, italics mine, quoting *J. & R.* III, p. 613.
69 Hefner, op. cit., p. 41.
70 Mueller, op. cit., p. 41.
71 ibid., p. 166.
72 For what follows, see ibid., pp. 167 f.
73 ibid., p. 168.
74 Tillich, *Systematic Theology* I, p. 7.
75 ibid., pp. 72–3.
76 *Supra*, pp. 87–88.
77 Mueller, op. cit., pp. 170 f.
78 Lotz, op. cit., pp. 124–5.
79 *J. & R.* III, p. 614.
80 op. cit., p. 163.
81 On this, see J. Macquarrie's paper 'Selfhood and Temporality', *Studies in Christian Existentialism*, pp. 59–76.

Index of names